THE TREFFRY FAMILY

DUM DEO PLACUERIT

The Treffry arms: *Sable a chevron between three hawthorn trees eradicated argent. Crest on a wreath, a Falcon's head erased sable, in the beak a sprig of hawthorn proper.* Motto: *Dum Deo Placuerit.* Windsor College of Heralds, as copied from the records of the College of Arms.

The Treffry Family

Adelaide Rideout

Illustrations by Alice Broadbent Wesche

For Mary Sargent, a beautiful lady and
gracious hostess, to whom I give this book
with grateful appreciation for her interest
and her help while the work was in
progress.

affectionately,

Adelaide Rideout

Phillimore

1984

Published by
PHILLIMORE & CO. LTD.
Shopwyke Hall, Chichester, Sussex

ISBN 0 85033 545 0

Printed and bound in Great Britain by
THE CAMELOT PRESS,
SOUTHAMPTON.

CONTENTS

LIST OF PLATES

(between pages 82 and 83)

LIST OF TEXT ILLUSTRATIONS

FAMILY TREES AND CHARTS

ACKNOWLEDGEMENTS

My indebtedness of gratitude to the following:

Anne Treffry of Place for leading me to Cornwall's historic areas, and for showing me earlier Treffrys in each one; for her kind permission to use the records held at Place; for finding many out-of-print books for me; in my moment of greatest discouragement for sending word that she had found Lysons' *History of Cornwall,* 1814, but that I would have 'to come and fetch it'! Nothing could have told me more clearly that she wanted me to continue.

Anne Treffry's son John for his kind permission to use material from the Treffry archives on loan to the County Record Office at Truro: for his relentless collecting and taking of pictures, filling in bits of family history, and for devoting several days of criss-crossing Treffry-trod territory in mid-Cornwall with me. His daughter, Peregrine, guided me through Devon and Cornwall, wherever I wished to go. Anne Treffry's daughter, Elizabeth Blair, verified points in the family history and identified people in old photographs.

Anne Treffry's nephew, David Treffry, introduced me to new sources to search for Treffry history; his guidance, and most of all, his constant encouragement have been invaluable.

Thanks are due to the talented author and illustrator, Alice Wesche, who has so ably prepared all the illustrations and maps; for her help in research and editing; for her deep interest in English history and the part the Treffrys had in it; and for being a joy to work with. Without her constant help this book would not have been.

To Mr. H. L. Douch, Curator, Royal Institution of Cornwall, for kind permission to use material from the archives and for the many willing hours he generously gave in searching and selecting Treffry-related material for me.

To Dr. A. L. Rowse for permission to quote from several of his books pertaining to the history of Cornwall with references to the Treffry family.

To Malcolm Thomas of the Society of Friends, London, for assisting in collecting all their records of the Roger and Mary Veale Treffry family.

To the County Archivist, Mr. P. L. Hull, and the staff of the Cornwall Record Office, Truro, for the many days they helped me with the Treffry records on deposit there.

To the staffs of the Devon County Record Offices in Exeter and Plymouth for assistance with their records.

To the staff of the Public Record Office in London for helping with their ancient archives.

To Mr. T. L. Stoate for kind permission to use material from his published works.

To Mr. T. Woodcock, Somerset Herald of the College of Arms, for searching their official records relating to the Treffry family and their coat of arms.

To Dr. Charles Treffry and his sister, Alice Treffry Parsons, for sharing all their family records pertaining to the John Treffry family, emigrants to Canada in 1834.

To Mr. Philippe Treffry, eldest son of eldest son, back to Robert Treffry of Landrake, Cornwall, in 1714, for sending records, photographs and history of his direct line.

To Marguerite Treffry Johnson and many other descendants of Roger and Mary Veale Treffry who sent their family records.

To Dennis Beadell of St Budeaux, member of the Devon Family History Society, who relentlessly searched Plymouth area archives with excellent results.

To Mary Sargeant for searching the records of Amy Jane Toulmin, artist, in Exeter and the Isle of Wight.

To Harry Lysons for his deep interest in the history of the Treffry family and for photographing family charts and sending pictures and records from his collection.

To John Treffry from Australia for sending the history of his emigrant family.

To David Trefry (spelt with one 'f') for briefing me on his family, emigrants to Australia.

To my brother, Eugene Rideout, for sharing the results of his Treffry family research and reports of his visits to our Columbia, S.A., cousins.

To my sister, Sara Condie, and her daughter, Claudia, who came to my rescue when I needed typing, and who followed the book's progress all along the way.

To Madeleine Gleason for her expert skill in editing.

To Marcella Wark for editing, typing and complete preparation of the manuscript; for her endless willingness to do whatever she could to help, and for her joyful and happy spirit. For John Wark's deep interest, proof reading and suggestions.

To Betty Farrell for searching in out-of-the-way places in Cornwall for answers to puzzling questions.

To Kevin Coleman of Keeble and Shuchat Photography for assistance in the preparation of copies of old photographs and portraits for the book.

To Dr. Jean Nelson for final editing and proof reading.

To the editorial staff of Phillimore for advice, assistance and splendid cooperation in the preparation and production of this work, I wish to give special thanks. To Mr. Charles Tucker, Manager of the Research Department of Phillimore, for digging deeply in record offices for old legal documents, wills and church records with fine results.

To the many other authors whose books I have used; to the many other libraries and librarians who have helped me, I am indebted. My special thanks to Mrs. Susan Start of the Woodstock Public Library, Ontario, Canada, and to Mr. Ed. Phelps of the Weldon Library, University of Western Ontario, London, Canada.

I should like to thank the following for their permission to reproduce illustrations in the plate section: nos. 2-9, *Country Life* Publications; no. 10, Don

PREFACE

Thomas Carlyle said 'All that mankind has done, thought, gained or been; it is lying as in magic preservation in the pages of books'. One might say the same of the history of the ancient Celtic Treffry family of Place, Fowey, in Cornwall, England, as much of their history is to be found in books on Cornwall, one of the most written-about counties in England.

Added to this is more that was discovered by many years of research in original parish registers, wills, indentures, various other documents, old directories and family archives. The very early history of the Treffry family lies in the mists of Celtic Cornwall, but the family legend is that the Treffrys were in Cornwall long before the Norman Conquest. Centuries later the family came into prominence when Sir John Treffry was knighted at the Battle of Crécy (26 August 1346) which was the first notable triumph in the Hundred Years War. His family remained on the edge of English history for many generations, serving their kings and their government.

Besides the recorded history of the Treffry family there are the living members, certainly with some physical likeness to, and certain characteristics of, their ancestors. There are the communities where they lived and helped to build or change in their time. There are the people whose lives have been influenced in many ways. There are artefacts and architectural structures remaining which tell us something of these earlier people, their achievements and way of life. There are memorials and monuments all along the way. To find the traces left by one's ancestors in their environment adds to one's understanding of these earlier family members.

No book I have found describes in detail the manor of Rooke which came into the Treffry family by marriage into the Killigrew family in the 16th century. Nor have I found a book that describes in detail Bere Barton, where one branch of the Treffry family settled in the mid 1700s. I have visited both. To be a guest at Place in today's comfort belies the difficulties of living there in bygone days.

In meeting members of the family and studying family portraits, of which there are many, one notes the fine light complexion and prominent blue eyes. Several elderly Treffry women whom I have known had unwrinkled faces into their late 80s and 90s. From early portraits of men in the related Killigrew family one finds that a cleft chin is characteristic. Hugh Peter, a Killigrew great-grandson had it; my great-grandmother's brother, George Treffry, had it; my mother's younger brother, Rolland Burdick, had it, as does my youngest brother.

In following many centuries of family history one notes that spellings of most proper names have changed as did spellings of common words. Thus the long history of the Treffry family contains various spellings of their name in historic documents and in the charts from the Place records—for instance, 'Austin' for 'Austen' in the name of Joseph Thomas (Austin) Treffry. However, Austen was the spelling he used. There may be found a few other discrepancies in spellings and dates on the charts which I have attempted to correct in the text. As spellings of family names have changed over the years, so have spellings of geographical names. Tamer has changed to Tamar; Beer Ferris has changed to Bere Ferrers; Foye, Foy and various other spellings of the town name have changed to Fowey. (Fowey rhymes with boy.) Treffry, as most words of Celtic origin, is pronounced with the accent on the last syllable, Trĕ-ffŕy. (Ffŕy rhymes with tie.)

As there are many spellings even today of some who carry the Treffry name, this does not necessarily prove or disprove relationship to the line followed here. Last names came into use in England around the time of the Norman Conquest, and as Treffry is a Celtic name, meaning 'house on the hill or slope', it is classed as a place-name, indicating that the Treffry family name was taken from a place. Over many centuries, it is possible that various unrelated families took their names at different times from the same place. To say that everyone with the same name is related is a statement without a basis in fact unless it can be proved. Many Treffry families are not included here because of insufficient records. I would be pleased to receive Treffry lineage charts which show proof of relationship to the charts included here for updating a future edition. As this book only shows the direct line of descent of the Treffry family of Place and Rooke, it is hoped that their records will be of help to those seeking to complete their Treffry family lineage.

As spellings of family names have changed over the centuries, so has the description of the heraldry in the Treffry coat-of-arms. The coat-of-arms of the Treffry family as shown in this book (as recorded in the College of Arms in 1850), is described as having a falcon's head in the crest. Other descriptions have placed a raven's head or eagle's head there. However, the earliest bird in the crest as recorded by the College of Arms in 1620 is the now extinct Cornish chough, and that is the bird still recognised by the family of Place as belonging in their crest. It is unknown how a falcon's head happens to be shown in the Treffry crest now, or why it was changed. The branch in the bird's beak has been called oak, laurel, or hawthorn. Hawthorn it is. The motto in Old English is 'Whyle God Wyll'.

The early history of the Treffry family of Place is based on records kept by that family which are considered the most accurate. Their records trace the family to Treffrize in Lincolnhorne, which means in Celtic, 'enclosure of the iron chief'. Could a Treffry have been the iron chief?

California, 1984   ADELAIDE RIDEOUT

For
ANNE TREFFRY
of Place

Chapter One

CELTIC CORNWALL

BEYOND THE TAMAR RIVER is the County of Cornwall in the most south-westerly corner of Great Britain. It is almost completely surrounded by water, as it reaches out into the Atlantic Ocean on the north and the west, with the English Channel on the south. On the east the Tamar River, rising five miles from the northern coast, divides Devon from Cornwall. It it were not for this five-mile strip of land, Cornwall would be an island instead of a peninsula.

This peninsula is a land of great enchantment, superb beauty and intense mystery: mystery that lies in great antiquity. Stories abound of King Arthur, Tristan and Isolde, piskies, pirates, and privateers. Through the ages this land has been trod by many famous people, including the Black Prince, Sir Francis Drake, Sir Walter Raleigh, Queen Victoria, Prince Albert, and many others down to Queen Elizabeth II, Prince Philip and the Prince of Wales, their son. Over the years writers and artists have chosen Cornwall as an inspiring homeland because of the beauty of the hills and valleys, moors, rivers and sea shores, magnificent trees, flowers and plants; and not least of all, for its mild climate.

To be born into a Celtic family of the greatest antiquity in Cornwall aroused my curiosity as to whom the members were, how and where they lived, how for many centuries they stayed in a very small area of Cornwall and then why some of them left for other continents. The history of a family is intertwined with the history of the times and places in which it lived. This is the story of the Treffrys of Cornwall and branches that emigrated to Canada in the 1800s, to the United States and elsewhere.

From the time that I was a small child I had heard stories of the Treffrys of Cornwall from my mother, whose grandmother was Elizabeth Treffry, born at Cosawes Barton, Ponsanooth, near Penryn, Cornwall, in 1829. What was there about this enchanted land that kept a family in one area for hundreds of years? Why were those who left always drawn back to it either in person or in thought? I had pondered these questions for many years as I searched for history of the Treffry family and stories of Cornwall and its people.

In June of 1950 I boarded a train in Liverpool that took me to Plymouth, Devon, and then on to Lostwithiel where I changed trains for Fowey, Cornwall, to visit Place, the seat of the Treffrys since the 13th century, and to meet the lovely Anne Treffry, whose home it was.

Leaving Plymouth, the train was soon to cross the Royal Albert Bridge, designed by Isambard Kingdom Brunel, and opened by Prince Albert on 2 May 1859. From a height of 100 feet above high water, the view out over Plymouth Harbour to the English channel was breathtaking on this bright and sunfilled June day. Now that I had crossed the bridge and was at last in Cornwall the hills seemed steeper, the foliage a deeper blue-green, casting a spell over me of being in a magic land. The train that I had boarded at Lostwithiel wound itself along the bank of the Fowey River through a grove of the most colourful and largest rhododendron trees that I had ever seen. Cornwall was indeed enchanted. (Unfortunately this train has now been discontinued.)

I left the train at the Fowey station where I was met and driven by car through ancient shoplined streets, so narrow that pedestrians had to stand in the doorways to let the motor cars pass. My room at the *Fowey Hotel* looked out over the harbour filled with sailboats, yachts, and a freighter waiting to pick up China clay. How very similar this sight was to the view from my home in California, overlooking the San Francisco Bay. The major difference was that this was a miniature replica, a stage setting in comparison, perfect in every detail to the hills that rose from the water's edge on both sides of the estuary. Fowey is a very beautiful town; I felt that I belonged there, that I had always belonged there, and I knew at once that I would always be drawn back to it. This was at last the Fowey that I had heard and read so very much about, but I found a quality and feeling about this place that escaped description. Perhaps that is the secret of its magic.

The name of 'Treffry' that had led me to this delightful place means 'homestead on the hill or slope'. It is Celtic in origin, and one of the oldest Cornish names. Little is known about the prehistoric times that brought the first Celtic immigrants to Cornwall beginning around 900 B.C. Similarly, any records of the arrival of the first Treffrys in Cornwall are lost in the history of the dimmest past. However, it is legend within the family that they were there long before the Norman Conquest. And, as prehistoric written records of the Celts are non-existent there is no way to prove or disprove this. As the Celts were in England hundreds of years before the Romans, it is within the realm of possibility that the Treffrys were among the early arrivals.

It appears that the Celts were a mixture of many races, rather than a people identified solely with one country. However, they are generally thought to have been fair-haired and tall. Families banded together forming tribes which over many centuries developed a culture, religion and language long before the Roman Empire came into existence. The Celts occupied all or part of the mid-European Continent west of the Rhine, Spain, Northern Italy and the British Isles.

The earliest Celts from 1100 B.C. are classified as 'Hallstatt Celts', named after a village in Austria which is 32 miles south-east of Salzburg, in a salt-mining area. The salty soil is credited with preserving many artifacts from prehistoric times. Among Celtic items found there in the mid 1800s were fine jewellery, war implements, bronze vessels and pottery. The later iron-using Hallstatt Celts flourished between 700 B.C. and 450 B.C. With the knowledge of iron, tools were made that could cut down forests, making land travel possible in addition to travelling by water.

Since the first Celtic immigrants were arriving in Cornwall around 900 B.C. they would have fallen into the classification of Hallstatt Celts. The 'La Tête Celts' who followed the Hallstatt Celts into Cornwall about 250 B.C. were not a different ethnic group, but a people with a changing culture and a higher level of development. They were named for La Tête, a place on Lake Neuchatel, Switzerland, where several prehistoric Celtic settlements were discovered in the mid 1800s. The artefacts found at La Tête were more sophisticated than those found at Hallstatt. Among the arms were swords, sheaths and shields. Also found there were bridles, brooches, mirrors, pottery and bronze containers. Many were beautifully ornamented, some with coral and enamel, others with intricate and detailed patterns hammered into the metal. The Celts worked in gold, silver and bronze. Sometimes the designs showed styles in furniture and clothing, revealing something of their life-style. Their craftsmanship and artistic ability ranks with the best of any civilisation.

During the 1st century B.C. the Romans were fighting against the Celts on the Continent. Although Julius Caesar invaded England in 55-54 B.C., he made no attempt at a permanent occupation. It was not until A.D. 43 that the Romans secured a foothold in Britain. However, there were remote areas left unconquered in Scotland, Ireland, Wales, Brittany and Cornwall. The Celts west of Exeter in Devon and in Cornwall kept their language, art and traditions, touched, but not moulded, by Roman culture.

The Celts were a people who liked to wander, travelling by sea, river and land. One of the earliest important trade routes in Cornwall which was used by the pre-Celtic people to reach eastern England or France was by sea to the Camel River in Cornwall, then across land at what is now Bodmin to Lostwithiel, then by the Fowey River to the English Channel. The Celts from the Continent used this same trade route when seeking copper and tin in Cornwall. Tin was an important component for making bronze. Ireland had gold which the Celts were also seeking. The Celts naturally established themselves along the trade routes. There were, of course, no towns, only small settlements; one was on the southern edge of Bodmin Moor where Bodmin is today, not far from Fowey. It is within this area that the Treffry family has lived for centuries. Fowey on the Fowey Harbour has been the home of the Treffrys of Cornwall for the last 800 years.

The Celts built round huts or houses with granite walls, as this rock is very plentiful in Cornwall. In other places, however, huts were made of wood. The structures usually were anywhere from six to 30 feet across, with central hearths. The conical roofs had an opening for the smoke to escape.

The Celts cleared land for farming and understood the importance of rotating crops. They had strong farm tools made of iron, including a wheeled plough pulled by oxen. They used bronze cauldrons for cooking and baking. They ground grain into flour, made butter and cheese, spun wool, wove and dyed cloth.

The Royal Institution of Cornwall's booklet, *Cornwall County Museum*, pictures and describes their fine collection of Celtic artefacts, including two

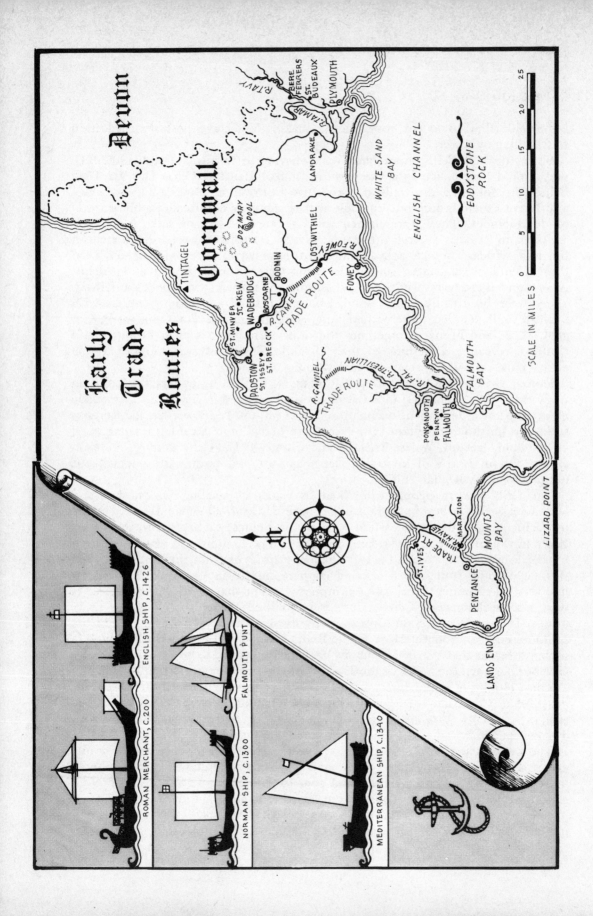

Early Trade Routes

Devon

Cornwall

TINTAGEL
ST. KEW
ST. MINVER
WADEBRIDGE
BOSCARNE
ST. ISSEY
ST. BREOCK
PADSTOW
DOZMARY POOL
BODMIN
R. CAMEL
TRADE ROUTE
LOSTWITHIEL
R. FOWEY
FOWEY
LANDRAKE
BERE FERRERS
ST. BUDEAUX
PLYMOUTH
R. TAVY
R. TAMAR

R. GANNEL
TRADE ROUTE
R. RESTLLIAN
R. FAL
PONSANOOTH
PENRYN
FALMOUTH
FALMOUTH BAY

WHITE SAND BAY

ENGLISH CHANNEL

EDDYSTONE ROCK

TRADE RT.
R. HAYLE
ST. IVES
MARAZION
PENZANCE
MOUNTS BAY

LANDS END

LIZARD POINT

SCALE IN MILES
0   5   10   15   20   25

ROMAN MERCHANT, C.200
ENGLISH SHIP, C.1426
NORMAN SHIP, C.1300
FALMOUTH PUNT
MEDITERRANEAN SHIP, C.1340

beautiful early Bronze Age gold collars found at Harlyn Bay near Padstow. An Early Bronze Age axe was also found there, and another was found at St Juliot. This museum also holds some Middle and Late Bronze Age artefacts, including burial urns found near Perranporth. A beautiful bronze bowl found at Warbstow, east of Tintagel, is of an uncluttered design except for an animal with fish-like eyes and ram's horns; a missing ring through the animal's nose would probably have served as a handle. A Celtic mirror found at Trelan Bahow on the Lizard is now in the British Museum in London. In the museum's collection are Bronze Age tools and weapons, some similar to those used until the 17th century. There you can see an iron-tipped oak shovel found at Luxulyan, near Fowey. Also discovered near Fowey was a beautiful amber-headed Celtic pin.

In the study of Celtic culture there seem to be many more questions than answers. So, when one tries to define Celtic religion it is most difficult. Since Celtic was not a written language in Cornwall, the Druids (or priests) taught only by word of mouth; they were looked up to as intellectuals and acted as inter-mediaries between the superstitious Celtic people and their gods. The Celts had great reverence for the head as they believed it contained the immortal soul. They often used the human head or face as a design pattern. Birds and animals were also held in various degrees of significance in Celtic mythology and used as art motives.

Forces of nature were worshipped as gods. If these gods were angry, human sacrifices were made at ritual sites, using criminals if there were any; if not, using innocent people. Gods varied from one area or tribe to another. They were very important to the everyday life of the people, and they were feared and respected.

Teaching of the young men was done by the Druids; it sometimes took over 20 years for the youths to memorise all that had to be taught orally. Verse forms were used to pass on history, traditions and genealogy of the tribes. The augurers or seers foretold the future. Eventually class structures developed within the tribes with the Druids being among the highly privileged. The ablest male was selected to lead in war or as king; warriors were ranked as nobles. Men of art and craftsmen who forged iron and fashioned bronze were also a distinct and highly respected class. Celtic learned men included doctors. On the Continent a warrior doctor's surgical instruments dated to c. 200 B.C. were found, including a probe, surgical saw and retractor, all acceptable to 19th-century doctors! Wherever the Celts settled they brought a more advanced culture with them.

In 1813 Joseph Thomas (Austin) Treffry was working on the remodelling of Place, and while excavating for a new foundation discovered various skeletons with their coats of mail, chained armour, spurs, rings, old coins and a very fine urn. (Some Celtic tribes cremated their dead and buried them in urns.) At the time of his discovery it was difficult to date these items, and since they are now lost there is no way to tell the exact period to which they belonged. Like so much of the very early Treffry history it has to be left to conjecture. It was not until the 8th century A.D. that the Christian scribes started to write down the Celtic oral history. Thus it is no wonder that there are no written records to tell us when our Treffry ancestors first appeared in Cornwall.

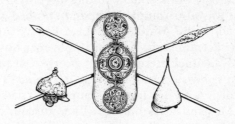

Chapter Two

TREFFRYS IN KING ARTHUR'S CORNWALL

CORNISH PEOPLE claim King Arthur, traditionally thought of as the great Christian Celtic king, as their own. They claim he was born at Tintagel, which is on the north coast in the eastern section of Cornwall. A defended structure stood there from very remote times, but the ruins one finds today at Tintagel are of buildings built centuries after King Arthur's time. The location in any period of time was ideal for protection from enemies coming either by sea or by land. The coastline is high and rugged, with the castle partly on the mainland and partly on a peninsula connected to the mainland only by a narrow ridge. According to legend, King Arthur used this fortress stronghold at Tintagel as one of his homes throughout his lifetime—late 5th century to early 6th century A.D.

The area from Padstow and Wadebridge on the Camel River to Boscastle on the northern coast and southward to the English Channel is the section most often associated with Arthur in central Cornwall. Here one can find on a current travel map of Cornwall, Camelford (Camelot), Slaughter Bridge, Dozmary Pool into which Sir Bedivere is said to have thrown King Arthur's sword Excalibur, King Arthur's hall on Bodmin Moor, King Arthur's Hunting Seat and many Celtic hill-forts.

The areas of central Cornwall associated with Arthur are in very close proximity to the early trade routes and to the places where the Treffrys and related families have lived for centuries. However, there is no way of knowing if the Treffrys were in Cornwall at so early a date as in the age or time of Arthur.

Many stories of Arthur are doubtless fables. The basic story of Arthur, a great leader in the struggle against the Saxons, is fully historical. In later centuries this history has been greatly embellished by poets. Many of the tales of Arthur were invented, but the places where the tales are set are real. In the spring of 1980 when I stood with Peregrine Treffry on the edge of Dozmary Pool, on a grey and bleak day, it was not at all difficult to imagine King Arthur riding by on the far side, followed by his loyal knights, all disappearing in the distant mist.

In my research I have found in the Domesday Book a place or manor called Trefrize that existed before 1066. Again it is mentioned in the *Minister's Accounts of the Earldom of Cornwall 1296–1297* under Treffris, Trefize or Trefry's Manor in parishes of Linkinhorne, Lewannick, and Northill, then held in 1300 by Thomas Arcedekene and given as Treuerys or Trenerys. Linkinhorne, less than eight miles due east of Dozmary Pool, was the seat of the Treffry family long before the Norman Conquest, and the earliest known dwelling place of the Treffrys.

The next place where the Treffrys are found is at Treffry in the parish of Lanhydrock, within a mile or two of Bodmin. Treffry is shown on a map in Lysons' *History of Cornwall* (1814). Although it is not shown on my current travel map, there is still a place there named Treffry. It is midway between Wadebridge and Fowey, and appears on the Ordnance Map Sheet 200, 1: 50,000 series.

A bit northeast of Lanhydrock is Cardinham, where there

Arthur's castle in legend, and Tintagel in ruins today

is an ancient Celtic hill-fort. Caradigan is prominent in Arthurian lore and was considered by E. G. B. Phillimore, who was an authority on Welsh literature, to be Cardinham. This is one of the places where Arthur was said to have held court. It is smaller than some of the other hill-forts and therefore was more appropriate for a fortified residence than a place of military encampment.

We next find the Treffry family at Fowey about nine miles south of Cardinham. The family lived at Lanhydrock only a short time before they acquired Place, the manor of Fowey, by marriage in the late 12th or the beginning of the 13th centuries, which remains the seat of the Treffry family in Cornwall.

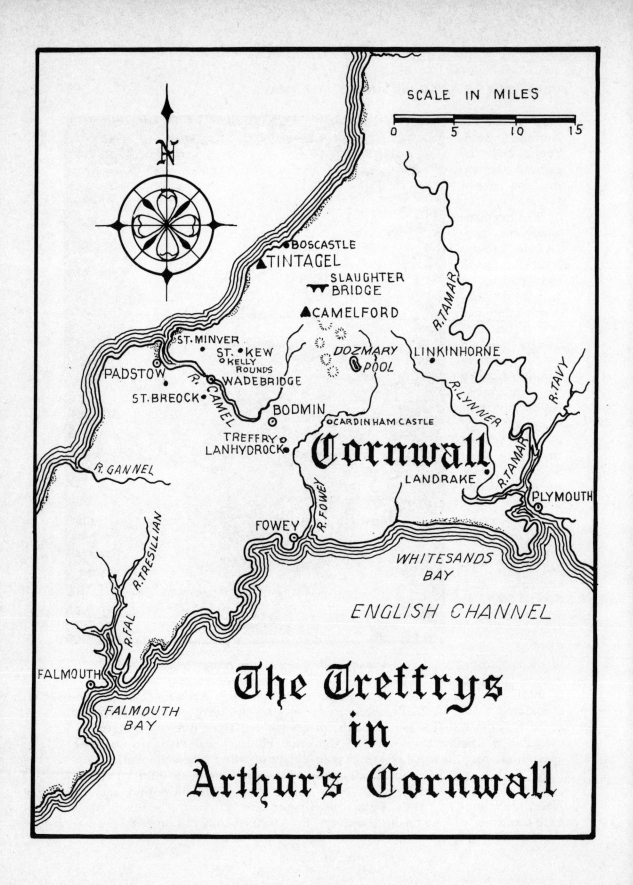

SCALE IN MILES

0   5   10   15

N

BOSCASTLE
▲ TINTAGEL
SLAUGHTER
BRIDGE
▲ CAMELFORD

R. TAMAR

ST. MINVER
ST. • KEW
KELLY
ROUNDS
WADEBRIDGE

DOZMARY
POOL

LINKINHORNE

PADSTOW

R. CAMEL

ST. BREOCK

BODMIN

CARDINHAM CASTLE

R. LYNHER

R. TAMAR

R. TAVY

TREFFRY
LANHYDROCK

Cornwall.

LANDRAKE

PLYMOUTH

R. GANNEL

R. FOWEY

FOWEY

WHITESANDS
BAY

R. TRESILLIAN

ENGLISH CHANNEL

R. FAL

FALMOUTH

FALMOUTH
BAY

The Treffrys
in
Arthur's Cornwall

When Thomas Treffry married Elizabeth Killigrew in 1505, the manor of Rooke in the parish of St Kew came into the Treffry family, where it remained until 1711 when it was sold to an Edward Treffry. In this parish were born many generations of the family. How long the Killigrews had held Rooke prior to 1505 I do not know, but they are a very ancient Celtic family, whose main seat was at Arwennack, Falmouth. An ancestor from the Killigrew line may bring a bit of Arthurian lore to the heritage of the Treffrys, for in the Killigrew family history is a connection with the Carminows, who claim to trace their history back to Arthur's time, and some say even to Arthur. In the 12th century the Carminow family brought legal action against a Norman knight who was wearing their coat of arms. The Carminows claimed that their grant of arms had come from the time of King Arthur's court. The belief in King Arthur was so strong at that time that their claim was upheld by the court, and they won their right to sole use of their arms! So if the Treffrys were not in Cornwall before or during Arthur's time, there may have been other ancestors of our family who were.

The following chart shows the Killigrew and Treffry connection to the Carminows and also back to the Plantagenets:

Carminow coat-of-arms with motto and supporters

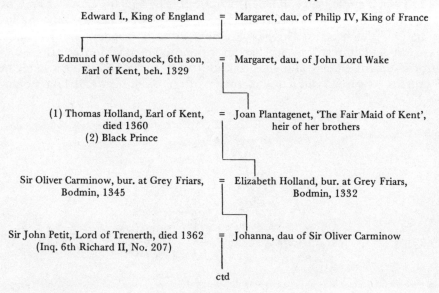

Edward I., King of England	=	Margaret, dau. of Philip IV, King of France
Edmund of Woodstock, 6th son, Earl of Kent, beh. 1329	=	Margaret, dau. of John Lord Wake
(1) Thomas Holland, Earl of Kent, died 1360 (2) Black Prince	=	Joan Plantagenet, 'The Fair Maid of Kent', heir of her brothers
Sir Oliver Carminow, bur. at Grey Friars, Bodmin, 1345	=	Elizabeth Holland, bur. at Grey Friars, Bodmin, 1332
Sir John Petit, Lord of Trenerth, died 1362 (Inq. 6th Richard II, No. 207)	=	Johanna, dau of Sir Oliver Carminow

ctd

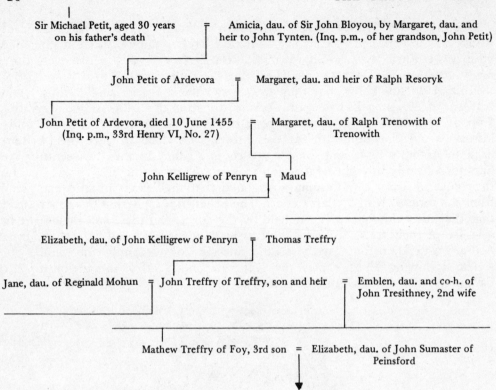

Sir Michael Petit, aged 30 years = Amicia, dau. of Sir John Bloyou, by Margaret, dau. and
on his father's death   heir to John Tynten. (Inq. p.m., of her grandson, John Petit)

John Petit of Ardevora = Margaret, dau. and heir of Ralph Resoryk

John Petit of Ardevora, died 10 June 1455 = Margaret, dau. of Ralph Trenowith of
(Inq. p.m., 33rd Henry VI, No. 27)   Trenowith

John Kelligrew of Penryn = Maud

Elizabeth, dau. of John Kelligrew of Penryn = Thomas Treffry

Jane, dau. of Reginald Mohun = John Treffry of Treffry, son and heir = Emblen, dau. and co-h. of
                                                                                      John Tresithney, 2nd wife

Mathew Treffry of Foy, 3rd son = Elizabeth, dau. of John Sumaster of
                                                    Peinsford

Two Celtic crosses in this area are of great interest to the Treffrys, the Carminow Cross and the Treffry Cross, both near Lanhydrock. The Carminow Cross
adjacent to Bodmin Moor at a crossroads junction near Bodmin is a tall stone
with a cross in a circle, the emblem of Cornwall. The Treffry Cross was discovered
in 1896 in the hedge at Treffry Crossroads near Lanhydrock. Only the broken
upper half of the head of this very ancient cross is original. Lord Robartes of
Lanhydrock had it restored and set up in its present position at his estate. In a
romantic moment one would like to think that Arthur may have knelt before
these crosses, as surely, did many members of the Carminow and Treffry families.

Although Tintagel may be the most popular and best-known area associated with King Arthur in Cornwall, a greater claim may be made to him by the beautiful parish of St Kew. Here are two very ancient earthworks or rounds. Kelly Rounds, thought to be 'Kelliwic' of King Arthur's time, is on the Wadebridge-Camelford Road. 'Kelliwic' was believed by the ancient Welsh to have been the site of one of Arthur's main palaces. A road now cuts the earthwork in two with only one side of Kelly Rounds remaining. The location is strategic, protecting the area from raiders coming by sea into the Camel River.

Tregeare Rounds, in the northern part of the parish, is considered to be a near-perfect example of an ancient Celtic fort. It has double ramparts and ditches. This is thought by some to be the 'Damelioc' of the Arthurian legend where Gorlois, Duke of Cornwall, fortified himself against Uther Pendragon, King of the Britons. It is only a short distance from Tintagel, on the way to St Endellion.

Slaughter Bridge and Camelford are quite close together just south of Tintagel. To the Cornish, Arthur held court at Camelford (Camelot), even though some historians place it elsewhere. In reality he probably ruled from many places as there was no centralised government at that time.

Slaughter Bridge is quite accessible today on a narrow road leading north from Camelford. There I climbed down a rather steep bank overgrown with wild foliage, to stand at the water's edge to photograph the ancient stone bridge that spans the narrow beginning of the Camel River. I could imagine this as really the place where King Arthur and Mordred met their deaths.

In the nearby St Kew parish church are found many monuments to the family of Thomas Treffry. One states:

> Sacred to the Memory of Thomas Treffry, Esqr., of Rooke, and Place in Fowey, and Elizabeth his Wife, Daughter of John Kelligrew, Esq.; he dyed the 31st of January, 1563.
> John Treffry, his Son, Married Jane, Daughter of Reginald Mohun, Esqr., had one Daughter; his Second Wife, Emblyn, Daughter of John Tresithyne, Esqr., Nine Sons And Seven Daughters; he Dyed 28th January, 1590.

A grandson of Thomas, and the third son of John and Emblyn, named Mathew, has his burial place in the St Kew church marked by a floor stone in front of the left pew facing the pulpit. In May of 1982, John Treffry of Place and I visited this church and located Mathew's marker, which read 'Matthew [sic] Treffry and Elizabeth his wife, Daughter of Sumester, he Dyed in the Reign of King James the First.' He died in 1626. His original will is extant and on loan to the Public Record Office in Truro, Cornwall, and the contents are included in Chapter 6. From this Mathew Treffry are descended the Treffrys of Place and the Treffrys who emigrated to Canada in the early 1800s, whose lines are followed in this history.

The line of Treffrys at Place is descended from Mathew Treffry's oldest son, Thomas. The marker for him in the St Kew church says 'Thomas Treffry and Jane his Wife, Daughter of John Vivian: Trewan, Esqr.; he married 1641.'

William, Mathew Treffry's second son, married and settled in St Minver, which is about three miles west of St Kew, or halfway between St Kew and Padstow, still in the romantic King Arthur area. William is the progenitor of the Treffry family in Canada.

Before leaving the Arthurian area, note should be taken of the Tristan stone that stands just outside of Fowey. It is traditionally said to commemorate a mid-6th century British knight who lived at Castle Dore three generations after Arthur. Tristan was the son of King Mark, not his nephew, as represented in the tragic legend of Tristan and Isolde. Tristan, King Arthur and others of their time are part of English legendary history, as are the settings that still have the same place-names today.

There are many references to the Treffry family of Place in the time of the Plantagenets (1154–1485) and continuing through the Tudor period (1485–1603) to the present day. One can hardly pick up a book on Cornwall without finding references to the Treffrys or to Place. In trying to track down the earliest Treffry records there are a number of sources that are helpful; as there are no census records as such until the 1800s, the following lists may serve as a guide. On the 1569 *Muster Roll* for Cornwall, as edited and transcribed by H. L. Douch, the following Treffrys are listed (we learn where they lived and what they furnished for military service):

Fowey	John Treffrie, esquire: a light horse: furnished 2 pair of corselets: 10 pair of Almayn Rivets: 20 pikes: 4 long bows: 4 sheafs of arrows: 3 harquebuts: 3 halberds
Endellion	John Treffrye: 4 arrows
	John Treffrye: 4 arrows
St Tudy	Henrye Treffreye: 2 pair of Almayn Rivets: harquebuts: bow and sheaf of arrows: sallet skull: pair of corselets
	Richard Treffrye
	Ambrose Treffrye, harquebuts

In 1641 all males over 18 years of age were urged to sign a Protestation against all 'popery' but supporting the Reformed Protestant Religion. Treffrys were as listed: from *Cornwall Protestation Returns,* edited and published by T. L. Stoate 1974.

Fowey	**John Treffry, Esq.**	Egloshayle	Nicholas Treffrye
Gwithian	Daniel Trefery	St Endellion	James Trefry
Lanivet	Thomas Trefrye		Rich Treffry
St Breock	Robert Trefery	St Kew	John Treffry
St Columb Major	Thomas Trefrye	St Tudy	Nicholas Treffry
Bodmin	Robert Treffrye		Joyce Treffry
St Minver	**William Treffry**		Grace Treffry
	Roger Treffry		John Treffry did not sign being feeble
	John Treffrye		in body and past his senses

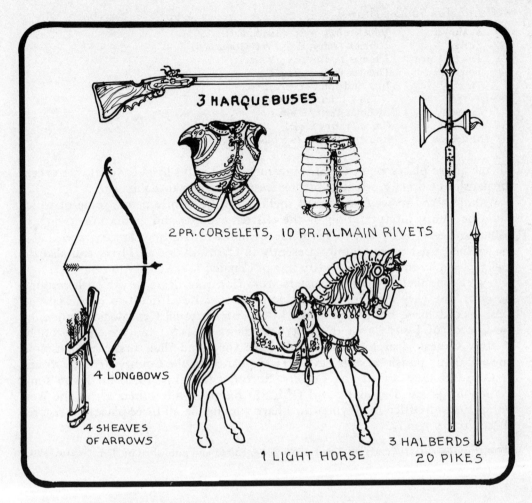

Arms supplied by John Treffry, Esquire, for 1569 muster roll

All the above places are in central Cornwall area except Gwithian, which is further west on the north coast of Cornwall. John Treffry, Esq., of Fowey, is the one from whom the line at Place inherited the Treffry estates. The William Treffry of St Minver, on this list is the ancestor of the Treffrys who settled in Canada.

The *Poll Tax of 1660* shows:

St Austell	John Trefrye
Fowey	Thomas Trefry, Esq. £10

Free and Voluntary Present 1661 shows:

St Kew	Thomas Treffry, Esq., of Rooke £10

Hearth Tax 1662–4 shows:*

St Minver	John Trefrey 1 esc. (Examined)
St Kew	Thomas Trefry, Esq. 7 ret. (Returned)
Fowey Town	Thomas Trefrey, Esq. 9 esc.
Fowey Parish	Thomas Trefrey, Esq. 1 esc.
Tregony	Joan and John Treffry 2 esc.
	(now John Trewry)
Cornelly	Nicholas Trefry 1 esc.
Advent	Grace Trefrey 2 esc.
St Breock	Robert Trefry 5, two blockt up

All the above places are in the area in which the Treffys lived for centuries except the parish of Cornelly, which is further west and nearer to Falmouth.

Within these lists we find various spellings of the family name, some of which could be faulty interpretation of the written records and errors in copying. In 1626 Mathew Treffry signed his name on his will 'Mathew Treffry' and that is the spelling used by the family presently in Cornwall and of Place, and also the spelling used by the William Treffry line of Canada.

A great number of parish registers from Cornwall begin in the 16th century. However, the very early records are sometimes quite difficult to read. Many of these records have been filed in the I.G.I., International Genealogical Index, by the Church of Jesus Christ of Latter-Day Saints (L.D.S.) and are on microfiche at their Genealogical Library in Salt Lake City, and their branch libraries. In England many parish records have been deposited in the County Record Offices. In Cornwall they are at the County Record Office in Truro. In Devon some records are at the Devon Record Office in Exeter, while others are at the West Devon Record Office in Plymouth. I have searched in all three places for records of the Treffry family.

*From *Cornwall Hearth and Poll Taxes 1660-1664,* edited and published by T. L. Stoate, 1981.

Chapter Three

HISTORY OF THE TREFFRY FAMILY THROUGH THE 16th CENTURY

THERE IS NO QUESTION that the Treffry family has a history of great interest covering many centuries of living in Cornwall. Family names are written in ancient parish registers, beginning as early as 1536 when records of birth, marriages and deaths were first required to be kept. Preceding that there were memorials carved in stone and some made of brass, in the St Fimbarrus church in Fowey. The earliest Treffry records kept by the family were carved in Old English lettering on oaken wall panels that were installed at Place over 550 years ago. These now have been copied in a manuscript book for permanent record. Also, there are a few 13th-century tax, land and legal records referring to the Treffrys that indicate dates and places of residence, and relationships within the family.

While searching for history of the Treffrys one realises that the magnetism of Cornwall that has captured the hearts and trapped the souls for centuries, is still there. One hears it as the sea crashes against the rocky shore. One feels it in the summer sea breeze. One scents it in the fragrance of the flowers. One sees it in the rolling green hills and valleys, in the moors, in the gently flowing rivers, in the clear blue sky, or in a grey winter day. All of this was there when the first Treffrys came into Cornwall. When one reflects on this, then it becomes easier to put each Treffry in his proper place, in his time, as far back as one finds records and memorials and discovers ancient legends about the family. Did a Treffry actually lead a body of troops to oppose the landing of Julius Caesar in 54 B.C.? There is a legend within the family that such has been said, but by what authority is unknown. But one should not disregard legends, because sometime, somewhere, in another age, another time, the legend may be authenticated.

Neither do we know if the Treffrys were in Cornwall in King Arthur's time, but without a doubt the name is of great antiquity in the county of Cornwall. The Domesday Book and documents kept by the Treffry family record that the Treffrys lived at their mansion home of Treffrys, 'Trefrize', in the parish of Linkinhorne prior to the Conquest of Duke William of Normandy in 1066. On an old oak panel that was in the library at Place in Fowey over 550 years ago was a description of this ancient mansion written in Old English script that indicated that the family was in Linkinhorne until Henry II's time, about 1154.

The manor of Trefrize or Treffrys was a manor of considerable size and importance extending into three parishes and including six tenements in Lewanick, eight in Northill, six in Linkinhorne. Within the manor of Treffrys was a famous consecrated Holy Well, dedicated to St Mary Magdalen, with a nearby chapel where members of the family of the great Lord Treffry were married, baptized and buried. The family had their own chaplain who lived in the adjacent chapel house, which with the chapel, was about a quarter of a mile from the mansion. When the Treffrys lived at Trefrize a spacious house of freestone stood there. In 1728 part of the east wall of the great hall with church-like windows was still standing. Near the ruins of the great hall there were walks 10 or 12 feet wide with trimmed hedges on both sides where the family and friends might walk for recreation.

About the middle of the 12th century Trefrize was carried in marriage by a female heiress, Eva Treffry, to the Arundells. Her husband thereafter was called 'Sir R. Arundell, Knight of Treffry'. A grand-daughter of theirs, named Eva, married William Roscarrock of Roscarrock. The Treffrys of Linkinhorne then settled at Treffry in the parish of Lanhydrock. This property extended into the parishes of Bodmin, Lanivet and Fowey. The Treffrys had a family mansion at Treffry which has been taken down. A smaller house is on the property now. The Treffrys lived at Treffry in Lanhydrock only a short time, although they held this house for many generations, until it was sold by William Treffry in 1620 to Sir Richard Robarts. It became part of that family's estate called Lanhydrock which is now a National Trust property open to the public at certain times. The manor of Tregwyned, formerly the property of the Treffrys, also went to the Robarts family.

About the end of the 12th or beginning of the 13th century the Treffrys acquired Place, the manor of Fowey, by a marriage with the Bonifaces of Piworthy of Devonshire. Place, or 'Cuni Court' as it was called anterior to the Norman Conquest, was according to tradition one of the ancient seats of the British kings and subsequently the seat of the Earls of Cornwall. Few mansions in the county are of greater interest than this very ancient building. In the Cornish language 'place' means 'palace'.

The early history of Place prior to the 13th century is unknown as is, also, the exact date when the Treffrys first settled there. However, the manor and barton of Treffry in Lanhydrock extended into the parish of Fowey as one estate, so the family had a Fowey connection before the Boniface marriage.

First, Second, Third Generations.

According to the Treffry family charts (shown in Chapter 4) there were three generations of the family recorded at Linkinhorne from *c.* 1100; Treffry de Treffry, Roger Treffry de Treffry, and John Treffry de Treffry. John is the first of these whose wife's name has been recorded. She was Ibatt, daughter of Sir Nicholas Le Flamank of Treglothnow, knight, and lived *c.* 1179. The ancient family of Flamank (an old French name) was among the early landholders in the county of Cornwall. A Robert Le Flamank received the honour of knighthood soon after the Norman Conquest. They remained an important and respected family in Cornwall for centuries.

Fourth Generation

John and Ibatt's son John married Johanna, daughter and heir of John de Kelligrew of Arwennack, c. 1210. Arwennack, close to the sea, is in the present-day Falmouth, but little remains today of their ancient house. Killigrew is an early Celtic name meaning 'grove of the eagles'. A later member of the Treffry family also married a Killigrew.

Around the time of the first Treffry-Killigrew marriage other records of the family begin to appear. In 1283, John Aston, the Escheator, took an inquisition at Bodmin, ex-officio, under the oaths of Stephen Glynn, Henry Cavell, Roger Treury (Treffry) and others. It was found that the Prior of Plympton held of the King 'in Capite' two carucates of land (240 acres) in Lannoseynt and that Robert, sometime Prior of Plympton, had granted the same to John 'Treury' (Treffry), Richard and Roger his sons and others without license of the King, for their whole lives. The jury said that John Treury and Richard Treury were dead and that Roger Treury was still alive, that the value of the land was £4 4s. 4d. per annum, and that the Escheator had taken it into the hands of the King. (*Escheats 6, Rich. II, no. 185*).

Fifth Generation

John and Johanna's son Roger married Senata, daughter and heir of Peter Polgreen, Esq., c. 1240. The Polgreens were also a very ancient Celtic family. The name in Celtic means 'gravel pit'. It may be that this family took its name from Polgreen in Lantegloss, near Fowey; families often took their names from places in early days.

Sixth Generation

Thomas Treffry, the son of Roger and Senata, married Elizabeth, daughter and co-heir of Robert Boniface of Piworthy in Devon. This is the marriage that brought Place at Fowey to the Treffry family. The Boniface family, according to family legend, were lords of the manor of Piworthy, Devon, from the latter part of the 3rd century and for many centuries thereafter. It is thought that the Bonifaces acquired Place from the representatives of Robert de Cardinham, either by marriage or purchase. Boniface was the name of a 3rd-century saint martyred at Tarsus, and was also the name of a number of Popes.

Seventh Generation

Thomas Treffry, the son of Thomas and Elizabeth Boniface, married Alice, daughter and co-heir of Serle of Penverane, Esq., c. 1310. The name Serle is frequently found in Cornwall.

Eighth Generation

The son of Thomas and Alice was the first of the Treffrys to gain prominence. It is a matter of history that John Treffry distinguished himself at the battle of Crécy, and was one of the glorious army of Englishmen, who under Edward the Black Prince fought and won the battle of Crécy, 26 August 1346. Sir John captured the Royal Banner of France in a hand-to-hand fight with the French Standard Bearer, who was slain. For this achievement, and in recognition of his valour throughout the battle, he was created a Knight Banneret on the battlefield.

John Treffry knighted by the Black Prince at Crécy, 1346

On one of the wainscot panels at Place were the arms of Sir John Treffry with a helmet suiting the degree of a Knight Banneret quartered with the Royal Arms of France with the motto 'Whyle God Wyll'. The following inscription was carved underneath in old ornamental text hand: 'John Treffry Esquire for his achievements under Edward the Black Prince was made a Knight Banneret by the King's own hand in the field'. To substantiate this, there is a Flemish account of the battle of Crécy that describes the loss of the Royal Banner of France, 'The great Banner of the King was stricken down, and fell into the hands of Sir John

Dereffry, a British or Breton Knight'. The name Dereffry is merely a Continental mis-spelling of the Treffry name.

The tradition has existed for many centuries that Sir John's service at the battle of Crécy was honoured by the King, who ordered that Sir John and his heirs should quarter the Arms of France with their own achievement and add supporters to the said arms. However, Edward III retired from the field at Crécy leaving his eldest son, the Black Prince, only 16, in command. The Black Prince, the first Duke of Cornwall, immediately after the battle of Crécy, created Sir John a Knight Banneret, and gave him liberty to quarter the arms of France with his own, and for supporters a wild man with a bow, and a wild woman with an arrow in her hands. I like to believe it was the Black Prince who knighted Sir John, and not his father, Edward III.

Also, it is a matter of record that Edward the Black Prince actually visited Sir John Treffry at Place. In commemoration of this visit Sir John Treffry had a magnificent stained glass window put up. To be seen today in the large window on the staircase in very old but brilliant stained glass is the badge of the Black Prince, the ostrich plumes, along with his initials 'E.P.' (Edwardus Princeps). This is a portion of the identical window placed in the old Hall upwards of 650 years ago.

It is quite plausible that the Black Prince did, indeed, visit Place, for besides his residence at Tintagel the Black Prince also used on his visits to Cornwall the fort-like Castle Restormel, the ruins of which one sees today near Lostwithiel just upriver from Fowey. I had often seen Restormel from the train, but it was not until the spring of 1982 that I explored the castle ruins. It is a large circular structure on the crest of a hill adjacent to a higher hill. On entering one finds a large open courtyard encircled by many rooms two storeys high with windows facing into the courtyard. All the rooms are named to indicate their use, such as cooking, dining and sleeping, as well as meeting rooms and a chapel, and, of course, a dungeon without which no castle would be complete.

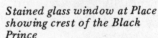

Stained glass window at Place showing crest of the Black Prince

The Black Prince lived here in style, entertaining the local gentry. Over the ancient trade routes from France into the Fowey Harbour came fine wines and many delicacies to add to the festivities of the Prince. It is reasonable to believe that Sir John Treffry, honoured at Crécy and living so nearby at Place was often a welcome guest. On 20 August 1354, the Prince, then a young man of 24, arrived at Restormel. He was accompanied by many of the knights who had fought with him at Crécy, and undoubtedly Sir John was among them. The Prince stayed only a fortnight on this trip.

The Council Book of the Black Prince shows that on 7 February 1356-57 a payment of three marks was directed to be made to John Trevry (Treffry) for

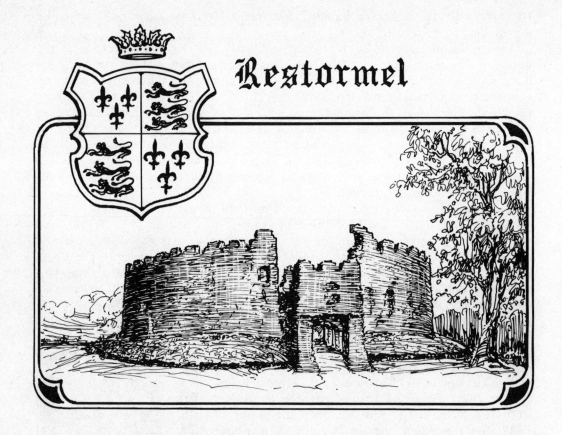

Restormel

remaining with the Prince's Council in Cornwall during the time of their session. The Black Prince came to Restormel again in 1363. It was on one of these trips, no doubt, that he visited Sir John Treffry at Place. The Public Record Office holds the Council Book of the Black Prince with references to the time he spent in Cornwall. The Black Prince was the last of the royal family to use Restormel. Eventually Tintagel and Restormel were neglected. The latter stands today roofless at the crest of well-kept grounds commanding a 360-degree view of the surrounding valley.

Here we can note another connection of the Black Prince with the Treffry family history. He was the second husband of the widowed Joan Plantagenet, the Fair Maid of Kent, his first cousin once removed. Joan and her first husband, Thomas Holland, were ancestors of Elizabeth Killigrew who married Thomas Treffry on 29 September 1506. Their chart is shown in Chapter 2.

In 1363 when the Black Prince wanted to marry his cousin, a Papal dispensation was required. The price of this was the founding of a chantry chapel in the crypt of Canterbury Cathedral. This was funded by the Manor of Vauxhall which the Black Prince gave for the purpose. In his will he directed that he be buried in Canterbury Cathedral. There his magnificent tomb is to be found in the Trinity Chapel. In 1978 when I visited it I thought his monument the most beautiful I had ever seen, a proper tribute to the most spectacular figure of the Middle Ages. After the battle of Crécy, he was known as the Black Prince, because he wore a suit of black armour.

Sir John Treffry married Joanna, the second daughter and co-heir of John Le Petit. There is a record of a legal suit in 1360 pertaining to them whereby lands were settled on them and the heirs of their bodies. Joanna was the daughter of John Le Petit, who was from an ancient and very illustrious Cornish family of Ardevora, dating from c. 1100. Various members of the family served at Court and in Parliament for the County of Cornwall. The Petits also married into the Killigrew family, linked to the Treffrys. It is thought they were originally from France where the name is still common.

Ninth Generation

Sir John and Joanna's son, John—styled John Treffry the younger—married Elizabeth, the second daughter of Nicholas Colan, Lord of Colan. John Treffry still held Treffry at Lanhydrock, but resided only at Place. Other than this, not a great deal is known about him. The Colans were also an ancient family which became extinct in the male line about the latter part of the 15th century. They were not of Celtic origin. The following lines by the historian William Camden may help you identify the Cornish surnames:

> By Tre, Ros, Pol, Lan, Caer, and Pen
> You may know most Cornishmen.

Tenth Generation

John Treffry and Elizabeth's son Roger married Maud, daughter of Richard Juyll of Bodmin in the third year of the reign of Richard II (1380). Richard Juyll was the founder of the elegant chapel of St Thomas the Martyr in the churchyard of Bodmin. In 1398 a jury found that Roger held some land in the parish of St Bruered by military service.

Eleventh Generation

Roger and Maud left a son and heir, also named Roger Treffry of Treffry in Lanhydrock and of Place in Fowey, who married a co-heir of Sir John Rosecassa of Rosecassa of St Just in Roseland, near Falmouth. As there were no heirs of this marriage, the estate went to his brother Thomas, the twelfth in line of inheritance. Thomas Treffry was a minor when his father died. When he came of age, he married Amicia (also called Avisia and Avisie), daughter and sole heiress of John Michelstowe of Rescaptwith in the county of Devonshire, by Margary, eldest daughter of Robert Boniface. By this marriage the Treffrys acquired a good deal of Boniface property. However, Place at Fowey had already been acquired when Elizabeth Boniface married an earlier Thomas Treffry five generations before. The Michelstowe family became extinct later.

In the year 1433 Thomas was appointed Collector of Customs for the Port of Plymouth and the County of Cornwall. Fifteenth-century references to the Treffry family can be found in the card file of the Society of Genealogists in London. References continue through the 18th century with a very few in the 19th century. Altogether, there were over 250 listings in this card file under 'Treffry'.

Twelfth Generation (Thirteenth in Line of Inheritance)

Thomas, the son of Thomas Treffry and Amicia Michelstowe Treffry, married Elizabeth, daughter of John Colyn of Helland. As early as the time of Richard II, *c.* 1377, the Colyns were of Boscarne and of Helland. Helland is about two and a half miles north of Bodmin. There is a bond of £100 in the Treffry archives pertaining to the marriage of Thomas Treffry and Elizabeth Colyn, granting part of the manor of Penvrane to them and to the heirs of their body, dated 25 Henry VI (1447) at Bodmin. This property still belongs to the Treffry estate.

Thomas Treffry's wife, Elizabeth Colyn, is credited with saving Place and much of Fowey from the French in 1457. The background of the situation that caused the French to attack Fowey started about 100 years before, during the warlike and troublesome reign of Edward III, father of Edward, the Black Prince. The port of Fowey at that time had 'sixty talle shippes of Warre'. This port contributed to the siege of Calais 47 warships, manned by 770 mariners, which was the greatest number contributed by any port in the kingdom except perhaps Great Yarmouth. Edward III granted commissions to the chief commanders of the Fowey ships to take French prizes during his wars with the French nation. In a few years the Fowey men grew immensely rich and formidable by taking French prizes. By force of arms the Fowey men would enter many ports of France and take all the ships they could, burning those they had to leave. When French prizes grew scarce they would turn pirate and take, plunder and destroy all ships that they could regardless of the country of ownership. This practice continued for about 100 years.

In July of 1457 the French invaded in retaliation; they sacked and partially burned Fowey by arrangement of Jean, the King of France. The French marine soldiers and seamen approached the south-west end of Fowey where they killed all persons they met, and set fire to the houses, burning half of them to the ground. The women, children and weaker people fled for safety into the hills.

At the time of this attack, Thomas Treffry was at Court, where he was Chamberlain to King Henry VI. Elizabeth Colyn Treffry, his wife, with the help of the strongest men at Fowey, fortified themselves in the mansion house, Place, where they stoutly opposed the assaults of the Frenchmen. The attack lasted so long that all the missiles and ammunition at Place were exhausted, without driving away the assailants. As a last effort, Dame Treffry led her people to the top of the house where they stripped off the lead which covered the

Elizabeth Treffry routs French raiders at Place, 1457

roof and melted it in large cauldrons brought up for the purpose. They then kept up a continual rain of molten liquid on to the heads of the Frenchmen below. This method of warfare soon proved successful. The Frenchmen quickly gave up the attack and fled, completely routed. While the engagement was going on at Place, the French sailors still in the town were plundering the houses that had not been burned. Eventually, fearing an uprising of people from the country-side, the rest of the Frenchmen hastily left.

John Leland, a 16th-century historian, later wrote 'Thomas Trevry builded a right fair and strong embatelid tour in his house, and embatelling all the waulles of the house, in a manner, made it a castelle and unto this day it is the glorie of the town building in Faweye'.

Richard Nevil, Earl of Warwick, Lord High Admiral of England, was persuaded to grant new commissions for privateering, and for taking French ships. Consequently, in a few years the residents of Fowey began to repair and rebuild their town with the wealth they gained from this activity. After the siege of Place, Thomas Treffry paid part of the cost of building a block-house to protect the harbour. This is now called Fowey Outer Castle, or St Catherine's. Another square tower or block-house was built about a quarter of a mile in, on the west side, with a big chain attached that crossed the harbour to a similar block-house near Polruan.

Thomas Treffry and the Earl of Warwick almost entirely rebuilt St Fimbarrus church and its tower. Thomas also built two large Gothic houses for his sons in the centre of Fowey, one of which was later demolished, and the other became the *King of Prussia* inn. These houses were enriched with many arches, oriel windows, coats of arms, splendid cornices and plaster work in the angles of the vaulted ceilings. They were built of stone from the same quarries that furnished materials for his rebuilding of Place and repairing the church and tower.

According to record in the De Banco Rolls, 15th Edward IV Easter, M.126, Thomas Treffry had been appointed Groom of the Chamber to King Henry VI and had a grant of the collectorship of the King's Customs and Subsidies in the Port of Fowey, 1439. He also served at court during the reign of Edward IV. Thomas Treffry died in 1475, on 20 January.

Thirteenth Generation

Thomas and his wife Elizabeth had three sons, John, William and Thomas, as well as two daughters, Janet and Jane. The two daughters doubtless led quieter lives than their brothers. Jane, the younger daughter, married John Becket, Esq., of Cartuther in Cornwall. The Becket family became extinct before 1620.

Janet, the elder daughter, married John Trevanion of Carryhayes in 1483. The Caerhays Castle one sees today on Veryan Bay some nine miles south and west of St Austell replaced the old original manor house early in the 19th century, and is not open to the public, although on certain occasions the beautiful gardens can be seen. The Trevanions, like the Treffrys, are a very ancient Celtic family with a remarkable and romantic history. An Elizabeth Trevanion nursed Charles I. Another Trevanion lady, Sophia, was a friend of Dr. Johnson. The name Trevanion comes from 'Tref' and 'Enion', a personal name. Together they mean 'homestead of Enion', the Celtic owner.

The Caerhays property had come to the Trevanions through marriage with an heiress of Arundell at a very early period. *The Byrons and Trevanions* by A. L. Rowse gives a very interesting duo-biography and history of the Trevanion and Byron families and their connections over the years which eventually produced Lord Byron of 19th-century fame. It was most often Trevanion women marrying a Byron, thus submerging the Trevanion name in the marriage. However, there were many men who carried the Trevanion name with distinction over the years. Sir Hugh Trevanion was said to have been knighted at Bosworth Field. Sir Charles

Trevanion, a loyalist during the Civil War, lost his son during it. A Richard Trevanion was a distinguished naval officer. Some Trevanion men were sea captains. However, the male line of the elder branch of this ancient family became extinct about 1768. There are monuments to the Trevanions in St Michael's parish church.

At the death of the elder Thomas Treffry in 1475 he was succeeded in the family estates by his eldest son, John, who also became executor of his will. He was fourteenth in line of inheritance. John was later sued by his mother for recovery of her dower of a third part of the manors of Tregnyed and Treffry in Lanhydrock. Litigiousness was a Cornish trait.

In January of 1476 it is recorded that an agreement between John Treffry and William Mohun granted free passage forever to all Treffrys on ferries to Bodinnick and Polruan from Fowey. In 1962 while being a guest at Place in Fowey, I was introduced by Anne Treffry to the ferry attendants as a 'Treffry cousin', and so crossed Fowey Harbour free of charge because of a privilege granted almost 500 years before!

John Treffry and his brothers, William and Thomas, together with the Arundells, Edgcumbs, and Nanfans, were among the Cornish gentry who supported the Lancastrians in the War of the Roses. Richard III confiscated all their lands and possessions, and drove them into exile in Brittany. On 7 August 1485, the three brothers returned to England with the Earl of Richmond and fought in his company at the Battle of Bosworth Field. Soon after Henry Tudor was established on the throne, he knighted John Treffry and granted supporters to the Treffry coat of arms, together with other honours and benefits, and restored to them all their previous lands and possessions. On 4 March 1485-6, Henry VII granted to Sir John Treffry in tail male the manor or lordship of Rode Langham (Redelaghan) in Somerset and Wiltshire, also the manor or lordship of Launden in the County of Bucks, which were in the hands of the King by reason of the attainder of John Lord Zouche who had supported the claim of King Richard III in the late war. Sir John was much involved in public affairs throughout his lifetime. Among other responsibilities, he was several times Sheriff of Cornwall between 1482-1500

Sir John Treffry married Anna, daughter of Sir Hugh Luccorn of Stockley Luccorn, Devon. There were no children of this marriage. Sir John died in 1501 (16th Henry VII), and his will dated 24 June 1500 was proved on 19 February 1501. He left numerous legacies, including one to the church of St Fimbarrus. His estates devolved on his brother William.

William Treffry, the fifteenth in line of inheritance, was like his brother, Sir John, active in public affairs and greatly favoured by King Henry VII. The King granted to William for life the Offices of Surveyor of Customs and Subsidies within the City of London, a very lucrative appointment. William was also an Usher of the Chamber of the Office of 'Controllers of the tunnage of Tynne' for the counties of Devon and Cornwall, and had custody of the gaol of Lostwithiel. He became an Usher of the King's Chamber in 1485. On 27 January 1489 he was granted in tail male forever the manors of Pedington, Avenscourt and Wike in Gloucestershire for services rendered at great expense. These manors had been forfeited by John Kendate for treason. In 1500-1501 William served as High Sheriff of Cornwall.

William Treffry married Margaret (parentage unknown), and died childless in 1504. His will was proved on 25 November 1504. As can be seen from this will, which is held by the Public Record Office in London, William died a very wealthy man. (*See* will in Chapter 4.) It appears from this will that William continued the rebuilding of Place which his father had started in 1457. The tomb of Purbeck marble with images of himself, his wife, and his brother, that he had instructed in his will to be erected was not created. In its place in St Fimbarrus church in Fowey is a large flat stone with pictures of three men scratched in it. A photograph of this stone can be seen in the plate section of this book.

William was succeeded by his brother Thomas, third son of Thomas Treffry and Elizabeth Colyn Treffry, and sixteenth in line of inheritance. Very little of historical interest has been recorded about this younger Thomas except that he was a soldier, supported the Lancastrian cause, and fought at Bosworth Field. But he is of notable importance in this family chronicle as it was he with his wife Janet, daughter and heir of William Dawe of Plymouth, Devon, who continued the male line of the family by producing three sons. All three of these sons were named in their Uncle William's will in 1504.

Thomas survived his brother William by only five years, dying in 1509. By the end of the 15th century predominantly Celtic-speaking Cornwall was being gradually absorbed into English life. Over the years members of old Cornish families had been serving in Parliament, bearing arms and rendering various services to their English King. The Treffrys were outstanding among them.

Fourteenth Generation (Seventeenth in Line of Inheritance)

Thomas, the eldest son and heir of Thomas and Janet Dawe Treffry, was prominent in his time in public affairs both in Cornwall and in London, even as his uncles, Sir John and William, had been. Employed under the crown he devised and built St Mawes Castle to protect the entrance to Falmouth Harbour. St Mawes Castle or fort was one of a series of castles or forts ordered to be built by Henry VIII between 1539-45 to protect England from invasion from the Continent. St Mawes is one of a pair, as Pendennis Castle on the opposite side guards the entrance to the estuary of the River Fal.

St Mawes Castle is strategically located adjacent to the water of the English Channel. It is protected on the land side by a ditch, gatehouse and drawbridge. Built of native shale and granite, it is four storeys high. Designed in a clover-leaf plan, the heart of the castle is a circular keep that rises above three semi-circular bastions designed to hold guns. The entrance is on the first floor, with the kitchen and mess room below. The building is relatively small and compact, adequate for the guns and the men required to man the fort. Soon after the forts were built the threat of invasion ended leaving the forts untested in warfare at that time.

St Mawes was, however, used for coastal defence in World War I. In 1920 it was declared an historic building.

On my first visit to Cornwall in 1950, Anne Treffry, with her deep interest in the history of Cornwall and the active part the Treffry family had played in it, introduced me to historic St Mawes Castle. I was impressed by its simplicity, its curvilinear plan, similar to early Celtic designs. The building was bare of furnishings. Anne Treffry called my attention to the fact that the fort had been planned and built almost 400 years before by Thomas Treffry, who was the King's clerk of works and the fort's first appointed captain. She also pointed out the verses in Latin that had been carved on the outside stone wall at the request of Thomas. They are given here in translation.

> O Henry! thy honour and praises shall always remain,
> May happy Cornwall rejoice in her chief,
> May Edward resemble his father in deeds and reputation,
> May the soul of King Henry VIII live for ever, who in the thirty-fourth year of his
> reign commanded this to be built.
> Honour to King Henry VIII, the most renowned of England, France, and Ireland.

As Anne Treffry and I stood in this ancient fort, my thoughts reflected back to World War II so recently ended. I asked myself, 'Had the world changed so very much in the past 400 years?' St Mawes had been built because of the fear of invasion. Four hundred years later Anne's two sons, along with other descendants of Thomas Treffry, were serving in the military forces to protect England again from invasion.

Besides being greatly involved with St Mawes, Thomas Treffry also sat on a commission constituted by Henry VIII to inquire into the abuses of the monasteries as Henry VIII wanted evidence to suppress them. Thomas was a commissioner for investigating the complaints made against the prior of Bodmin.

In 1547 when Edward VI succeeded to the throne, he commissioned Thomas Treffry of Fowey, captain of the King's Majesty's Fortress of St Mawes, ordering him to 'kill, slay, sink, burn and destroy all the enemies of the Republik'. Under Henry VIII and Edward VI, Thomas was in charge of superintendence and outfitting government ships from Fowey and Falmouth. As he remained employed under the crown, he was greatly involved in public affairs. He sat in Parliament for Cornwall in the first Parliament of Queen Mary, 1553. However, being opposed to her marriage to King Philip of Spain, he had to flee the country, remaining a political refugee until Mary was forced from her throne in 1558, losing many of his extensive estates.

In 1506 Thomas Treffry married Elizabeth, daughter of John Killigrew of Penryn, by Maud, daughter and co-heir of John Petit of Ardevora. The marriage settlement was 29 Sept. 21 Henry VII. The following document relates to this settlement.

1 March 1548/9
3 Edward VI

John Kyllygrewe of Arwennek esquire, son & heir of John Killygrewe formerly of Penryn esq. decd, after reciting an indenture made between Thomas TREFFRY the elder, esq. deceased, and the said John Kyllygrewe, 'patrem meum, of covenants upon the marriage intended between Thomas TREFFRY, junior, esq. then son & heir apparent of the said Thomas TREFFRY the elder and Elizabeth, one of the daughters of the said John Kyllygrewe his father, dated 29 Sept. 21 Henry VII 1505.

In accordance with and by the way of implementing such covenants, gives, grants, and confirms to the said Thomas TREFFRY the son all those messuages, mills, lands, tenements, rents, reversions & services with weirs, leats & etc. in Rowcok in the County of Cornwall, habendum to the sd. T. TREFFRY and the heirs of bodies of the same Thomas and the said Elizabeth (formerly his wife, but now dec., lawfully begotten forever), Warrants the same against all people.

William Lowre [Lower] of Saynt Wenowe, esq. & John Bere, Gent. attorneys to give seisin.

[was missing from seal-tag]   per me Johannem Kyllegrewe'

In dorso: Certificate of livery of seisin
Attested by: William Carnsuyowe the younger
                John Tregodyck
                Wyllyam Swetland
                John Smythe the yongeste
                Thomas Collyffords
                Thomas Woffe

Docketed: Rouck in St. Kew   *(From the Treffry Collection,*
                                              County Record Office, Truro)
[Damaged by vermin & damp.]

By the marriage settlement the Treffrys acquired the manor of Rooke in the parish of St Kew. Elizabeth Killigrew brought the family a royal line of descent from Isabella, daughter of King John, who married Sir Richard Fitz-Ivor, as well as from King Edward I (*see* Chapter 2).

Of all the families that married into the Treffry family, the Killigrews may have had the most romantic and colourful history. Over the centuries they contributed to the history of their country with diplomats, warriors, courtiers, writers, poets, and Oxford scholars. Some distinguished members of the family are buried in Westminster Abbey. The Killigrews were originally from Killigrew in St Erme parish (five miles north of Truro). They have been traced to the reign of Henry III (1216-72). They held this property until 1636. The tradition is that they were descended from a natural son of Richard, Earl of Cornwall and King of the Romans by Joan de Valletort. In the manuscript history of the Killigrew family, their arms were said to have been given by that prince to Ralph de Killigrew, the first of the family mentioned in the manuscript.

The Killigrews acquired Arwennack near Falmouth Harbour by Simon Killigrew marrying the heiress of that house and name, Jane, daughter of Robert, Lord of Arwennack, sometime in the reign of Richard II (1377-1399). The Killigrew arms are argent an eagle displayed with two heads Sable, a border of the second bezanty. The crest is a demi-lion Sable, charged on the body with three bezants in pale. The arms of the city of Falmouth were taken from the Killigrew arms, being argent, an eagle displayed, with two heads Sable, with a castle on each wing, and a rock with a pole on it on the body. A major street in Falmouth is named after the Killigrews.

From Simon Killigrew is descended Elizabeth, who married Thomas Treffry. She was a sister of Sir John Killigrew, the first Captain and Governor of Pendennis Castle that John Treffry had helped him build on John Killigrew's own property in the time of Henry VIII. Sir John Killigrew was heir to the Killigrew estate, worth £6,000 per year. Arwennack Manor House in the 16th century was said to be the 'finest and most costly' house in Cornwall with many beautifully decorated rooms. It was built like a castle and surrounded by a wall with lawns continuing down to the edge of the sea. Captain John Killigrew, who died in 1567, added to the manor house. In 1646 during the Civil War the manor house was set fire by the royalist troops from Pendennis in order to keep it from falling into the hands of the Cromwellian forces.

Arwennack is said to be an old Cornish name meaning 'beloved still cove' or 'upon the marsh'. The Arwennack property is thought to have extended from the Falmouth area to the mouth of the Helford River, five or six miles along the coast. The Killigrews remained at Arwennack from 1385 for over 400 years. During that period they governed Pendennis most of the time. They served at court during the reigns of Henry VIII, Elizabeth I, James I, James II, Charles I, Charles II, and William III. They were loyal, able and trusted servants. There is a brass in the Gluvais church near Penryn, to Thomas Killigrew and his two wives, Joan and Elizabeth, and their children, dated to the late 15th century. Thomas is wearing a long, handsome, fur-trimmed robe.

John Killigrew, the first Captain of Pendennis, is represented by a brass in St Budock church near Falmouth. He is dressed as a warrior in plate armour. In 1551 this John with Francis Godolphin surveyed the Islands of Scilly and built a fort there under the direction of Henry VIII. He was also Sheriff of Cornwall.

Sir Walter Raleigh, on his return from his unfortunate voyage to Guiana in 1595, landed at Falmouth and was entertained at Arwennack. Raleigh was greatly impressed by the natural situation of Falmouth Harbour and was responsible for instigating the building of additional houses, as there was only one other than Arwennack at the time.

Fifteenth Generation

Thomas Treffry and Elizabeth Killigrew Treffry were parents of John, Sibyll and Agnes. Sibyll Treffry married into the Gayer (Geares) family of Trembraise, one of the fine old families of Cornwall. Her sister, Agnes Treffry, married William Lower of St Winnow, who was originally from Polscoe. The Lowers trace their family 13 generations before 1620. Over the years they had married into the Moyle, Tresithney, Upton, and Reskymer families. William and Agnes Treffry Lower were parents of two sons, Thomas, who was baptized 27 January 1543, and Edward, who married Mary, daughter of Humfry Nicoll of Tremeure.

(*See* pedigree of Hambly, Billing, and Lower families in Chapter 4.) This chart shows that Agnes Treffry and William Lower were the great-grandparents of Thomas Lower, M.D., born in 1633 and who died in 1720, who became a Quaker. He was a nephew of Loveday Billing Hambly, who was considered a Quaker 'saint' of Cornwall. Thomas Lower was a medical doctor, practicing in London when Loveday died. A few months after her death he returned to Cornwall to visit her grave, as he had been as devoted to her as to his own mother. While he was taking care of legal matters pertaining to the property she had left 'in trust for Friends', he was arrested and put into Launceston gaol. He was kept there for almost two years with other Quakers. After he was released he returned to his wife and children and to his medical practice in London. Many years later Dr. Lower again returned to Cornwall where he gave Tregangeeves burial ground to the Quakers. One marker states 'The Land For This Burial Ground Was Given By Richard Edgecumbe Esquire of Mount Edgecumbe Park to Thomas Lower By Deed Dated the 6th. Day of 8th. Month 1706 And Transferred By Thomas Lower To Trustees By Deed Dated 12th. of 1st. Month 1711'.

When a road was cut through this burial ground, soil was thrown up on both sides of the road covering the earliest graves of the 17th century. All one sees now is a rolling hillside blanketed in green. A marker there reads, 'Society of Friends [Quakers] site of Tregangeeves Burial Ground 1664-1965'. A marker to Thomas Lower states, 'THOMAS LOWER, Became a member of the Society of Friends After Visiting GEORGE FOX When He Was Imprisoned In Pendennis Castle Falmouth'.

John, the son of Thomas and Elizabeth Killigrew Treffry and brother of Agnes Treffry Lower, became the 18th in line of inheritance of the Treffry estates on the death of his father on 24 January 1563. In the manuscript history of the Treffry family he is described as the eldest son. However, on the lineage chart no other sons are listed, and if there were any I have not been able to identify them.

Elizabeth I was in the fifth year of her reign when John came into his inheritance. These were exciting years to be alive in England and especially to be living in Cornwall and Devon. The first 10 years of Protestant Queen Elizabeth's reign (1558-1568) England lived peacefully within the Anglo-Spanish alliance. However, in 1568 John Hawkins, one of the Queen's officers, was fired on when his ship was in a Spanish port. When his brother back in Plymouth heard a rumour that John had been killed he demanded from his government that the cargo be seized from Spanish ships that were protecting themselves from French piracy in the safety of Saltash and Fowey Harbours. The ships contained £400,000, a loan from Genoese bankers on the way to pay the Spanish troops fighting in the Netherlands. With the approval of the government, orders were given under the guise of friendship and for the protection of the money to unload it. Mr. Champernowne and Mr. Killigrew were in charge. Champernowne thought this great treasure should belong to his Queen. The officials of the government thought so, too. Then he asked government officials for permission to have John Treffry assist in the commission of removing the treasure from the

Spanish ships in Fowey Harbour. He knew that John Treffry would be willing and co-operative.

Spanish gold comes to Fowey

As the treasure was unloaded from the ships by the Spaniards themselves, every case was opened in their presence and in front of the officials of Fowey and some Fowey merchants. Each bag from the cases was weighed on a merchant beam, then numbered and its contents recorded in a book. The Spaniards, thinking their treasure was being taken to safety, willingly carried it up the steep hill to Place, the home of John Treffry. There 32 cases were locked and sealed. Several of the Spaniards stood watch with the Cornishmen. Fifty pounds were taken from the treasure to provide for the sailors while they were in the town. Later Champernowne took the treasure by land to the Tower of London. For this long trip by land he had the protection of 50 horsemen, 50 footmen, and artillery. Thus began the age of Anglo-Spanish feuding. (From A. L. Rowse, *Tudor Cornwall*.)

John Treffry was the Sheriff of Cornwall in 1579 and High Sheriff in 1583. In 1585 the Twenty Years War with Spain began. Historical evidence indicates that John was active in the military in the mature years of his life. The Muster Roll of 1569 shows that John Treffry was the best armed man in Cornwall with a light horse, two pairs of corselets, 10 pair almayn rivets, 20 pikes, four long bows, four sheaves of arrows, three harquebuses, and three halberds. Recalling the deeds of his great-grandmother, Elizabeth Colyn Treffry, in defending Place and the people of Fowey, he recognised the great need for a well-armed and trained household. Cornwall at this time was sparsely populated and being remote as the most south-westerly county, it was the most vulnerable part of England in those troublesome times. Therefore, the fortifications of St Mawes and Pendennis with other forts along the coast were strengthened. Sir Walter Raleigh was in supreme command as Lord Warden of the Stannaries and Lord Lieutenant.

During the course of this active public life John Treffry was twice married. His first wife was Jane, daughter of Sir Reginald Mohun of Hall in Lanteglos, across the river from Fowey. The Mohuns, who came from Somersetshire in the reign of Edward III, had acquired considerable property in Cornwall by the marriage with a Fitzwilliam heiress. Hall, Bodinnick and Tolcarne by Fowey were theirs. However, only Hall and Bodinnick were used as early residences. Living so close to Fowey, the Mohuns and Treffrys had undoubtedly known each other for almost two centuries. The free passage on the ferry between Fowey and Bodinnick had been agreed upon by their families about a hundred years before the marriage of John and Jane. As John courted Jane he probably made many trips by ferry across the Fowey River. Being a gentleman, he was surely grateful to his great-uncle, Sir John Treffry, for the free passage agreement.

'Hall' in Cornish means moor. John and Jane undoubtedly spent many hours strolling on the then-famous walk at Hall, cut in the side of a steep hill bordered on both sides with trimmed hedges and planted with beautiful and fragrant flowers. The walk was wide enough for five or six to stroll side by side, and was about half a mile long. There were turnings off the path here and there, and places for the walkers to stop and rest. Summer-houses along the way gave protection from sudden Cornish showers, or were used for recreation and refreshment. At the far end of the walk one could see ocean ships coming and going on the Channel, as well as the local barges and fishing boats cruising along the coast. And always, there was the view over Fowey haven to Fowey, where Place stands on a hillside overlooking the church and the town.

At the foot of the walk the ground had been levelled to make a bowling green covered with sand to soak up the frequent rains. During their courtship the young couple, besides strolling on the beautiful walk and bowling on the green, undoubtedly went horseback riding over the hills and moors, never out of sight of the harbour or the sea. It was a very romantic place for a courtship.

Besides the property inherited from the Fitzwilliams, the Mohuns later purchased the Boconnoc estate from the Russell family. Other property was acquired by the Mohuns through marriage with co-heiresses of Courtney, Earl of Devonshire and Reskymer.

John and Jane Mohun Treffry were parents of only one child, a daughter called Lora, who married Trenwith of Trenwith.

The manor house at Hall came to an early end as it was destroyed during the Civil War.

The Mohun family became extinct in the male line with the death of a William Mohun, Esq., last of that ancient name and family. There is a monument to him dated 1737 in the parish church of St Ewe, about six miles south of St Austell.

The romantic courtship and marriage of John and Jane Mohun Treffry came to a sad end with the death of the young bride and mother. John, left a young widower with an infant daughter, married again. His second marriage was to Emblen, daughter and co-heiress of John Tresithney. There were 16 children of this marriage, nine sons and seven daughters. The Treffrys of Place and Canada are descended from this marriage.

The Celtic Tresithneys married early into ancient families of Cornwall as is shown by their arms, quartered by Treffry, Beville, Trefusis, and others such as the Lord Clinton family, Arundells of Lanherne and Beville of Gwarnicke in St Allen. The Tresithneys had also married heiresses of Bossoham and Rostylian. There is no question of the antiquity of the Tresithney family as there was a very ancient chapel called Tresithney in St Columb Major. It is now gone and the adjacent cemetery has become a garden and orchard. In later times the Tresithneys were of Penryn. The arms of Tresithney are: Arg: a chevron Sable between three roses, Gules.

John Treffry died on 28 January 1590. His tombstone in the St Fimbarrus church, Fowey, is evidence that he was a soldier as was his father before him. John's effigy is represented there in a coat of mail with his spurs on, with a long sword on one side and a short one on the other. This flat stone is on the wall facing the Treffry pews.

Sixteenth Generation

John and Emblen Tresithney's first child was a daughter. Their second child was a son named William in the 16th generation of the family and 19th in line of inheritance. He succeeded his father in 1590, aged 31, as head of the family and owner of Place and Treffry in Lanhydrock among other holdings. However, Rooke in St Kew, which had come to the Treffrys through his grandmother, Elizabeth Killigrew Treffry, had been conveyed in 1589 to three of William's younger brothers, John, Mathew and Tresithney, to provide for their maintenance. John and Tresithney died without heirs, leaving Mathew in sole possession of the manor of Rooke.

A contemporary and close friend of William Treffry was the Oxford-educated and very erudite Richard Carew of Antony, who wrote the *Survey of Cornwall,* first published in 1602, twice reprinted in the 1700s and again in 1811. Lastly it was edited in 1952 for publication in 1953 and 1969 by the historian F. E. Halliday. The distinguished English naturalist and one of my favourite authors, William Henry Hudson (1841–1922), considered Carew's *Survey of Cornwall* 'the one very good book ever written by a Cornishman excluding living authors'. It is considered a minor English classic, a guide to the county which beautifully describes life in Cornwall in Elizabethan times. It is a unique record of Carew's life and that of his friends and their involvement in the political, economic, and social events in the age of Elizabeth.

William Treffry, being a close friend of Carew's, was asked for help in proof-reading the manuscript and making necessary corrections before publication. Another who helped in this way was Sir Walter Raleigh, Carew's cousin. William Treffry must have had a fine education to have been called on to proof-read and correct so important a manuscript, a publication that has stood the test of time.

In 1581 Carew was appointed a justice of the peace, which office required that he travel into mid-Cornwall. While on these duties he would visit the homes of his friends. These included the splendid home of the Treffrys overlooking Fowey, described by Carew as 'a faire and ancient house, castle-wise builded'. In 1584 both Richard Carew and William Treffry served in Parliament. It is very possible that William Treffry joined Carew at Antony to continue the 200 miles to London together overland by horseback on the 'uneasy roads' of mire or stones.

While William Treffry and Richard Carew served in Parliament they were very aware that troublesome times were developing between England and Spain. Besides being concerned for England, both men were especially worried about Cornwall as they realised how extremely vulnerable it was because of its strategic location in case of an attempted invasion of England by Spain. A sea power coming from Spain would reach the south coast of Cornwall first.

Because of the strategic location of Cornwall in the defence of England, the very capable Sir Walter Raleigh was appointed Lord Lieutenant General of Cornwall. The commanders and officers who served under him consisted of the local gentry, loyal and trusted, and well known to each other. They served as unpaid volunteers. They were expected to organise, to train, and to supply an efficient militia to repel any attempted invasion by the Spanish. Only when the threat of an invasion became imminent did Queen Elizabeth I furnish Cornwall with ordnance and ammunition. This added to what the local gentry had already supplied.

William Treffry was appointed Master of the Ordnance and his friend, Richard Carew, became Treasurer, serving directly under Lord Lieutenant Sir Walter Raleigh. As the threat of invasion by Spain intensified, both Treffry and Carew evidently felt they could better serve their country by aiding in defence of the south-west coast than by sitting in Parliament, so they remained in Cornwall to await the arrival of the Spanish Armada. The principal commanders and officers who served in Cornwall at this time were: (from *Survey of Cornwall*)

> *Lord Lieutenant General*: Sir Walter Raleigh
> *Deputy Lieutenants*: Sir Francis Godolphin, Sir Nicholas Parker, Sir Reynold Mohun, Peter Edgcumbe, Bernard Grenville, Christopher Harris, Richard Carew, or any three of them
> *Colonel General*: Sir Nicholas Parker
> *Marshal*: Bernard Grenville
> *Treasurer*: Richard Carew
> *Master of the Ordnance*: Will. Treffry
> *Colonel of the Horse*: John Arundell of Trerice
> *Sergeant Major*: Humphrey Parkes
> *Quarter Master*: William Carnsew
> *Provost Marshal*: John Harris
> *Sçout Master*: Otwell Hill
> *Corporals of the Field*: Osborne, Russell, Battenbury, Sled
> *Ammunition Master*: Leon. Blackdon
> *Trench Master*: Cooke

At the same time the forces of the shire were as follows:

Regiments	Com-panies	Number	Arm. Pikes	Muskets	Calivers	
Sir Fra. Godolphin	12	1,200	470	490	240	
Sir William Bevil	6	670	225	315	130	
Sir Reynold Mohun	6	600	200	210	190	
Bernard Grenville	10	1,000	370	390	240	
Richard Carew	5	500	170	300	30	For Cawsand Bay
Anthony Rous	6	760	270	320	170	
Charles Trevanion	5	500	180	190	130	
Will. Treffry	4	400	140	130	130	For Fowey
Sir Nic. Parker	2	200	60	80	60	For Pendennis
Hannibal Vivian	1	100	40	40	20	For St Mawes
Arthur Harris	1	100	40	40	20	For the Mount
Summa	58	6,030	2,165	2,535	1,330	

In retrospect, Carew felt that the gentry of Cornwall had exceeded its county's quota of men and supplies; that they had called up a greater number of men to fight, asking them to arm themselves beyond what the law required and sometimes beyond their ability to supply.

Sir Francis Drake, a year before the Armada, had brought back from Spain reports on the vast preparations being made for the invasion of England. His scouts continued the reports.

On 19 July 1588 the long-expected Spanish Armada was first sighted off the Scilly Isles south of the Cornish coast. It must have been a frightening sight to see the arrival of a fleet of 132 sailing ships in unbroken formation (one half supply ships and transports). They carried 21,621 soldiers and 8,065 seamen. Continuing along the Cornish coast this great fleet sailed past Land's End, the Lizard and the forts at Pendennis and St Mawes that were guarding the Falmouth Harbour. It was thought a landing might be attempted there. Earthworks had been built behind the beaches: beacons had been put on the hills in every parish; and all the forts built in King Henry VIII's time were well supplied and staffed. Overland messages could be sent by a system of foot-post or horseback that had been organised and was on the alert. The land defences were ready.

The excitement in the Cornish parishes must have been great as the Armada sailed the full length of the south coast. Fortunately, no landing was attempted at Falmouth. The Armada sailed on, passing Fowey Harbour in anticipation of making its landing at Plymouth. The rest is history.

William Treffry as Master of the Ordnance at the time of the Armada undoubtedly solicited the help of his brother Thomas in seeing that adequate supplies were wherever needed. If they were at lookout points guarding Fowey Harbour, their hearts probably jumped a beat as the great Armada passed. No one along the Cornish coast had ever seen such a large and spectacular array of ships in one collection.

The Cornish could not give up their vigilance even after the defeat of the Armada, for the Spanish, although no longer a great sea power, still hoped to invade England. It is quite evident from extant letters that William Treffry and his brother Thomas were employed by the government for quite some time to watch for Spanish and other ships along the coast and to report everything of a suspicious nature to Sir Robert Cecil, Elizabeth's chief minister. It is evident from letters that Thomas also acted as steward or overseer of some of Sir Robert Cecil's property or Duchy property in Cornwall.

In 1595 the Spanish made a surprise landing at Penzance. William Treffry on Cecil's orders was appointed a commissioner of the peace for his vigilance 'at the invasion of the Spaniards'. He had reported four Spanish warships scouting off the Cornish coast, picking up small boats to see what information they could find concerning the English fleet at Plymouth.

When Carew visited Fowey he gave credit to William Treffry for fortifying the town, and honoured him by saying that William was a gentleman who had devoted his rare gifts of learning, wisdom, and courage to the good of his country in many ways. He said that his notes were 'beholden to William's judicious corrections'. Carew also noted the antiquity of the Treffry tombstones in the churchyard—one was said to be 145 years old at the time.

A year after the Armada, on 3 April 1589, William married Ursula, daughter of William Tremayne. There was one son, John, and six daughters of this marriage. William died as a young man of 43 in 1603, a year before his mother, Emblen Tresithney Treffry, was buried at Fowey on 30 June 1604. William's death in 1603 was also the year that the colourful and exciting reign of Elizabeth came to an end. It was the period in time that saw the foundation of the British Empire; the blossoming of English sea power; the unparalleled literary outburst of writers such as Shakespeare, Spenser, Christopher Marlowe, Richard Carew, and others; and world explorations by Sir Francis Drake, who set out in 1576 to circumnavigate the world, reaching as far as the coast of California, and landing near San Francisco.

William and Thomas Treffry took an active part at this time in the glorious achievements of their country. They were polished and brilliant gentlemen, noted for their learning and statesmanship. With both serving in Parliament in London they certainly must have had numerous occasions to meet Queen Elizabeth.

Before moving on to the next generation, additional information should be noted about William's brother Thomas and other brothers and sisters of this large family. William's brother, Thomas, was a Counsellor at Law, one of three in the county. He served in Parliament and was three times Mayor of Lostwithiel. His portrait hangs in the dining-room at Place. He and his wife, Katherine Hellyer, had only two daughters and no sons.

It has been noted that both William and Thomas distinguished themselves in public affairs. But it is the third brother, Mathew, from whom the Treffrys of Place and the emigrants to Canada descend. Mathew does not seem to have made a name for himself in public service. At the time of the Armada he would have been 22 years old, so perhaps he was called upon to help his brother William in protecting the coast. From Mathew's will (*see* Chapter 6), we know that he lived at Rooke in St Kew. His five children are named in this will. Four or them were baptized in St Kew church; only William, his second son, was baptized at Fowey. This William is the ancestor of the Treffrys who came into Canada in the 19th century (*see* Part IV, Chapter 11).

Mathew's sister, Anne, married Edward Hearle of Prideaux. They were parents of Charles Hearle, who became a chaplain to Oliver Cromwell. Mathew's sister, Martha, married Thomas Peter and became the mother of Hugh Peter, to whom Chapter 5 is devoted. A younger brother of Mathew's named Abel, born in 1577, held an M.A. degree from All Souls College, Oxford, and had some of his poetry published. Several other members of this large and outstanding family of 16 children of John and Emblen Tresithney Treffry deserve of special research.

Chapter Four

EARLY TREFFRY WILLS AND GENEALOGICAL CHARTS

IT IS NECESSARY to keep the thread of this lengthy Treffry chronicle, covering hundreds of years, in an understandable order. To accomplish this the direct line of the Treffry family from the earliest records through the 1500s is included in this chapter in chart form. These charts are the records kept by the Treffry family of Place. Anne Treffry graciously gave me permission to copy them. Her granddaughter, Peregrine Treffry, assisted me in 1980 in copying and checking our copies for accuracy.

The original charts were quite colourful, with illustrations of the many coats of arms of the families who married into the Treffry family. A similar chart with coats of arms and some family history was prepared by Beryl Evelyn Blanch Treffry, daughter of Spencer Thornton Treffry, who wrote a family chronicle in 1891, which has not been published. A copy of her chart was sent to me by her nephew, Harry Lysons, and from these charts Alice Wesche prepared the coats of arms included here.

Continuing charts are included in Part II, Part III, and Part IV, bringing the family's history up to date.

See p. 40 for key

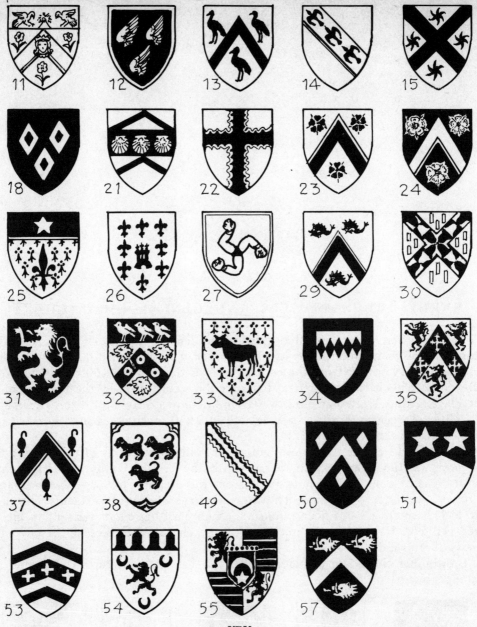

KEY

FAMILY TREES

Note: names of persons and places spelt as in original

1. Treffrys of Place, Fowey

TREFFRY de TREFFRY = *c.* 1100
in parish Linkinhorne
Sans date
County Cornub.

Roger TREFFRY de TREFFRY = *c.* 1140
in parish Linkinhorne
County Cornub. Sans date

John TREFFRY de TREFFRY = Ibatt, da. of Sir Nicholas Le Flamank
in parish Linkinhorne, *c.* 1179, of Treglothnow, Knight
County Cornub.

John TREFFRY, lord of the manor of = Johanna, da. and heir of John de
TREFFRY in parish of Lanhydrock Kelligrewe of Arwinnic,
County Cornub. Dead in 1283. County Cornub., Esq.
11th Edward I *c.* 1210 ?

Roger TREFFRY de TREFFRY = Senata, da. and heir of Peter   Richard TREFFRY
in parish Lanhydrock Polgreen of Polgreen, Esq.   1st son.
County Cornub. Son and *c.* 1240   Dead 1283.
heir. Living 1283   11th Edw. I

Thomas TREFFRY of TREFFRY = Elizabeth, da., co-heir of Robert
in parish Lanhydrock and of Boniface of Piworthy, County
PLACE in parish FOWEY, County Devon. *c.* 1280
Cornub.

Thomas TREFFRY of TREFFRY in parish = Alice, da. and co-heir of Serle of
Lanhydrock and of PLACE in parish Fowey, Penverane, Esq., *c.* 1310
County Cornub.

Sir John TREFFRY of TREFFRY in parish = Joanna, 2nd da. and co-heir of John Le Petit of
Lanhydrock and of PLACE, FOWEY, Knight Trangwainton
and Banneret. He was knighted by the King's
own hand on the battlefield of CRESSY
26 Aug. 1346

ctd

41

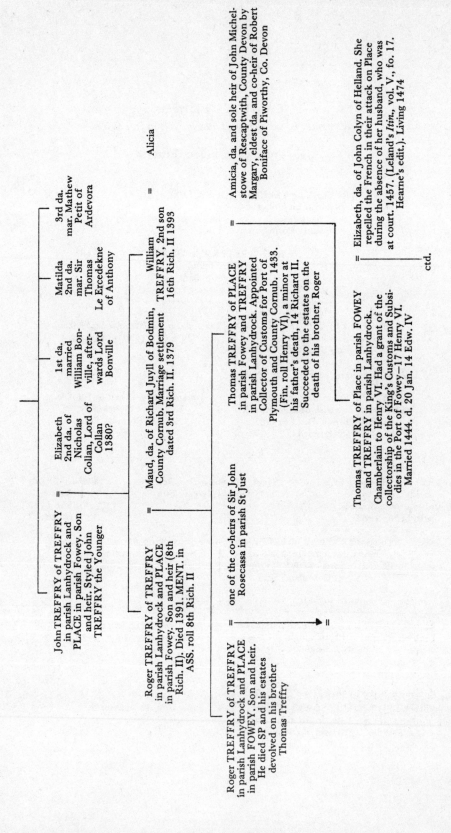

John TREFFRY of TREFFRY in parish Lanhydrock and PLACE in parish Fowey. Son and heir. Styled John TREFFRY the Younger

=

Elizabeth 2nd da. of Nicholas Collan, Lord of Collan 1380?

1st da. married William Bonville, afterwards Lord Bonville

Matilda 2nd da. mar. Sir Thomas Le Ercedekne of Anthony

3rd da. mar. Mathew Petit of Ardevora

Alicia = William TREFFRY, 2nd son 16th Rich. II 1393

Roger TREFFRY of TREFFRY in parish Lanhydrock and PLACE in parish Fowey. Son and heir (8th Rich. II). Died 1391. MENT. in ASS. roll 8th Rich. II

=

Maud, da. of Richard Juyll of Bodmin, County Cornub. Marriage settlement dated 3rd Rich. II. 1379

Roger TREFFRY of TREFFRY in parish Lanhydrock and PLACE in parish FOWEY. Son and heir. He died SP and his estates devolved on his brother Thomas Treffry

= one of the co-heirs of Sir John Rosecassa in parish St Just

→ =

Thomas TREFFRY of PLACE in parish Fowey and TREFFRY in parish Lanhydrock. Appointed Collector of Customs for Port of Plymouth and County Cornub. 1433. (Fin. roll Henry VI), a minor at his father's death, 14 Richard II. Succeeded to the estates on the death of his brother, Roger

=

Amicia, da. and sole heir of John Michelstowe of Rescaptwith, County Devon by Margary, eldest da. and co-heir of Robert Boniface of Piworthy, Co. Devon

Thomas TREFFRY of Place in parish FOWEY and TREFFRY in parish Lanhydrock. Had a grant of the collectorship of the King's Customs and Subsidies in the Port of Fowey—17 Henry VI. Married 1444. d. 20 Jan. 14 Edw. IV

=

Elizabeth, da. of John Colyn of Helland. She repelled the French in their attack on Place during the absence of her husband, who was at court, 1457. (Leland's *Itin.*, vol. V., fo. 17. Hearne's edit.). Living 1474

ctd.

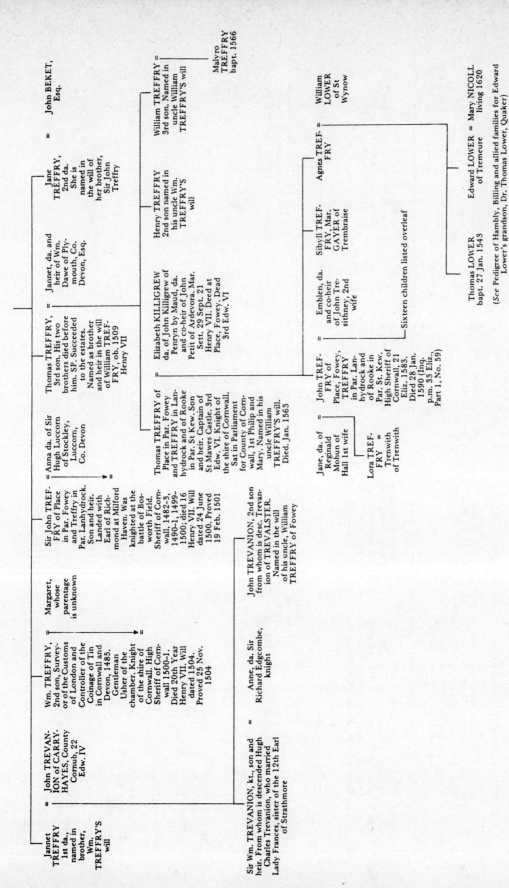

Jannet TREFFRY 1st da., named in brother, Wm. TREFFRY'S will

= John TREVANION of CARRY-HAYES, County Cornub, 22 Edw. IV

Wm. TREFFRY, 2nd son, Surveyor of the Customs of London and Controller of the Coinage of Tin in Cornwall and Devon, 1485. Gentleman Usher of the chamber. Knight of the shire of Cornwall. High Sheriff of Cornwall 1500-1. Died 20th Year Henry VII. Will dated 1504. Proved 25 Nov. 1504

= Margaret, whose parentage is unknown

Sir John TREFFRY of Place in Par. Fowey and Treffry in Par. Lanhydrock. Son and heir. Landed with Earl of Richmond at Milford Haven. Was knighted at the battle of Bosworth Field. Sheriff of Cornwall, 1482-3, 1490-1, 1499-1500; died 16 Henry VII. Will dated 24 June 1500. Proved 19 Feb. 1501

= Anna da. of Sir Hugh Luccorn of Stockley, Luccorn, Co. Devon

Thomas TREFFRY, 3rd son. His two brothers died before him. SP. Succeeded to the estates. Named as brother and heir in the will of William TREF-FRY, ob. 1509 Henry VII

Jannet, da. and heir of Wm. Dawe of Plymouth, Co. Devon, Esq.

Jane TREFFRY, 2nd da. She is named in the will of her brother, Sir John Treffry

= John BEKET, Esq.

Thomas TREFFRY of Place in Par. Fowey and TREFFRY in Lanhydrock and of Rooke in Par. St. Kew. Son and heir. Captain of St Mawes Castle. 3rd Edw. VI. Knight of the shire of Cornwall. Sat in Parliament for County of Cornwall, 1st Philip and Mary. Named in his uncle William TREFFRY'S will. Died. Jan. 1563

= Elizabeth KILLIGREW da. of John Killigrew of Penryn by Maud, da. and co-heir of John Petit of Ardevora. Mar. Sett. 29 Sept. 21 Henry VII. Died at Place, Fowey. Dead 3rd Edw. VI

Henry TREFFRY 2nd son named in his uncle Wm. TREFFRY'S will

William TREFFRY = 3rd son. Named in uncle William TREFFRY'S will

Malvro TREFFRY bapt. 1566

John TREVANION, 2nd son from whom is desc. Trevanion of TREVALSTER. Named in the will of his uncle, William TREFFRY of Fowey

Sir Wm. TREVANION, kt., son and heir. From whom is descended Hugh Charles Trevanion, who married Lady Frances, sister of the 12th Earl of Strathmore

= Anne, da. Sir Richard Edgcombe, knight

John TREF-FRY of Place, Fowey, TREFFRY in Par. Lanhydrock and of Rooke in Par. St. Kew. High Sheriff of Cornwall, 21 Eliz. 1583. Died 28 Jan. 1590 (Inq. p.m. 33 Eliz. Part 1, No. 59)

= Emblen, da. and co-heir of John Tresithney, 2nd wife

Jane, da. of Reginald Mohun of Hall 1st wife

Lora TREF-FRY = Trenwith of Trenwith

Sibyll TREF-FRY. Mar. GAYER of Trembraise

Agnes TREF-FRY

= William LOWER of St Wynow

Sixteen children listed overleaf

Thomas LOWER bapt. 27 Jan. 1543

Edward LOWER = Mary NICOLL of Tremeure   living 1620

(See Pedigree of Hambly, Billing and allied families for Edward Lower's grandson, Dr. Thomas Lower, Quaker)

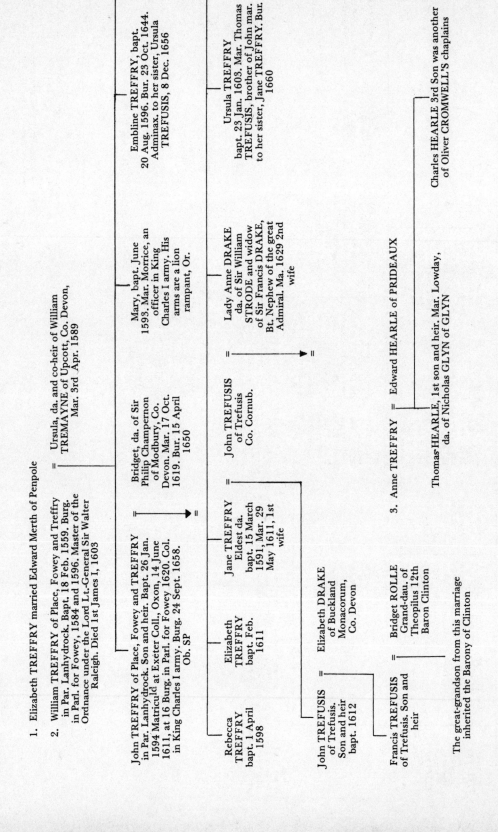

1. Elizabeth TREFFRY married Edward Merth of Penpole

2. William TREFFRY of Place, Fowey and Treffry = Ursula, da. and co-heir of William
   in Par. Lanhydrock. Bapt. 18 Feb. 1559. Burg.   TREMAYNE of Upcott, Co. Devon,
   in Parl. for Fowey, 1584 and 1596. Master of the   Mar. 3rd Apr. 1589
   Ordnance under the Lord Lt.-General Sir Walter
   Raleigh. Died 1st James I, 1603

Embline TREFFRY, bapt.
20 Aug. 1596. Bur. 23 Oct. 1644.
Adminax. to her sister, Ursula
TREFUSIS, 8 Dec. 1656

Ursula TREFFRY
bapt. 23 Jan. 1603. Mar. Thomas
TREFUSIS, brother of John mar.
to her sister, Jane TREFFRY. Bur.
1660

Mary, bapt. June
1593. Mar. Morrice, an
officer in King
Charles I army. His
arms are a lion
rampant, Or.

Lady Anne DRAKE
da. of Sir William
STRODE and widow
of Sir Francis DRAKE,
Bt. Nephew of the great
Admiral. Ma. 1629 2nd
wife

John TREFUSIS
of Trefusis
Co. Cornub.

Bridget, da. of Sir
Philip Champernon
of Modbury, Co.
Devon. Mar. 17 Oct.
1619. Bur. 15 April
1650

John TREFFRY of Place, Fowey and TREFFRY
in Par. Lanhydrock. Son and heir. Bapt. 26 Jan.
1594 Matricul'd at Exeter Coll., Oxon, 14 June
1611, at 16 Burg. in Parl. for Fowey 1620. Col.
in King Charles I army. Burg. 24 Sept. 1658.
Ob. SP

Jane TREFFRY
Eldest da.
bapt. 15 March
1591, Mar. 29
May 1611, 1st
wife

Elizabeth
TREFFRY
bapt. Feb.
1611

Rebecca
TREFFRY
bapt. 1 April
1598

3. Anne TREFFRY = Edward HEARLE of PRIDEAUX

Thomas HEARLE, 1st son and heir. Mar. Lowday,
da. of Nicholas GLYN of GLYN

Charles HEARLE 3rd Son was another
of Oliver CROMWELL'S chaplains

Elizabeth DRAKE
of Buckland
Monacorum,
Co. Devon

John TREFUSIS
of Trefusis.
Son and heir
bapt. 1612

Bridget ROLLE
Grand-dau. of
Theopilus 12th
Baron Clinton

Francis TREFUSIS
of Trefusis. Son and
heir

The great-grandson from this marriage
inherited the Barony of Clinton

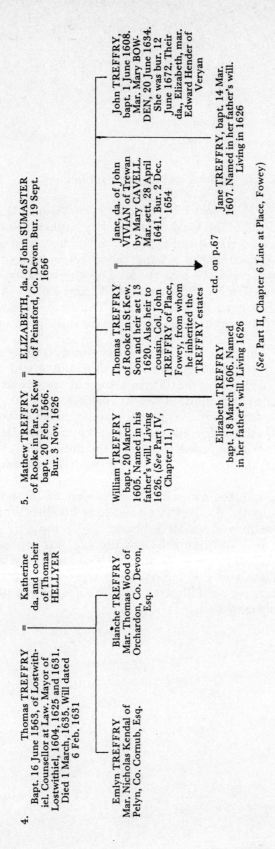

4. Thomas TREFFRY Bapt. 16 June 1563, of Lostwithiel. Counsellor at Law. Mayor of Lostwithiel, 1604, 1625 and 1631. Died 1 March, 1635. Will dated 6 Feb. 1631

= Katherine da. and co-heir of Thomas HELLYER

5. Mathew TREFFRY of Rooke in Par. St Kew bapt. 20 Feb. 1566. Bur. 3 Nov. 1626

= ELIZABETH, da. of John SUMASTER of Peinsford, Co. Devon. Bur. 19 Sept. 1656

Emlyn TREFFRY Mar. Nicholas Kendal of Pelyn, Co. Cornub, Esq.

Blanche TREFFRY Mar. Thomas Wood of Orchardon, Co. Devon, Esq.

William TREFFRY bapt. 20 March 1605. Named in his father's will, Living 1626. (See Part IV, Chapter 11.)

Thomas TREFFRY of Rooke in St Kew. Son and heir aet 13 1620. Also heir to cousin, Col. John TREFFRY of Place, Fowey, from whom he inherited the TREFFRY estates

= Jane, da. of John VIVIAN of Trewan by Mary CAVELL. Mar. sett. 28 April 1641. Bur. 2 Dec. 1654

John TREFFRY, bapt. 1 June 1608. Mar. Mary BOWDEN, 20 June 1634. She was bur. 12 June 1672. Their da., Elizabeth, mar. Edward Hender of Veryan

ctd. on p.67

(See Part II, Chapter 6 Line at Place, Fowey)

Elizabeth TREFFRY bapt. 18 March 1606. Named in her father's will. Living 1626

Jane TREFFRY, bapt. 14 Mar. 1607. Named in her father's will. Living in 1626

6. Sara TREFFRY, bapt. 25 June 1568. Mar. Lewis Cruis of Cruis MOREHARD. Living 1620.

7. Deborra TREFFRY, bapt. 30 April 1570. Mar. 1609 Henry PETER, M.P. for Fowey in the last Parliament of James I.

8. Tresithney TREFFRY, bapt. 23 July 1571. Ob. SP.

9. Martha TREFFRY, bapt. 14 March 1572. Mar. Thomas DICKWOOD, alias PETERS, June 1594. Mother of Hugh PETERS, chaplain and chief advisor to Oliver Cromwell. Beheaded for high treason on the accession of Charles II, 1660. She was bur. at Fowey1598. (See Part I, Chapter 5, Hugh Peters.)

10. John TREFFRY. Ob. SP.

11. Henry TREFFRY, bapt. 2 Feb. 1575.

12. Abel TREFFRY, bapt. 15 Oct. 1577. M.A. of All Souls' College, Oxford.

13. Rebecca TREFFRY, bapt. 29 March 1579.

14. Mary TREFFRY, bapt. 1 Apr. 1581.

15. Henry TREFFRY, bapt. 20 June 1583.

16. Benjamin TREFFRY, bapt. 26 June 1585.

2. Pedigree of Hambly, Billing and Lower Families

Roger Treffry (described in Part IV, Chapter 13) became a very staunch Quaker after marrying Mary Veale, who came of a Quaker family. Her mother, Elizabeth Hingston Veale, was also from a long-established Quaker family. Many Veales and Hingstons were buried in the Quaker burial ground called Tregangeeves, near St Austell, Cornwall. Dr. Thomas Lower, who gave the land for this burial ground, was the great-grandson of Agnes Treffry, who married William Lower. Agnes appears on the Treffry charts as the daughter of Thomas Treffry and Elizabeth Killigrew Treffry. Agnes was a great-aunt of Hugh Peter, who is the subject of the next chapter.

There are many wills, some quite early, in the Treffry family archives. To include them all would take a great deal of work and time and would fill a separate book. The very early wills are quite difficult to read as they are all handwritten in old-fashioned script with quite different spellings of words. The wills that I have examined nearly always include bequests to the church, provision for the needy, gifts to various friends, relatives and immediate family. The eldest son, or next in line heir male, usually received the bulk of the estate. In this way many parcels of land, manors and family treasures have remained in the Treffry estate for centuries.

The earliest will that I have selected to include here is that of the second brother, William Treffry, who inherited the Treffry estates from his elder brother, Sir John Treffry, whose will was proved on 19 February 1501, and who died without children. William also died without children; his will was proved on 25 November 1504. He left his estate to the third brother, Thomas, who was the progenitor of the Treffrys of Place and the Treffrys who went to Canada. So this is a significant will in the lines we are following. A copy of a section of the original is shown with William's signature.

Pedigree of HAMBLY, BILLING and LOWER Families

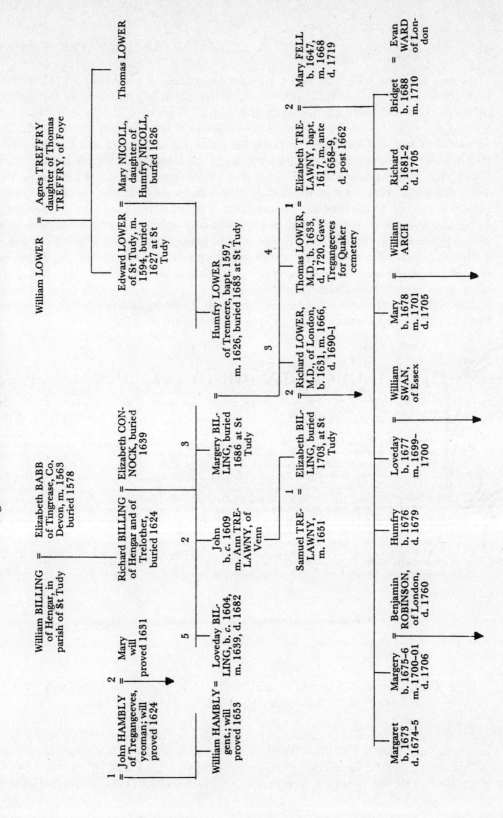

As you read the will, you will note that he wanted a tomb of Purbeck marble with three images to be built. However, in its place is a tomb with the images of these three brothers scratched in the stone. (A picture of this is in the plate section.) From this will we learn who William's friends were; he mentions his relationship to the Trevanions through his sister Jannet's marriage. He also refers to his brother, his nephews, etc. In the study of a family, wills are important in identifying various members. William wanted to ensure that certain properties and possessions remained in the family. He mentioned that the house at Fowey (Place) was to go to his brother Thomas and to his children.

We discover that William was a very wealthy man. He was a religious and kindly person, who remembered the poor, and his servants, as well as his friends.

He gave gifts of velvet, silks, damasks, tapestries and clothes to the latter, as well as jewels—diamonds, rubies, pearls, amethysts and sapphires. He also gave silver, plate, candlesticks and dishes.

The will indicates that he had a home in London besides his residence at Fowey, and he also owned Treffry Manor at Lanhydrock.

Facsimile of part of the will of William Treffry, 1504

Transcription of the will of William Treffry, of Fowey, 1504; will proved 25 November 1504 P.C.C. (Holgrave 21)

In the name of God, amen. The yere of our Lord god a thousand fyve hundreth and fowre. I William Treffry beyng of hole mynd make my testament in this world, ffirst I bequeth my soule to Almighty God and to our lady Seynt Mary, and to all the Sayntz in heven, and my body to be buryed in the Amlatorye

on the South side of our lady chapell, in the church of Saynt Barre, of ffowy, if
it please God I dye ther, and assone as the Almatorye ys made I will myn
executo^{r}s cause to make a tombe w^t three ymages, oon for my broder, another
for me, and another for my wif, after their discrecions, and lyke vnto a tombe
which lyeth on Mr Browne in the Croched freers of london, w$_t$ the pitie of
Saynt Gregory, and such scriptures as ye myn executo^{r}s can devise after the
apparell of the same. Also I bequeth principally vnto my lord Broke a bordcloth
conteynyng in brede iij yerdes, and in lenght x yerdes of damaske wark, and to
cutt oute of a hole pece, also to the said lord Broke another pece of Taptarye of
Arys Riche conteynying but a flemysch steke which ys in a Chist w^t shetes in
my grete Chambre in my house at london of the childhood of our lady, Also to
S$^r\cdot$ John Aroundell another pece of cloth of Dyaper of Damaske wark conteynyng
in brede thre yerdes, and in length ten y,erdes. Also I will, that another pece
conteynyng xiiij yerdes shall rest in the grossery at london w^t other plate which
I shall reherse hereafter to the use of Thomas Treffry my nevewe. They to haue
a hundreth shillinges of money or as myn executo^{r}s and they can agree. Also I
bequeth to the said Thomas Treffry my nevew, and eldest son of my broder
Thomas Treffry my best basyn and my best ewer of silver, two pottes of silver
parcell gilt, three candilstikkes of silver parcell gilt with priketts for waxe, and
ther sokettes for talowe, also a Smoth stonding cup clene gilt w^t a couer, also myn
best praunge for grene gynger, also a Spaynysch disch of silver all gilt on the yn
syde, also a whit laer pounst of siluer, also a dosen spones of the apostelles their
names written on the bak side w^t enamell and on spone of our lord longing to the
same which makth xiij. The which plate I will shuld rest in the Grocery forsaid
vnto the tyme the said Thomas my nevew come to the age of xxj yeres, by the
best advise of myn executors That is to sey Maister William Holybrand Mr. Robert
Rydon and my nevew John Trevanion that may better attend then these other
two gentilmen. How be it I make my lord Broke and Mr. Sr John Arundell of
Cornwall ouerseers of my testatment, Also I beqeth to William Holybrond my
felowe my best gowne Mr. Rydon the seconde, and my nevew Trevanyon the
third, Also I will Mr. Rydon chese my best couerlet of silk verdur because Mr.
Holybrond chosed my best gowne, and the said Mr. Holybrond to have my
second coverlet of silk verdour, Also I bequeth to my nevew Henry, broder of the
said Thomas my nevew, and my broder Thomas sonne half a dosen Parys bolles
parcell gilt w^t their couers to the same and the halfe monethes of the yere con-
teyned w^{t}in theyme, Also my worse basyn and myn ewer of silver parcell gilt,
the said plate to Rest in the forsaid grocery tyll the said Henry come to his age
of xxj yeres by the advise of my said executors. Also I bequeth to William the
third sone of my broder Thomas Treffry and my godson a gret gilt stonding cup
of siluer which ys chaest w^t a couer all gilt, also a dosen sponys of siluer and gilt
of the xj appostells and our lorde in all but xij, Also another praunge of siluer
for grene gynger, the said plate to Rest in the said grocery till the said William
come to the age of xxj yeres. Also I bequeth to my eldest suster Genet a great
playn flat Parys boll w^t a cover of siluer to be delivered Immediately after my
deth to her by hir sone John Trevanion and by other myn executors, Also I will

that my broder Thomas wif have a litell cuppe w^t a cover of siluer and clene gilt w^t a litell law foote, to be delivered Immediately after my deth to her, she neuer to doo it away but to remayn to her children after her decesse, Also I will that all the said plate which resteth in the grocery forsaid shall remayn from child to childe, if any of theym should happen to dye, Also I will that my neuew John Trevanyon shal have a litell flate cvpp of silver and half a dosen of small litell sponys, a goblett w^t a couer w^t enamell of violettes on the couer w^t other broken siluer which ys in a standart* of yron in my Counter at London. Maister Holybrond I toke out of the kyngs money xli and a noble, the whiche I pray you take out of my fee Reward gederying money for the clothes and botehyre money. ffor I have taken no peny of the said parcelles of all this yere past, and the Rest of the said money my accompte made I will be departed betwene you Maister Holybrond, Mr. Rydon, and John Trevanyon. It^m I pray you to geve my maydens specially Marget xx^{ti} mrc at her mariage, and to Alys myn other mayden xx nobles for the good service she hath doon to me. Maister Holybrond ther ys two hundreth pounds of Royalls lakyng xx^{ti} whereof I will that ye make it upp fully the number of the said some of ijeli w^t parte of my woddes as I shall reherse vnto you; that is to say of woode xliiij or xlvj bales wherw^t I will ye refurnyshe the said ij^{c}li lakkyng xxli of Royalles to the hole some of CCli or w^t my money of my fees and Rewards of the Custom hous. Also Mr. Holybrond ye have my two chynes in the said Coffer of fine duket gold w^t the other old Henry nobles Crusados and dukettes and ij souerayns which ys in value Chynes and all Cli, and three poundes or ther aboute which is in the said Chiste ther the CCli ys. Also ther lyeth in the same place two colers of gold whereof oon hath xviij peryll and fyue Rubyes, as I vnderstand, the other coler black enamell w^{t}oute any stone. Mr. Rydon, I haue in my Chiste a pece of purpell veluet conteyning xxiiij yerdes whereof I pray you to deliuere to the parson or the Wardens of the parisshe Church ther as I dwelled, that ys to say the parisshe of Saynt Olyf in London asmoche as will make theym a frounte for the high Aulter, oon aboue the Aulter, another before the Aulter, and the Remenent of the said veluett, I will ye geve it to the croched ffreers they to make a coope and a vestment thereof, if it will stratche thereto. And they to haue me in ther prayers both in the said parisshe Churche and also in the freers after yor discrecions. Maisters and Executo^{r}s, I beseche you at the Reuerence of God, and in the way of charitie that ye will dispose of the said money, chynes and colers to be sold to the value of theym and to be disposed after the maner and forme as I shall reherse, that is to say to the Church of St Barry of ffowy xxli to be deliuered mediately after my decesse of the said money chynes, and colers, M^r. Holybrond, M^r. Rydon, w^t my nevew John Trevanyon, I pray you to purchase asmoche lands as will come to fynd a Preest to syng perpetually ther as I am buryed and for the reparacion of the said lond yf ye may let yt the same tenements house and gardyn ther I dwell in london or in some other good soile w^{t}in london, and that to the

---

*Standard, a large chest generally used for keeping plate and jewels and sometimes for linen. (Halliwell.)

intent to pray for my fader and my moder and my broder Sr John and my wif
my fader in law and me. Also I beseche you at the Reuerence of God to convey
a tombe to be made, and send to ffowy oute of the yle of Purbek after the fo^rme
and the patron of the Tombe ther Maist^r Browne lyeth in the Croched freers,
if it be my fortune to dye at fowy. Also I bequeth to the towne and parisshe of
ffowy xli to be distrabutt and geven at two tymes to the poore peopel and
householders ther vli to be disposed of at the discrecion of the Vicar and
Wardeyns of the Churche of the said toune w^tin the yere. Also at Tregwyte
to such poore tenants as I have in that quarter iijli, also to Synvepe parisshe
amonges my tenants and poore people there iijli. Also to Trefryes and Lanhedryk,
Tywardreth iijli, in Seynt Penek parisshe xls, also to the Churche of Lansawlowes
to be delivered to the poore peopull after the discrecion of the Wardeyns and
parson there xls, and all the money to be ordered after my Executo^rs that know
my will, that ys to say all the money that I have bequethed to euery of the
townes and parisshes abovesaid, Also I will that Thomas Clark my servant have
my best horse after the Vicar w^t xls of money to be paied continent after my
decesse besides his wages and his wynter clothing, Also my horskepar John
Penhale to haue my third horse he to chese hym and xls of money and his quart'
wages and his wynter clothing, Also to Thomas Haktherope my servant another,
to chese hym, next, and xls of money, his wages and his wynter clothing, Also
to Thomas of my kechen at home at london his wynter gowne and four nobles
of money. Myn Executo^rs at the Reverence of God I beseche you that ye will
see that w^t my money, that is to say my Chynes and Colers and wode and other
goods that my bielding at ffowy may goo furth according as it is begonne and my
nevewe, John Trevanion can shew you the playnness thereof. Also I will and pray
you that non of my goodes which ys w^tin my house of ffowy be distributed or
geven fro the place, but that it remayne w^tin the same to my younger broder
and so to his children. Also I bequeth to Maistres Holybrand of London a flour
wheryn is a pointed diamond w^t three Rubyes three perills to the value of
iiijl^l which is in a littel coffer or standart in my counter. Item I bequeth to my
ladye wif of John Aroundale a pawnce w^t diamondes w^t a gret perill hangine
vnder, she to pray hir husband to be special goode frende and helpar of myn
Executo^rs and he beying oon ouerseur hymself. Also I will that my lord Broke
shall haue an Vche* for his pleasur a hert enameled, wrapped in a towell whereyn
is coched a fare dyamond, a Rubye and a perell. Also I will that Maistres Rydon
have a Rubye in a whit fleure w^t three perylls hangyng vnder to that entent that
she pray her husband to be speciall good frende to my nevewe Thomas Treffry
and to his brethren. Also I will my suster Genat Trevanion have a pomander of
Gold which ys in my standart w^tin my Counter as I vnderstand, Also I will that
Genat my brothers wif haue a litell Vche of Gold w^t a ametest, a saffer and a
peryll. Also I will my suster Trevanion haue a girdell best harnest w^t gold w^t
a bonet of black veluet. Also I will my nevewe haue to help hym to his mariage
a bonet of veluet w^t the best frontlet of gold w^t the next girdle of gold. Also I

---

*'Ouch' a jewel—the term was applied to various ornaments. The book of Exodus.

will my suster William Trevanion wife haue the third girdell of gold w^t a bonet
and a frontlet. Also I will my broder Thomas wif haue another girdell of gold w^t
a bonet and frontlet if ther be any mo lefte as I am [*sic.*] they be. Also my wyll
and my last mynd ys that Henry Pester haue the house that he dwellith yn which
hath be in debat betwene hym and me, paying to my broder after his conscience,
Also I will that Sr Thomas Haldman my Chauntrie preest of Barkley haue another
of my gildyns he to chuse after this other, also a gowne furred w^t blak buyge,
to chuse next after John Trevanion. Also I will my broder Thomas Treffry haue
my gowne lyned w^t Sarsenet, another of damaske, also my best dowblet of Tawny
saten. Also I will that the forsaid Sr Thomas, Chauntrie Preest of Barkeley, haue
three poundes of money for his Reward to pray for me to be delivered incon-
tynent after my decesse. Also I will he haue a pece of lyne cloth to the number
of xx^{ti} elles, price the elle xx^d, also other xx^{ti} ellys of lynne cloth price the elle
xiiij^d. Also I will that my felow Hugh Denys haue a pece of crymsyn chamlet
to have me in his memorye, Also I will that Mr. Weston of the Kyngs Chambre
haue another pece of fyne blak Chamlet, also I will Mr. Shereley, Clerk of the
Kechen haue a good pece of Chamlet oreles a gobet* of fyne lynne cloth. Mr.
Hugh Denys and Mr. Weston I besech you commaunde me onto my soueraine
lord the Kyng he to be good and gracious lord vnto my nevewes, and shew
his grace that I never had non of his money vntruely in all my life, and thus
I beseche you in the way of charitie to pray for me. Also I will that all such
moevable goodes as I haue in my hous at london and in the Kyngs place at
Wanstead that my nevewe John Trevanion haue it to garnisshe my place at ffowy
therew^t at his disposicion, except that, that ys bequest afore. Also I will that the
foresaid John Trevanion haue a salt of siluer couered parcell gilt which goeth
aboute in the house. Also I will that my nevew Thomas Treffry haue my best salt
with the covere all gilt, his broder Henry the second salt of silver w^t the couere,
his broder William another salt of siluer w^{t}oute a couer. Also I will that Thomas
Treffry my nevew haue my botyl chyne w^t a devise enameled which I were daiely,
and these parcells to be deliuered to the grocery foresaid w^t the other till the
children come to the age of xxj yeres. And moreouer as to the disposicion of
all my lands and tenements w$_t$in the Countie of Cornwall, Couentrie and Barkley
this is my last will that my feoffees of the same, Robert Willowby lord Broke,
John Aroundale, Knight, Robert Rydon and John Trevanion shall suffer Thomas
Treffry my broder and heir to haue and to occupye all the same londes and
tenements w^t their appurtenences for term of his life w^{t}out any interupcion or
lett, providing alwey so that my said broder aliane sell nor make none estate of
the said londs, nor of any parcell thereof, to any person or persones from the
Right heyres, and assone as the Right heyres come to their playn age my mynd
ys that ye my feoffees make relesse vnto them of all the said londs and tenements
as ye fynde them of discrecion whosoever happen to be heyre thereof &c. Item I
will that mynne executours incontinent after my decesse shall fynde a preest to
pray for me and Margaret my wif with my fader and moder with all my frends as

*'Gobet', 'goabet', a morsel, a small piece. (Halliwell.)

is aforerehersed the said preest to haue for his stipendy and wages every yere vnto the tyme the said londs be purchased, as is before rehersed, for the continuance of the same. (Transcribed by Sir John Maclean, *Journal of the Royal Institution of Cornwall*, Vol. V, 1874-5, pp. 166-174).

The purpose of including genealogical charts and wills together in the same chapter, is to show that family members named in the wills can help to verify names in the lineage charts. Verification from more than one source helps to establish the authenticity of family history.

Thomas Treffry, who was the beneficiary of the preceding will of 1504, was the grandfather of John Treffry who married Emblen Tresithney. They were the parents of 16 children. A few things discovered in a legal document of John Treffry are of interest. In 1589 he granted one half-tenancy of the grange or barton of Trenent to his third son, Mathew Treffry and one half for the use of Mathew's mother, Emblen Tresithney Treffry. In this same year he granted the Manor of Rooke to his three sons, Mathew, Tresithney and John. After these grants, John Treffry still owned the Manor of Treffry in Lanhydrock, Tregoyde Manor, the Manor of Penvrane, and Hendra and Treleden in St Germans and Bodmin and Place at Fowey. John had purchased the Barton of Trenant in 1564 and it remained part of the Treffry estate until 1806 when it was sold to Philip Rashleigh, Esq., probably at the suggestion of Joseph Thomas (Austin) Treffry (*see* Part II, Chapter 7).

In his will John Treffry settled his estates in trust on his oldest son and heir, William Treffry, and also provided for William's intended wife, Ursula Tremayne. Ursula and William had only one son, John, and six daughters. William's will was dated 23 February 1602. To his wife, he gave the house they dwelt in and closes in the town of Fowey, viz., The Culver House Close; Three Cornered Park; The Windmill Parke, and the Windmill; Saffron Close; and Fennell Stinche. He mentions four daughters, Jane, Bridget, Emblyn and Ursula, and his son, John Treffrie, the Queen's ward. Each daughter was to have £300. 'My purchased lands to descend to my daughters. My mother's annuity is £30. My brother's Thomas and Mathew, sister Rebecca and wife Ursula executrix.' He also mentions his brothers, Henry and Benjamin. William died the same day as his will was written. The only son and heir to the remainder of the estate, John Treffry, was aged eight years, five months and 10 days, at the time of his father's death.

Seventeenth Generation

When the above William Treffry died, John, his only son and heir, twentieth in line of inheritance, was under age, and by his father's will not entitled to enter into his inheritance until 24 years of age. His mother, Ursula Tremayne Treffry, had made John a Ward of Chancery. At the age of 17 he entered Exeter College, Oxford, on 14 June 1611. He served as a member of Parliament in the 18th year of James I (1621). As soon as he came of age he went into the army, rising to

the rank of colonel, and served in the royalist army in the Civil War. At that time he was living at Place. He followed his King to the end, and like many other Cornish gentlemen, spent a large part of his estate and fortune in the cause of his royal master.

On 17 October 1619 John Treffry had married Bridget, daughter of Sir Philip Champernoun of Modbury in the County of Devon. As there were no children of this marriage, and he had no brothers, the Treffry estates passed to John's first cousin, Thomas Treffry, the eldest son of Mathew Treffry of Rooke, and eldest grandson of John Treffry and Emblen Tresithney Treffry, who was therefore the eldest male heir. The Treffry family of Place descends from this Thomas (*see* Part II, Chapter 6).

Up to this time, through 17 generations, the Treffry estates had passed from father to son, or if no son then from brother to brother, always to a male heir. John Treffry had to decide whether he should follow the custom of the times which was also established tradition of the Treffrys (for the estates to pass to a male heir) or whether the estates should go to the son of his eldest sister. His decision was to give the estates to his eldest male cousin. This is the first time that the Treffry estates passed on to a cousin when there were no brothers.

One sister, Bridget (not Mary as shown on the chart) had married a man by the name of Robert Morrice, who served as an officer in King Charles I's army. Apparently Robert and Bridget were unhappy that John Treffry had left the Treffry estates to his cousin, Thomas Treffry. Thomas in a Bill of Complaint C.9/28/185 in P.C.C., 24 January 1662, stated that Robert and Bridget Morrice had endeavoured to nullify and make void John Treffry's will, and had even suggested that John Treffry had not been of sound mind and that the Treffry estates should descend to Bridget as the sole surviving sister in 1662. John had willed the lands belonging to his mother to be equally divided among his three sisters for their lives, but the estates John willed to Thomas seemed to be fair game for lawsuits by other blood relatives. However, cousin Thomas Treffry and his descendants have remained in possession of the Treffry estates.

Two other sisters of John Treffry married Trefusis brothers. Jane, the eldest sister, married John Trefusis of Trefusis, and her sister, Ursula, married Thomas Trefusis. Both Trefusis men were on the side of Parliament in the Civil War. The Trefusis family, like the Treffrys, were an ancient Celtic family. They have been traced as residents of Trefusis in Mylor four generations before 1292. During the course of 23 generations they married many heiresses and co-heiresses as, of course, did the Treffrys. Among the heiresses were those of Delechamp, Treviados and Balun; and co-heiresses of Martin–Halep, Tresithney, Colan, Trevanion, Gaverigan and Cotton.

The grandson of John and Jane Treffry Trefusis, named Francis Trefusis, married Bridget, daughter of Robert Rolle, Esq. of Heanton and his wife Arabella. She was the elder daughter and co-heiress of Theophilus Clinton, Earl of Lincoln. Their great-grandson, George William Trefusis, inherited the barony of Clinton in 1794. The title was fourth in the list of English barons. The seat of the family remained Trefusis Castle, Falmouth, Cornwall. If John Treffry had chosen to have the Treffry estates descend through his nephew, John Trefusis, the son of his eldest deceased sister Jane, who married John Trefusis of Trefusis, the heir-general to the Treffry estates would now be the heirs of the Right Honourable Charles John Robert, the 21st Baron Clinton, who died 5 July 1957. On his death the barony fell into abeyance between his daughters the Hon. Mrs. Fane and the Hon. Mrs. John Bowes-Lyon.

Three other grandchildren of John and Emblen Tresithney Treffry who were in the 17th generation are covered in this book. Two of them are Mathew Treffry's sons: one is Thomas Treffry, Mathew's eldest son, who was 21st in the line of inheritance, and the progenitor of the line at Place (*see* Part II, Chapter 6). The other is Mathew's second son, William, the ancestor of the emigrants to Canada (*see* Part IV, Chapter 11). The third is a cousin of Thomas and William, Hugh Peter, who is the subject of the next chapter.

Chapter Five

HUGH PETER(S) 1598–1660

'AFTER GOD HAD CARRIED us safe to New England, and wee had builded our houses, provided necessaries for our livili-hood, rear'd convenient places for Gods worship and settled the Civill Government; One of the next things we longed for, and looked after was to *advance Learning and perpetuate it to Posterity*; dreading to leave an illiterate Ministery to the churches, when our present Ministers shall lie in the Dust.'

These words describing the reasons for the founding of Harvard are carved on the wall near the university's Johnston Gates. They indicate clearly that from the time of the Pilgrims' arrival in the New World in 1620 they were desirous of continuing the culture and life style they had had in the Old World. The influence of this early foundation of the culture that developed in New England and spread throughout the country can be compared to that of Athens in creating the intellectual basis of Europe. Harvard was founded in 1636, only 16 years after the Pilgrims landed at Plymouth in the New World.

One man who had great influence in this infant colony—on its religion, on the development of its industries and economy, and in the founding of Harvard—was Hugh Peter. He arrived in Boston on 6 October 1635 with many other passengers in the ships *Abigail* and *Defence*. The dynamic effect he had in the short six years he spent in the colonies was of significant importance then, and has been of continuous importance in the cultural growth of the new nation that became the United States of America. Of the many members of the Treffry family before and after him, he has probably had the most lasting influence through his efforts on behalf of the colonies.

Hugh Peter, through his mother, Martha Treffry, belonged to the ancient Treffry family of Place. She was the ninth child of John Treffry and Emblen Tresithney Treffry. His uncle was William Treffry, the friend of Carew and Master of Ordnance under Sir Walter Raleigh. Hugh's mother died in the year that he was born, but his father, Thomas Peter, jr., remained in Fowey: he was from the Peter or Dickwoode family of Fowey. As Martha Treffry and Thomas Peter had been married in June of 1594, there were already two children in the family

* Chapter headpiece: the original Harvard College

when Hugh was baptized on 11 June 1598—his sister, Alice, born in 1595, and a brother Thomas born in 1596, in the twilight years of Queen Elizabeth I's reign.

The Dickwoode family, originally from Antwerp, left the Continent, probably for religious and business reasons, around 1543 during the turbulent times of the Spanish occupation. Settling in Fowey, they became prominent merchants and were classed as 'gentlemen'. They bought property from the old Peter family of Fowey. They may have found it simpler and safer on acquiring title to the property to take the name of the previous owner, the Cornish custom of the time.

Both the Treffrys and the Peters were wealthy at the time of the marriage of Hugh's parents. The Treffrys continued to hold the manor of Treffry in Lanhydrock, Tregoyd Magna, Polfuthen, Penvrane, Langurthow, and Place in Fowey. Hugh's uncle Mathew Treffry had by then inherited the manor of Rooke in St Kew. The Peter family owned tenements in the manor of Fowey and elsewhere, dwellings and quays in Fowey, merchant vessels, and a thriving import/export business.

Hugh, born into a family of considerable abundance, had a privileged, cultured and presumably happy childhood. The place of his birth, the present *King of Prussia Inn* in the heart of Fowey, where he probably lived as a young child, was only a short distance from the spacious grounds of Place, where Hugh could play with cousins of his own age. There, when tiring of looking for the piskies and goblins of Cornish folk-lore, they could go down· to the harbour to watch the cargo ships being loaded and unloaded, and to question the sailors about the outside world. There were always fishermen around the harbour, too, as fishing was a major industry in Fowey, and fishermen are always ready to tell tall tales of the sea to eager listeners. There was also shipbuilding to watch, and no doubt Hugh had his own small boat for exploring the bay and river. He could ride the ferry across to Polruan or Bodinnick since, being of the Treffry family, he had no fare to pay. From Hall-Walk on the other side he could watch the great ocean-going sailing ships plying the Channel as he dreamed of the day when he too might travel to far lands. It must have been a fine life for an adventurous and inquisitive boy.

Little is recorded of the boy's elementary education in Fowey. There were now other children in the family besides his older sister and brother, who were children of Martha Treffry Peter, as his father had re-married after his mother's death, and there were a number of younger ones. Perhaps they had a tutor, or shared one with their cousins nearby. Hugh's early education must have been good, as at the age of 14 he was admitted to Trinity College, Cambridge. There, to obtain his B.A. degree in 1617–18, he would have spent his time in study of logic and theology along with mathematics, ancient languages, geography and perhaps astronomy.

During his student days in Trinity Hugh Peter became aware of a number of able and influential Puritans, who believed the Church of England needed further changes beyond those introduced during the Reformation. Among the many famous Cambridge Puritans were William Ames and John Cotton. Thomas Hooker, another who shared these beliefs, was still at Cambridge. Hugh was influenced by the thinking of these Puritans and later joined them. In 1622 Peter returned to Cambridge to receive his Master's Degree, which required three or more years of study *in absentia* on ancient languages, theology and philosophy. Deeply interested in religion, he spent much time in London completing his studies and listening to sermons by learned men. He did some preaching himself, as he had been ordained by Bishop Montaigne of London and appointed lecturer at St Sepulchre's. His eloquent lectures attracted many followers, and he estimated that he persuaded over 100 souls a week 'from sin to the ways of Christ'. The powerful Puritan Earl of Warwick, Robert Rich, was so attracted by Hugh Peter's preaching that he became his patron and lifelong friend.

In 1624 Hugh Peter married Elizabeth Cooke Reade, much his senior, and the widow of Edmund Reade of Wickford and daughter of Thomas Cooke. The Reades' daughter, Elizabeth, now Hugh Peter's step-daughter, married John Winthrop, jr. In the late 1620s Peter had difficulties with the British government because he would not conform to the doctrines and disciplines of the Established Church. Consequently, in 1629 he decided to move to Holland, where William Ames led him towards the principles of independence and Congregationalism. When Archbishop Laud tried to make English churches in Holland conform to the doctrine of the Anglican Church, the English ambassador to Holland informed him that Peter was not conforming strictly. Because of these complaints Peter was on the point of being expelled from Holland, so he decided to emigrate to New England.

Because of his relationship with John Winthrop and his friendship with the Earl of Warwick, who was President of the Council for New England, Hugh Peter became very interested in the early Massachusetts settlements and was one of the earliest promoters of the Massachusetts Bay Company. With the Massachusetts Patentees he had signed their instructions to John Endicott, and was the first clergyman to contribute funds (£50) in 1628. While still in Holland he had served as their material as well as their spiritual advisor.

In 1635 Henry Vane, John Winthrop, jr., and Hugh Peter arrived in the Bay Colonies together as agents for the Connecticut Patentees, and remained there for the winter. Mrs. Peter followed them in the latter part of 1637, but died a short time after her arrival. The date of her death is not recorded. The bitter winter of 1635–36 was a severe trial for the struggling little colony. The cold was extreme even for New England weather; an early freeze had taken much of their gardens; gales swept the coast, keeping their small craft in harbour. Many of the colonists were discouraged and desperate, and their supporters in England were impatient for a return on their investments. With no industry and no trade, the situation seemed hopeless. Many were talking of returning to England.

As agent for the Patentees, Peter had no assignment, as yet, to preach, so he devoted all his attention and energies to improving the economy of the colony. The colonists needed a promoter to improve their material needs and economy. They had not been able to produce products that could be traded in world markets. Peter's first thought was to build up an active fishing industry. From his early years in Fowey he knew how profitable this could be, so he put every effort into raising funds, in England and locally, for more and better equipment for the work. Within a few years large and active operations were thriving in Gloucester and other ports, where fish were caught, processed for shipping, and marketed, with a good return to the colony. As a necessary part of this industry more suitable ships needed to be built, so the men of the colony began busily cutting timber in nearby forests while, under the direction of those colonists who knew the trade, serviceable cargo ships were built. Peter's own money helped build the *Desire,* Salem's first vessel, which was referred to as 'his' ship.

Sheep were brought in from colonies farther south, and from the West Indies, and flocks established so the colony could produce its own wool for the women to spin and weave and sew into warm clothing for all, or for export. No doubt Peter believed, as did our grandmothers, that 'the Devil finds work for idle hands' and hoped this useful occupation would keep the women-folk from slipping into evil ways.

While all these new industrial ventures were getting under way, in April of 1636 the ship *Charity* docked with a cargo of meal, malt, peas, prunes and aqua vitae. Peter bought most of this cargo with his own money and distributed it among the colonists according to their needs, thus saving them considerable expense. Soon after his arrival in the Colonies Peter had been granted a two-acre plot of land in Salem. A little over a year later he was ordained as minister of the Salem church.

At the time of Peter's ordination religious matters in Salem and Boston were in a sorry state of discord. These early colonists were strong-willed men with deep-seated convictions. Being an eloquent speaker as well as an accomplished organiser, Peter made a strong effort to resolve some of these conflicts and to bring erring members back into the Salem Congregational church. Church rules of that time were strict by today's standards. Members were brought before the pastor and deacons if they failed to attend services, or to have their children baptized, forgot to give thanks at all meals, or committed similar irregularities. Records indicate that Peter, as pastor, was stern but just.

Peter saw the need for better inter-church organisation within the colony. Among his suggestions were that:

1. The scholarly John Cotton should compose marginal notes on the scriptures.
2. That a new *Book of Martyrs* should be compiled.
3. That a new form of church government should be planned, based on the scriptures.

As a result, the synod meeting of 1637 contributed greatly to cohesion in the spiritual guidance of the colonists.

The Salem church grew rapidly under Peter's ministry. The great Puritan migration was under way and scores settled in Salem, joining Peter's church— 38 in 1637 alone. In that year 20 children were baptised. By 1639 the church building had to be enlarged. The popular young pastor was a forceful speaker and attracted many to his congregation.

He did not forget the economic projects he had helped to start on his arrival in the colony. The fishing industry in 1640–41 sent some 300,000 processed fish to market, and salt cod had become a staple diet on the Atlantic seaboard. Other port towns developed important fishing industries, including the little village of Foy, later known as Marblehead. Lumber and dried fish were being shipped to the West Indies. Shortly after a printing press arrived in the Bay Colony Peter offered printing services to the people of Bermuda!

Hugh Peter seems to have had a finger in any project that might benefit the young colony. He helped one of his deacons build a water-mill. He persuaded the town folk to set up a glass works and brought craftsmen from Holland to operate it. He provided a set of scales for the town of Salem. He engaged in the beaver trade, and invested in sheep. No other person, with the possible exception of Governor Winthrop, spent more time or money on behalf of the Massachusetts Bay Colony than did Hugh Peter.

With homes, commerce, church and civil government now well established, our attention must next turn to Peter's influence in the advancement of learning in the colony. Hugh Peter became a prime mover in the founding of Harvard College 'to advance learning and perpetuate it to posterity'. The General Court of the colony appointed Peter as one of the six members of the first Board of Overseers. He was also one of three men assigned the responsibility for the construction of the first college building, and was no doubt influential in the selection of the first President of Harvard, and of the first college motto *Christo et Ecclesiae*.

Peter was also responsible for sending a number of young men to England for training to return to the colony as teachers. He had been involved in every phase of the founding of Harvard from the very beginning and never ceased to work for its benefit, begging persistently throughout England and locally for more funds and books. However, when John Harvard died in Charlestown, leaving his library and half his estate to the infant college, the General Court of 1638-9 ordered that in recognition of the gift it should be named Harvard.

If Peter could see today the accomplishments, growth and influence of this one-building college he had helped to start, he would surely be pleased. Besides providing a literate clergy, Harvard has sent six Presidents to the White House, several Justices to the Supreme Court, and furnished cabinet officers, senators, congressmen and governors. Added to the list over the years would be scientists, lawyers, doctors, business leaders, writers, and educators. Nor is there yet an end to the momentous influence of this one small college which has grown to be one of the great universities of the world. For this Hugh Peter should be given his due credit as one of the principal founders.

In contrast to Hugh Peter's very active and successful public life, his private life was more troubled than he might have wished. His wife's untimely death soon after her arrival in the colony left him deeply grieved and depressed. He sought comfort with old friends, including the family of William Ames. He had come to the aid of this family when Dr. Ames died, and had helped them get settled in Salem. His long friendship with the family had given Ames's daughter Ruth an opportunity to become attached to him, and the family assumed that a marriage settlement was imminent.

However, Mrs. Deliverance Sheffield, a widow recently arrived in Boston from England, became interested in this popular widower, and the people of Salem believed them to be 'contracted'. The Ames family brought the situation to the attention of the members of the Salem church. Peter was able to convince his congregation that, because of his well-meant kindness to them over the years, the Ames family were assuming more than was warranted.

Mrs. Sheffield was a determined woman, as strong in her opinions and convictions as Peter himself. So it was with some doubts about a happy outcome and somewhat against his better judgement, that Peter and Deliverance were married in the late summer of 1639. Peter's only child, his daughter Elizabeth, was born in March of 1640. Little Elizabeth Peter was but an infant when Peter was sent to England as an agent for the Massachusetts Bay Company in 1641. His new wife became mentally unbalanced after his departure, and his friends looked after the mother and child for a time. But in Puritan thinking insanity was considered to be 'possession by the Devil', so Deliverance was excommunicated and sent to her husband in England. The child went to the care of the Rev. Thomas Shepard's family.

As agents for the Bay Company, Peter and his companions, Thomas Weld and William Hibbins, were expected to pacify the colony's creditors, to use any opportunity for the good of the colony, and to raise funds and collect books for Harvard, while 'supporting the reformation of church and state'.

When the three arrived in England in September of 1641 they found a country torn by strife and grown somewhat out of sympathy with the constant requests for help from the colonies. Hugh Peter seized every opportunity to plead the cause of the Bay Colonies before Parliament, but results were less than hoped for. With the help of John Winthrop, jr., he raised funds for an iron works in Massachusetts, and collected other moneys and supplies to the value of £2,000 as well as £150 for books for Harvard, all of which was duly sent back to New England. However, less than a year after their arrival the Civil War began, making it almost impossible to raise any additional funds for the colony. As a result the colonial government, being disappointed in the amount sent them by their agents, took over Peter's investments and properties in the Bay Colony. They confiscated his three Salem houses and farms and the 500 acres granted to him by the General Court. Peter decided to stay in England and preach for the Parliamentary cause.

The Royalists contended for the supreme authority of the monarch. The opposition acknowledged the King but insisted that Parliament should have more say in government. Hugh Peter spoke firmly and often on Parliament's behalf. He eventually became chaplain and chief advisor to Oliver Cromwell. As in any Civil War, families were divided. John Treffry of Place was a Royalist, but his sisters' husbands, John and Thomas Trefusis, were for Parliament, as was their cousin, Charles Hearle. This did mean, however, that Place had protection from both sides.

At the beginning of the strife Fowey was garrisoned by the King's men, but fell to Parliamentary forces in March 1646. Several serious engagements were fought at Castle Dore, near Fowey, where Peter's first cousin, Colonel John Treffry, a staunch Royalist, led a troop of cavalry. Boconnoc, the Mohun property, was used as headquarters alternately by the contending forces. King Charles I stayed for a short time at Place, then moved to Hall across the river where it is reported that once while walking on Hall-Walk he was shot at, but escaped unharmed.

When Cromwell's forces took Fowey St Finbarrus's church was used as a stable. But the manor of Place was not harmed, possibly because of Peter's connection with the Treffrys, or because John Trefusis, who was also a strong Parliamentarian, spent much of his time there.

In 1650 Oliver Cromwell appointed Hugh Peter Chaplain to the Council of State, a position comparable to that of Archbishop of Canterbury previously. It appears that in this position Hugh Peter had many conferences to counsel King Charles I before his execution, and had tried to be of service to his Majesty during his confinement in prison.

On the Sunday following Oliver Cromwell's death in 1658 Hugh Peter preached at Whitehall a touching sermon on the text 'Moses my servant is dead'. In the procession at Cromwell's public funeral on 23 November 1658, he was appointed to wear mourning.

At this point Peter was in poor health and took little part in public affairs. After the restoration of the monarchy he left the country for a short time, but returned, believing that as he had had no part in the death of King Charles I, he would have amnesty under the general pardon. Despite this, his arrest was ordered and he was sent to the Tower. Declared guilty and condemned to death, he was executed at Charing Cross on 16 October 1660.

As he was about to be executed a bystander accused Peter of the death of the King and asked him to repent. 'Friend', replied Peter, 'you do not well to trample on a dying man. You are greatly mistaken: I had nothing to do in the death of the king.' Cook, a friend of Peter's, was hanged first in front of Hugh. 'Sir', said Peter, 'you have here slain one of the servants of God before mine eyes, and have made me to behold it, on purpose to terrify and discourage me; but God hath made it an ordinance to me for my strengthening and encouragement.' Thus Hugh Peter met his death, a martyr for his convictions.

A number of portraits, pictures and cartoons exist of Hugh Peter. One fine oil portrait is owned by the Treffrys of Place. One is in the residence of the President of Queen's College, Cambridge. I have been privileged to take photographs of both. However, the picture I have selected for use in this book was acquired by my brother Eugene Rideout while serving in World War II. As a student at Harvard he had become interested in the life of Hugh Peter and the important part he had in the founding of Harvard. While stationed in London in the midst of World War II he visited the British Museum, where he asked if it would be possible to obtain any pictures of Hugh Peter. He was advised that for safe keeping most of their valuable collections were stored in Wales, but they would see what could be done about it. As this would take time, he left a forwarding address. Later while serving in France, with the war still raging, he received a package from the British Museum with copies of two pictures, one of Hugh Peter, and one of Oliver Cromwell surrounded by his chief advisors, including Peter. The former of these can be seen in the plate section.

Hugh Peter was the author of many sermons, tracts, articles and books, but the treatise of his life that he wrote for his daughter while he was in prison in the Tower is one of the most often quoted from. Its title is *A Dying Father's Last Legacy*. From all the accomplishments of his busy and turbulent life, Hugh Peter should perhaps most be remembered for his interest 'to advance learning and perpetuate it to posterity' in the founding of Harvard.*

*For further information, *see* R. P. Stearns, *The Strenuous Puritan: Hugh Peter, 1598–1660.*

PART II

*

THE FAMILY OF THOMAS TREFFRY, ELDEST SON OF MATHEW TREFFRY (from 1604)

Treffrys of Place, Fowey—*continued from page 45*

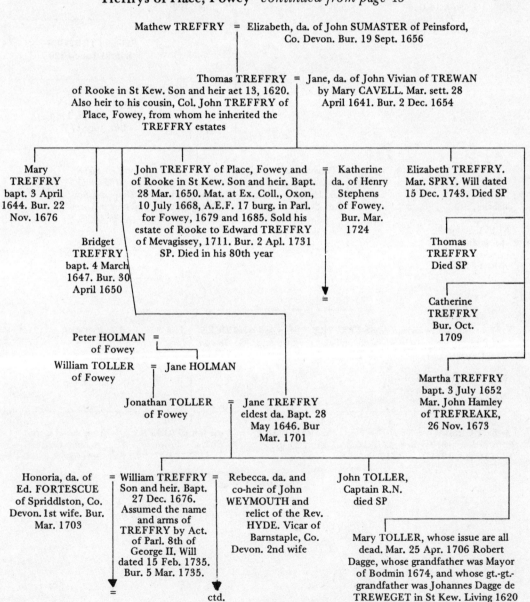

Mathew TREFFRY = Elizabeth, da. of John SUMASTER of Peinsford,
Co. Devon. Bur. 19 Sept. 1656

Thomas TREFFRY = Jane, da. of John Vivian of TREWAN
of Rooke in St Kew. Son and heir aet 13, 1620. by Mary CAVELL. Mar. sett. 28
Also heir to his cousin, Col. John TREFFRY of April 1641. Bur. 2 Dec. 1654
Place, Fowey, from whom he inherited the
TREFFRY estates

Mary
TREFFRY
bapt. 3 April
1644. Bur. 22
Nov. 1676

Bridget
TREFFRY
bapt. 4 March
1647. Bur. 30
April 1650

John TREFFRY of Place, Fowey and = Katherine
of Rooke in St Kew. Son and heir. Bapt.   da. of Henry
28 Mar. 1650. Mat. at Ex. Coll., Oxon,   Stephens
10 July 1668, A.E.F. 17 burg. in Parl.   of Fowey.
for Fowey, 1679 and 1685. Sold his   Bur. Mar.
estate of Rooke to Edward TREFFRY   1724
of Mevagissey, 1711. Bur. 2 Apl. 1731
SP. Died in his 80th year

Elizabeth TREFFRY.
Mar. SPRY. Will dated
15 Dec. 1743. Died SP

Thomas
TREFFRY
Died SP

Catherine
TREFFRY
Bur. Oct.
1709

=

Peter HOLMAN =
of Fowey

William TOLLER = Jane HOLMAN
of Fowey

Martha TREFFRY
bapt. 3 July 1652
Mar. John Hamley
of TREFREAKE,
26 Nov. 1673

Jonathan TOLLER = Jane TREFFRY
of Fowey   eldest da. Bapt. 28
May 1646. Bur
Mar. 1701

Honoria, da. of   = William TREFFRY =   Rebecca. da. and
Ed. FORTESCUE   Son and heir. Bapt.   co-heir of John
of Spriddlston, Co.   27 Dec. 1676.   WEYMOUTH and
Devon. 1st wife. Bur.   Assumed the name   relict of the Rev.
Mar. 1703   and arms of   HYDE. Vicar of
   TREFFRY by Act.   Barnstaple, Co.
   of Parl. 8th of   Devon. 2nd wife
   George II. Will
   dated 15 Feb. 1735.
   Bur. 5 Mar. 1735.

John TOLLER,
Captain R.N.
died SP

Mary TOLLER, whose issue are all
dead. Mar. 25 Apr. 1706 Robert
Dagge, whose grandfather was Mayor
of Bodmin 1674, and whose gt.-gt.-
grandfather was Johannes Dagge de
TREWEGET in St Kew. Living 1620

=   ctd.

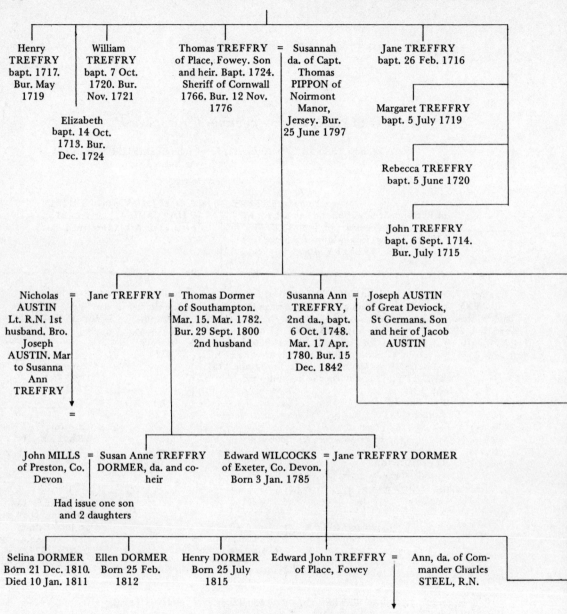

Henry TREFFRY bapt. 1717. Bur. May 1719

William TREFFRY bapt. 7 Oct. 1720. Bur. Nov. 1721

Elizabeth bapt. 14 Oct. 1713. Bur. Dec. 1724

Thomas TREFFRY of Place, Fowey. Son and heir. Bapt. 1724. Sheriff of Cornwall 1766. Bur. 12 Nov. 1776

= Susannah da. of Capt. Thomas PIPPON of Noirmont Manor, Jersey. Bur. 25 June 1797

Jane TREFFRY bapt. 26 Feb. 1716

Margaret TREFFRY bapt. 5 July 1719

Rebecca TREFFRY bapt. 5 June 1720

John TREFFRY bapt. 6 Sept. 1714. Bur. July 1715

Nicholas AUSTIN Lt. R.N. 1st husband. Bro. Joseph AUSTIN. Mar to Susanna Ann TREFFRY

= Jane TREFFRY =

Thomas Dormer of Southampton. Mar. 15. Mar. 1782. Bur. 29 Sept. 1800 2nd husband

Susanna Ann TREFFRY, 2nd da., bapt. 6 Oct. 1748. Mar. 17 Apr. 1780. Bur. 15 Dec. 1842

= Joseph AUSTIN of Great Deviock, St Germans. Son and heir of Jacob AUSTIN

=

John MILLS of Preston, Co. Devon

= Susan Anne TREFFRY DORMER, da. and co-heir

Had issue one son and 2 daughters

Edward WILCOCKS of Exeter, Co. Devon. Born 3 Jan. 1785

= Jane TREFFRY DORMER

Selina DORMER Born 21 Dec. 1810. Died 10 Jan. 1811

Ellen DORMER Born 25 Feb. 1812

Henry DORMER Born 25 July 1815

Edward John TREFFRY of Place, Fowey

= Ann, da. of Commander Charles STEEL, R.N.

See Part III, Chapter 8 (13 children). Folio 5

William Esco TREFFRY
of Place, Fowey. Son and heir. Survived his father three years, dying SP in
1779. He settled his estates on his sister, Susanna Ann and her issue. Bur.
19 Nov. 1779

Joseph Thomas AUSTIN. Bapt. 1 May 1782. In 1808
purchased of the two daughters of Thomas DORMER
and Jane TREFFRY and of their husbands, JOHN
MILLS and Edw. WILCOCKS their undivided moiety
of the TREFFRY estates. By Royal Licence 23 Feb.
1836 he assumed the name and arms of TREFFRY.
Sheriff of Cornwall 1836-7. Bur. 29 Jan. 1850. He
died SP and divined his estates to his kinsman, Edward
John WILCOCKS on condition that he assumed the
name and arms of TREFFRY. (*See* Part II, Chapter 7.)

Susanna AUSTIN
born 7 Jan. 1784.
Bur. 14 June 1800

Sarah Shaw TREFFRY
born 20 Feb. 1788, died
young

Charles TREFFRY DORMER
Born 12 June 1821

Thomas Austin TREFFRY DORMER
Born 21 Sept. 1819

St · Kew

Chapter Six

THOMAS TREFFRY FAMILY OF ROOKE AND PLACE (from 1604)

THOMAS TREFFRY, son of Mathew and Elizabeth Sumaster Treffry, was christened on 21 October 1604 in St Kew. His birthdate is either omitted or incorrectly given in some printed records. However, the above date is given in the original St Kew parish register. Also, in his father's will he is described as the eldest son.

At the time of Thomas Treffry's birth, his father was in possession of the Manor of Rooke. Mathew, with his brothers Tresithney and John, had received Rooke by Conveyance of Deed from their father in 1589. The income from Rooke was to provide for their maintenance. Tresithney and John died unmarried, leaving Mathew in sole possession of Rooke. Mathew lived at Rooke from the time of his marriage (*c.* 1603) to Elizabeth Sumaster of Peinsford, County Devon. The baptisms of four of their children—Thomas, Elizabeth, Jane and John—took place in St Kew; only William, the second son, was baptized in St Fimbarrus church, Fowey (*see* Part IV, Chapter 11).

Little is recorded of Mathew Treffry's activities, although we know a great deal about several of his brothers (q.v.) and his nephews, Hugh Peter (q.v.) and Charles Hearle. As Mathew lived at Rooke Manor, which was a property of considerable extent covering a large area of St Kew parish, he undoubtedly was busy with farming activities and managing the manor, as we see from his will of 1626, which follows:

In the name of God Amen I Mathew Treffry of St. Kewe in the Countie of Cornwall present the 20th day of August in the yeare of our lord god 1626 being sick of bodie but god bee praised of perfect memory doe make and ordaine this my last will and testament in manner and forme following Imprenis I bequeath my soule to my Redeemer and Savior Jesus Christ and my body to Christian buriall And for my goods and chattels as there may be a blessed quietness forever hereafter I give bequeath and bestowe them in manner and form following: *Item* I give and bequeath to the poore of Fowey twentie shillings *Item* I give and bequeath to the poore of the parish of St. Kewe xx s which few giftes and bequests to be paid by my brother —— within one year after my decease *Item* I give to my daughter Elizabeth one cowe in liewe of one which I had of her which was given her by her Aunt Kent *Item* I give and bequeath to my daughter Jane one heifair two years of age *Item* my will and

70

Testament is my younger children that is to say William Treffry my second sonne and John Treffry my youngest sonne and Elizabeth Treffry and Jane Treffry my two daughters shall have the sum of 200 £ to be paid and divided amongst them in such manner and forme as is mentioned expressed and declared in a certaine paire of Indentures made the XXVIII day of October in the yeare of the Raigne of our Late Soveraigne Lord King James that is to say of —— land France and England the XXth and of Scotland the sixth anno di 1622 betweene me the same Mathewe Treffry of the one partie —— John Benoke of —— Freshford in the said countie of Cornwall gent of the oth —— parte amongst other graunts and demises therein doth more at large appear and further my Will and Testament is that my said children shall have all such further some and somes of money as is expressed & declared in the forenamed Deed Indenture according to the uses and limitations —— of the said deed *Item* I give and bequeath unto Jone Benoke my kinswoman 5 s to buy her a lambe Lastly my debts and legacies paid and my funerall expenses performed doe make Elizabeth Treffry and Thomas Treffry my eldest sonne joyntly and together my sole Executors hereby revoking and disallowing all former legacies and bequeathes and to this my last will and Testament have hereunto subscribed my name and day and yeare aforesaid

MATHEW TREFFRY

Sealed and subscribed as my last will and testament in the presence of

John Treffry

John Benoke
William Benoke

sign   Johns ⋀ Morrowe

Memorand that the within named Matthewe Treffry the eyghteenth day of October and on 1626 did in the presence of us whose names ar subscribed againe publish the within written will to bee his that said Matthewe Treffry's last Will and Testament and did revoke all other willes made by him whatsoever and that the word Thomas interlined over the fourth line in the ending of the said will was so interlined before this publication.

The sign of ⋀ John Morrowe
The sign of ⋎⋀ William Roake

On 16 November 1626 an inventory was made of Mathew Treffry's personal property. A partial list follows which gives a glimpse of his manner of living:

INVENTORY

His purse and girdle
His wearing apparel
His sword and armour
His books

Chattels in the Parlour
2 muskets, 2 fowling guns, a harquebut
4 table bowls, 3 forms, 4 chairs
6 stools, a carpet, 8 cushions
2 pr of playing tables
2 pr of iron dogs (andirons)
2 portments (?) (probably leather travelling cases for use on horseback)
12 silver spoons and a gilt bottle
Ivory (?) dishes and like vessels in the
   parlour cupboard
2 china basins and ewers

The Chamber over the Parlour
2 bedsteads with bed curtains and coverlets, blankets and cloth sheets (?)
3 chairs and 2 stools
2 trunks, chest, press and
2 little window boxes

The Chamber over the Hall
2 bedsteads with bedding, coverlets,
   blankets and sheets provided
Little table, chest and 3 boxes
Cupboard, a stool of pine (?) and a
   looking glass
In the cupboard china dishes, baskets,
bottles, glasses, storing jugs, and 2 brushes

The Chamber over the Buttery
2 bedsteads with beds, coverlets, blan-
   kets and sheets provided
Clothes, 2 cushions, chair
A still and a round mill
17 pairs of (?) spoons
Baskets and flasks (?)
Saddle and furniture.

The Hall and Kitchen
2 table boards, a cupboard, 3 forms
Pr of andirons, 3 spits, a bar iron
Dripping pan, 2 brandirons, a spit iron
Pewter, small pewter platters
Charcoal (?), 3 chamber pots
Candlesticks, pestle and mortar
Basin

The Buttery
10 beer barrels, a glass cage
a warming pan and 3 flesh tubs

The Dairy
4 pans, 3 great brass pans
A fillet, 2 frying pans
2 barrels, a cupboard, 3 shelves and
   cheesing (?) vessels

The Larder
Household provision of fine butter,
   cheese, tallow and grease
4 round (?) tubs, a pipe and timber
   utensils

The Workmen's Chamber
2 bedsteads and beds provided

The Stable
Cart, mares (?), with 6 saddles

The Weaving House

The Wagon House
Wheels, butts, harrows, yokes, chains
   and such utensils
Wood and fuel for fires

The Haymow
Wheat, barley, oats, hay
A hayrick (haystack)
Various (?) tools, hooks, shovels, and
   timber

The Mill House and Mill
Bunting (?) hurhes barrels
Bar iron and 2 millstones

Also listed
Corn in the field
23 acres of wheat
Poultry, 18 sheep
4 horses and mares
2 young colts
Oxen, bull and 2 beefs
80 young heifers and beefs
A young bull
8 cattle, and 30 pigs

As Thomas Treffry grew up at Rooke, he apparently helped with the farm and management of the manor. He was 22 in 1626 when his father died. Mathew's widow, Elizabeth, outlived her husband by 30 years: they are both buried in St Kew. The Aunt Kent mentioned in the will was Elizabeth's sister, co-heiress with her of their Sumaster father.

In the spring of 1980 Peregrine Treffry and I explored the romantic 'King Arthur' area, which includes the Manor of Rooke in St Kew. There we found a very old two-storey stone house which was open for Cornish cream teas. Whether this is the home used by the Mathew Treffry family or not, I do not know. Stone houses were characteristic of that period. The owner knew very little about the history of the house, but she showed us a bit of it. There was a large square entry hall with a smaller hall off it, with floors of Delobole slate. All the ceilings were quite low which is typical of 17th-century houses. The room in which we

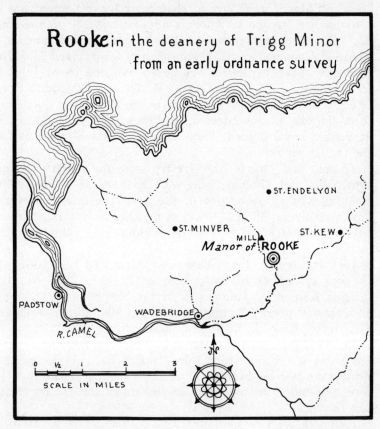

had tea was not a large room: the centre dining-table took up most of the space. From the outside there were signs that there had been some structural changes of doors and windows at various times. Not too far away, we found a place called Rooke Mill, apparently the one mentioned in the will. The area was sparsely settled with many open fields remaining in the countryside which was glowing with the freshness of spring.

While Thomas was busy at Rooke, his first cousin, Colonel John Treffry of Place, was fighting for his king in the Civil War. Colonel John Treffry had no issue at the time of his death in 1658 (*see* above, pp. 55-6). He chose to leave the Treffry estates to Thomas Treffry of Rooke. Thomas and John were in the 17th generation of descent, and Thomas became the 21st in line of inheritance from the beginning of the records on the Treffry charts.

As Place came into the Treffry family six generations after the beginning of the records, Thomas on his inheritance of the Treffry estates from his cousin became the 16th of Place. Thomas Treffry of Rooke married Jane, daughter of John and Mary Cavell Vivian. Their marriage settlement was dated 28 April 1641. I found a reference to Thomas and Jane in the *Henderson Calendars*, p. 325, no. 142. 'Thomas Trefrye of Rooke gent having married Jane sister of John Vivian the younger of St. Colombe gent & Received 500 £ in person bequeathed to her by John Vivian by her father assigned to sd John Vivian, Jun, W Inch Jo Benoke and Jo Carsen gents Rooke als Rongog & Rouke Mill in St. Kew.' The Jo Benoke whose signature is on the above document may be the same John Benoke who witnessed Mathew's will. Jane Vivian through her mother brought a royal descent from Edward I and Eleanor of Castile to this line of the Treffry family.

Thomas and Jane Vivian Treffry were the parents of six daughters and two sons, John and Thomas, who were all born at Rooke. After Thomas inherited Place and other properties of the Treffry estate, however, he moved with his family to live at Place. However, he lived only a short time after inheriting. He left this property and Rooke to his eldest son, John, who thus became the 17th of Place.

John entered Exeter College, Oxford, on 10 July 1668, aged 17, from Fowey. He was a Member of Parliament in 1678-9, 1679-81, 1681 and 1685-7. He married Katherine, daughter of Henry Stephens of Fowey. John Treffry wrote a number of poems, 'being the result of idle hours', to please some of his friends. They were printed in 1700, in London.

In 1711, John sold the Manor of Rooke to Edward Treffry of Mevagissey. I do not know his relationship. John Treffry lived to the age of 80, dying in 1731. Neither he nor his brother Thomas, who died before him, left any issue. Therefore, this ended the male line of descent of the Treffry family through Mathew's son Thomas.

Although Mathew's second son, William Treffry, left male heirs who would have been first cousins of John, John elected to leave the Treffry estates to his sister Jane's eldest son, William Toller, on condition that he took the name of Treffry. John Treffry bound his nephew by bonds of £4,000 to do so or forfeit that sum and also the estates. From the beginning of the Treffry family records until 1731, 18 generations and 22nd in line of inheritance, the estates had always descended only through male heirs, either sons or brothers, and once through a male first cousin.

William Toller assumed the name and arms of Treffry, by Act of Parliament, 8th George II, 1735, becoming the 18th of Place. The Tollers were a wealthy merchant family of Fowey, and William was involved in shipping. In 1727 he was appointed Collector of Customs for Fowey. William Toller Treffry married

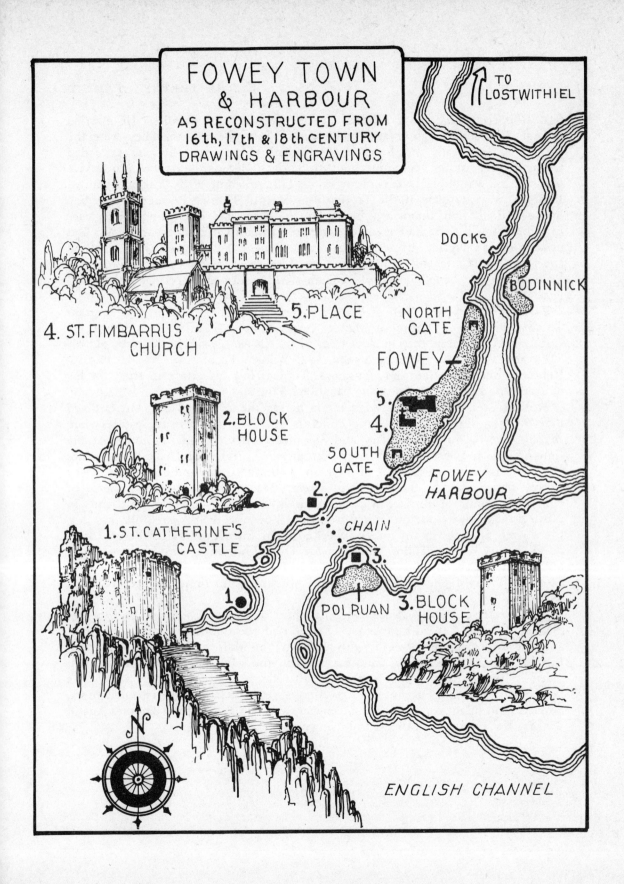

FOWEY TOWN
& HARBOUR
AS RECONSTRUCTED FROM
16th, 17th & 18th CENTURY
DRAWINGS & ENGRAVINGS

TO
LOSTWITHIEL

DOCKS

BODINNICK

5. PLACE

NORTH
GATE

FOWEY

4. ST. FIMBARRUS
CHURCH

5.

4.

2. BLOCK
HOUSE

SOUTH
GATE

FOWEY
HARBOUR

2.

CHAIN

1. ST. CATHERINE'S
CASTLE

3.

1.

POLRUAN

3. BLOCK
HOUSE

N

ENGLISH CHANNEL

first Honoria, daughter of Edward Fortescue, who died childless. He married second, Rebecca, daughter and co-heiress of John Weymouth. They were the parents of four sons and four daughters. The eldest son, Thomas, succeeded to the Treffry estates becoming the 19th of Place. He was the only son to survive infancy, and was only 11 years old when his father died in 1735. William's widow, Rebecca, was guardian of the Treffry estates until Thomas became of age. She had a difficult time financially in paying the debts and honouring the legacies in William's will as he had spent considerable amounts of money on repairs and upkeep of the Treffry properties. In order to meet the obligations she diverted the rent from Caffa Mill, Penventinue and Liskerwell in Fowey and property in Bodmin to the beneficiaries of William's will until they received their full legacies.

Thomas Treffry, the 19th of Place, married Susanna, the daughter of Captain Thomas Pippon of Noirmont Manor, Jersey. Thomas Treffry was Sheriff of Cornwall in 1766; and died in November 1776. His widow survived him by almost 21 years. They were parents of one son, William Esco, and four daughters—Rebecca, Elizabeth, Jane and Susanna. Thomas left his estate in trust for his wife and son and the two surviving daughters, Jane and Susanna.

William Esco Treffry succeeded his father as the 20th of Place, but outlived him by only three years, dying childless in 1779. The Treffry estates were therefore vested in Jane Treffry and Susanna Treffry in equal moieties. At the time of Jane and Susanna Treffry's inheritance in 1779 the Treffry estates besides Place consisted of the Barton of Trenant, with the tithes and advowson of the Fowey parish church, the Manor of Fowey, Manor of Langurthow, Manor of Penvrane, Manor of Borlase Wartha, lands in St Veep (near Fowey), lands in Lanteglos-by-Fowey, various rental houses in Fowey and St Austell. Besides this, there were holdings in tin mines inherited from Elizabeth Treffry Peter. Lands purchased by William Toller, added to the Treffry holdings, were Lescrow, Caffa Mills, part of Penventinue and Liskerwell in Fowey. Added to this was Nicholas Close in Bodmin. The Treffrys also held interest in tin mines in Gwennap and Kenwyn.

Jane Treffry, the eldest surviving daughter of Thomas, married Lt. Nicholas Austin, R.N. He died without issue. She married a second time, Thomas Dormer, and had two daughters, Susan, who married John Mills, and Jane, who married Edward Wilcocks of Exeter. Susanna Treffry, the second daughter of Thomas, married Joseph Austin, the brother of Lt. Nicholas Austin, R.N., her sister's husband. Joseph and Susanna Treffry Austin were the parents of two daughters, one dying in infancy and one as a teenager, and one son, Joseph Thomas Austin Treffry. He is the subject of the following chapter.

Chapter Seven

JOSEPH THOMAS (AUSTIN) TREFFRY

The Great Industrialist, 1782–1850

WHO WAS Joseph Thomas (Austin) Treffry? Who was this industrial and mining giant of remote Cornwall who had made a name for himself long before gold was discovered in California? Why is he still remembered and written about to this day? Is he remembered because of his success in mining, in business, his ingenuity in engineering, his far-sightedness, or his concern for those who worked with him? Perhaps he is remembered not because of any one of these qualities alone, but because of a rare combination of them all.

Hardly a book on the history of mining in Cornwall has been written that does not have some reference to Treffry's well-managed mines, and to his concern for his miners. He was one of the first to provide sick pay to a miner and medical attention not only to the miner, but also to his family.

What manner of man was he that at his death in 1850 the newspapers would write, 'We announce today a general calamity. Mr. Treffry is dead! The enterprise which no difficulty could damp is quenched; the energy which never slept is at rest; the public spirit which expanded itself in works of usefulness from which he could never look for a return is passed from among us'. What additional tribute can one add to this description of a hard working, creative, dedicated and concerned man? Why did he deserve such acclaim?

Born Joseph Thomas Austin, he was the son of Susanna Ann Treffry Austin and Joseph Austin, of the Austin family, formerly of Great Deviock in St Germans, Cornwall. Joseph was baptized on 1 May 1782 in St Andrew's church, Plymouth. After his father's death early in young Joseph's life, his mother moved back to Place at Fowey which she had inherited with her sister from their brother in 1779. Joseph's only two sisters died young, one as an infant and one as a teenager, leaving him as an only son and eventually as an only child in a fatherless home.

Joseph's childhood days were probably spent not too differently from the way Hugh Peter spent his time as a child in Fowey almost 200 years before. There were the same hills and woods to roam. The same harbour was busy with much activity as the war with France that began in 1793 was still raging. There were

* Chapter headpiece: Luxulyan viaduct

children of the naval officers for friends as well as visiting cousins to play with. As Joseph matured, being left the only child, he felt a great sense of responsibility for his widowed mother to whom he was completely devoted to the end of her days.

Just before his 19th birthday he entered Exeter College, Oxford, keeping up the Treffry tradition of being Oxford educated. From records he kept at Oxford it is apparent he had been trained by his mother to keep accurate account of his expenditures. Most items on his list for the first three months he was at Oxford are not too different from items one might find on a college student's record today—paper, quills, ink, soap, toothbrush, comb, nail brush, hair brush, clothes brush, wafers, stick (walking), and looking glass. In his first 15 months at Oxford, Joseph had spent nearly £40 on the mending and making of tailor-made clothes. Every three months in this period there was an entry of £1 for a haircut.

Not having made any great mark at Oxford, Joseph left after three years without obtaining a degree. He was 22 years old. Place and the other Treffry properties were much in need of attention. Now that he was of age, perhaps he felt that he should take over the responsibilities that had been on his widowed mother's shoulders for so many years.

During the fall after leaving college he visited the Meins, a naval family he had met in his childhood at Fowey. The following is from a letter he wrote to his mother from there.

> 18 October 1804
>
> My dear Mama,
>
> I received yours with draft £20. It is not enough.
> I shall return soon from the Meins.
> It is very gay with three balls with all the people of fashion coming from this and neighbouring counties. Riding and fox hunting.
> I remain with love and compts to all friends.
> Your Dutiful and Affectionate son

From Joseph's expenditures at Oxford it is apparent he liked fine clothes and was well groomed, indicating that he had some interest in a social life and in impressing the young ladies. However, after returning to Fowey, he shunned the social life with nearby gentry, turning all his efforts to estate matters and to repairing Place, which had been badly neglected for many years.

With the Napoleonic war on, there was a great market for farm produce at this time. The Treffrys being almost land poor, and the farms not too well managed, young Joseph went on horseback many times from Fowey to the north coast looking over all the family farms and establishing plans that put them on a paying basis. These farms were used for growing wheat, barley, oats and various vegetables. Cattle, sheep and pigs were also raised. Mrs. Austin had a dairy herd on the land at Place, producing butter which was sold at the local market as well as in Plymouth and London. After four years of turning his business ingenuity towards making the farms income-producing, young Joseph was able to buy out the moiety in the Treffry estate from his cousins, Susan Wilcocks and Jane Mills.

By 1812 Joseph, now aged 30, was in a position to purchase Penventinue Farm from the Boconnoc estate which at one time had belonged to the Mohuns.

With this purchase came Hillhay, which had been owned by the Peter family in Hugh Peter's day. On this property Joseph built a lime-kiln, for lime was much needed by the farmers, as Joseph had realised. It appears that he had the same ability to size up the economic conditions in Cornwall in the early 1800s that Hugh Peter had displayed in the infant Massachusetts Bay Colony in the early 1600s.

It was with great foresight that Joseph had turned his attention to interests other than farming in 1812, as when the war with Napoleon ended in 1815 farm prices plummeted. Fortunately, the Treffrys had held some interests in tin mines, and during the war with Napoleon there was a great search for copper in Cornwall. With Joseph's sharp eyes awake to everything that was going on around him, this activity caught his attention, turning his thoughts toward mining. Seeing several copper mines becoming quite prosperous, he began to invest. In 1816 he bought a sixteenth share in Wheal Treasure with other 'adventurers', as investors were then called. When some of the mines Joseph invested in later closed, he felt it was because of bad management, not because of lack of ore. In 1820 he persuaded the wealthy George Lucy, who had been involved in Fowey politics, to advance him some money so he could re-open Wheal Treasure mine completely under his own control, as in this way he believed the mine and other 'adventures' could be made profitable.

Joseph Austin showed good judgement in the person he chose to manage Wheal Treasure mine, Thomas Petherick. Petherick invented a machine for cleaning copper ore, and with William West patented an improved type of boiler. Austin was always looking for a better way to make mining more productive, efficient and easier for the miners. Austin, as one of the original investors in the four mines that eventually became part of Fowey Consolidated mines, was joined by others as his mining interests developed into a vast mining empire, including many mines throughout Cornwall. However, the greatest concentration of his mining interests was in the mid-Cornwall area around St Austell.

The Fowey Consols gave a profit of £220,000 in copper alone. Par Consols belonging to Austin produced a profit of £250,000 from copper and tin. In 1848 Joseph Thomas (Austin) Treffry was described in business journals as the greatest employer of miners and other labourers in the West of England. In Spencer Thornton Treffry's family history it is stated that Joseph Treffry was the largest employer of manpower in the United Kingdom—5,000 or more.

In attempting to make his mining interests more productive and profitable, many problems had to be solved, among them the transporting of the ore to the ships. The people of Fowey were unhappy having their narrow steep roads chopped up and rutted by heavy-laden wagons carrying Austin's ore to waiting ships in Fowey harbour. Consequently he decided to build a breakwater to create a harbour at Par. He sent for Isambard Kingdom Brunel, the famous engineer who later designed the bridge that spans the Tamar. Brunel told Austin that the place he had chosen to build the breakwater was impossible to use. Austin replied that 'impossible' was a word not in his vocabulary, so he undertook the work himself. Year after year winter storms tore down the summer's work, but at

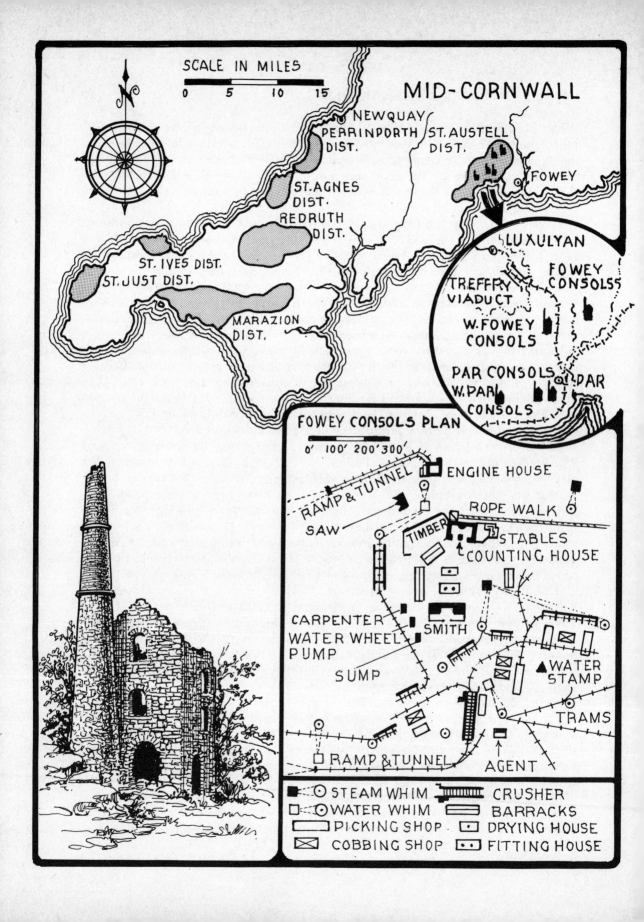

SCALE IN MILES
0   5   10   15

MID-CORNWALL

NEWQUAY
PERRINPORTH
DIST.

ST. AUSTELL
DIST.

FOWEY

ST. AGNES
DIST.
REDRUTH
DIST.

ST. IVES DIST.
ST. JUST DIST.

MARAZION
DIST.

LUXULYAN

TREFFRY
VIADUCT

FOWEY
CONSOLSS

W. FOWEY
CONSOLS

PAR CONSOLS
W. PAR
CONSOLS

PAR

FOWEY CONSOLS PLAN

0' 100' 200' 300'

ENGINE HOUSE

RAMP & TUNNEL

SAW

ROPE WALK

TIMBER

STABLES
COUNTING HOUSE

CARPENTER
WATER WHEEL
PUMP

SMITH

SUMP

WATER
STAMP

TRAMS

RAMP & TUNNEL

AGENT

STEAM WHIM   CRUSHER

WATER WHIM   BARRACKS

PICKING SHOP   DRYING HOUSE

COBBING SHOP   FITTING HOUSE

last he was successful. Soon after Par harbour was completed it filled daily with ships bringing coal and lumber for the mines, and loading ore for Welsh ports.

As interest in railways developed, Austin became actively involved for his own commercial use as well as for the benefit of all the people in Cornwall. He eventually became chairman of the Cornwall Railway. From the recently published *Barclay Fox's Journal,* which was written in Joseph Treffry's day, Fox noted after a railway committee meeting in January 1844, that 'Treffry made a capital, practical, statistical speech showing from his own experience how cheaply a railway may be constructed in Cornwall. His did not cost £3,000 per mile'. (By Act of Parliament Joseph Thomas Austin had changed his name from Austin to Treffry in 1836.) In February of 1844 Treffry chaired a railway meeting in Truro at which time he was appointed with two others to travel to London to raise capital and confer with the Great Western Railway directors. In August of that year with three other leading businessmen he journeyed to London carrying the decision of the Cornwall railway committee that they had agreed on going ahead with a railway for Cornwall. They were to meet with the directors in London 'to find out what assistance we may expect from them and on what terms'.

Needing a port on the north coast of Cornwall Treffry had purchased Newquay harbour, with the idea of connecting this harbour to his harbour at Par by railway. In 1844 Parliament passed the Bill authorising his Newquay harbour, which meant he could go ahead with this railway. Undoubtedly while in London on business for the Great Western Railway he was also carrying on negotiations for his own interests. The Cornwall Minerals Railway bought Treffry's line in 1874.

In addition to railways, Treffry constructed canals (now defunct) to carry ore between Fowey Consols and the wharves. He owned ships that carried his granite, coal, copper ore, lime, clay and culm. He established his own smelting plant at Par with a stack 235 feet high. His purpose in building this high stack was to have the natural wind pattern over the harbour carry away the harmful smelting fumes. Being concerned about air pollution at that time certainly makes him a very early environmentalist.

The greatest evidence today in Cornwall of Treffry's ingenuity is undoubtedly the beautiful and spectacular Luxulyan viaduct-aqueduct which still stands today in all its majesty with a narrow road running underneath. On my first trip to Cornwall in 1950 Anne Treffry told me the story of Joseph Thomas (Austin) Treffry's life and all that he had accomplished. She then took me to see this great structure spanning the Luxulyan Valley with its 10 magnificent 40-foot arches that he had had built in three short years from 1839-42. The viaduct was made entirely of granite from his own quarries. It is 700 feet long and 100 feet high. On its completion he was able to ship granite from the area as well as ore from his mines. As I stood in awe taking a picture of this vast structure, I knew that a great man had been there. Without a wide-angle lens my camera caught only three of the 10 arches. By 1982 when John Treffry took me to see the Treffry viaduct again, I found much heavier undergrowth than over thirty years before. On this last trip, late on a sunless day, the viaduct seemed even more impressive as it dwarfed the undergrowth and mammoth granite boulders. With my share of Cornish imagination, I wondered if Joseph Treffry had envisioned leaving this viaduct after it had lost its usefulness, to protect the valley below as a refuge for the piskies, goblins, and little folk that some Cornish say had been frightened away by the arrival of the railways that he had helped to bring into Cornwall.

When Joseph Treffry's industrial and mining enterprises were well under way he turned some of his boundless energy and engineering ingenuity toward repairing, remodelling and adding to Place. Fortunately, he kept a 'Memorandum Book' of this tremendous project on which he spent over £120,000.

Joseph Treffry's mother was in her mid-nineties at the time of her death in 1842. Her vivid memories of Place back into the mid 1700s had undoubtedly helped to spark her son's interest in the restoration and preservation of this ancient and historic building. Like most old houses, she recalled that Place had a 'dungeon cut in the solid rock. The lower room of the castle above the dungeon had the windows protected by stout iron bars only and was generally used by the gardeners for keeping their tools. The rooms above had diamond glass windows and the plastering bold and beautiful'. In one of the rooms the gardener kept fruit, and in the other Joseph's mother and sister kept pigeons.

Some very fine work had been done on Place in Joseph Treffry's grandfather's time by two men who had been employed to do work on the Palace at The Hague for the Prince of Orange. Very few structural changes had been made to Place since 1457, however, when the then Thomas Treffry partially rebuilt it, adding the strong embattled tower after the French attack. In 1740 the east side of Place was rebuilt. However, around 1770 the castellated tower fell down. In 1817, when Austin turned his thoughts to restoring Place, its structure was in a bad state of decay. As in all his other projects he took complete control. All the work was done under his direction and according to his plans and instructions. In order to replace the fallen tower it was necessary to excavate to make a proper foundation. At the depth of 20 feet was found a very thick stone wall built of solid masonry. At the base of this wall were found several bodies clad in coats of chain armour, with breast plates and large powerful spurs. Also found were some old coins, and very ancient curious rings, some of plain gold, and others set with precious stones, symbolic of both marriage and mourning. One was thought to have been made in Constantinople. Also discovered around the wall was a large quantity of splattered lead. Was this lead splattered in 1457 when Elizabeth Treffry poured molten lead onto the heads of the French invaders?

Joseph Treffry tried to preserve the ancient character of Place both inside and out. The present dining-room was the ancient 'Hall' and the oldest part of Place. It had a richly carved quarter-arch unpainted oak ceiling that had gradually sunk several inches in the middle. He had to take up the weight of the dining-room floor from the cellar and take up the ceiling from the floor, and by screws and purchases put in a new beam in the place of the decayed one. 'I raised the whole ceiling to its original sweep and to secure, opened the walls on the outside, and fixed on the ends of the beams strong iron casings firmly

1. Place, Fowey, Cornwall, c.1920.

2. Heraldry on the steps to the front door, Place

3. The granite tower from the west, Place.

4. The Porphyry Hall, Place.

5. The panelled library, Place.

6. The dining room, Place.

7. The drawing-room, Place.

8. The drawing-room door, Place.

9. Detail of the drawing-room cornice, Place.

10. Treffry Gate, Lanhydrock

1. (top right) Baptismal font—
t Kew.

2. (above) Slaughter Bridge.

3. (right) Monument in St
imbarrus church, Fowey to
ir John, William and Thomas
reffry, brothers.

14. (*left*) Hugh Peter, 1598-1660.

15. (*bottom left*) Joseph Thomas (Austin) Treffry 21st of Place.

16. (*bottom right*) Edward John (Wilcocks) Treffry 22nd of Place.

17. John de Cressy Treffry, 10th son of Edward John Treffry. Portrait at Place.

. Charles Ebenezer Treffry, 23rd of Place.

19. Anne Treffry, Place.

20.   Col. Edward Treffry, 24th of Place.

21. (*above*) Anne Treffry with Mayor and Mace Bearer after receiving the honour of 'Freeman of the Borough of Fowey', 1967.

22. (*left*) John Treffry, expert horseman, elder son of Col. Edward and Anne Treffry.

23. (*below*) Jonathan de Crécy Treffry, expert skier, elder son of John Treffry and grandson of Anne Treffry.

24. (*top left*) Ancient doorway, Bere Barton.

25. (*top right*) Bere Barton, 1984.

26. (*above*) Ancient steps between Bere Barton and the churchyard.

27. (*centre right*) Old section of house, Bere Barton.

28. (*right*) Fireplace in dining room, Bere Barton.

29. (*top left*) Philomene Chesnel Treffry, wife of Joseph William Leonard Treffry.
30. (*top right*) Philippe Treffry, eldest son of eldest sons back to Robert Treffry of Landrake, Cornwall.
31. (*centre*) Joseph William Leonard Treffry.
32. (*bottom left*) Mary Ann Horan Treffry, wife of Joseph Eveleigh Treffry.
33. (*bottom right*) Joseph Eveleigh Treffry, emigrant to Canada in 1876.

34. Robert John Treffry (1811-1879) of Colombia, S.A., 1870. Eldest son of John and Hannah Treffry.

35. George Treffry, c. 1870, Exeter. Third son of John and Hannah Treffry. Note the Killigrew chin.

36. Elford Eveleigh Treffry, younger brother of Joseph Eveleigh Treffry as a young boy in Liverpool. Living in Boston, Mass., U.S.A., 1878.

37. Anna Jane Fox, daughter of Benjamin and Sarah Treffry Fox.

38a. Hannah Hayward Treffry, 1788-1879.   38b. John Treffry, 1778-1849.   39. George Treffry, third son, 1814-1880.

Portraits of the Family of John and Hannah Hayward Treffry, emigrants to Canada, 1834

40. Emma Treffry, 1818-1860 and Edwin Treffry, 1820-1904.   41. Marianna Treffry, 1816-1842.

2. William Hayward Treffry, 1827-1910 and Elizabeth reffry, 1829-1912, the author's great-grandmother.

43. Anna Jane Treffry, 1822-1909 and Charles John Treffry, 1825-1908.

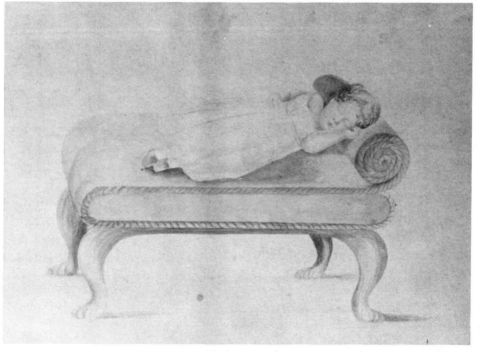

44. Henry John Treffry, 1830-1835.

45. (*top left*) Charles and Alice Corless Treffry, at their golden wedding, 11 Oct. 1904, Tree Lawn Home, Hawtrey, Ontario.

46. (*top right*) Dr. Charles Treffry, grandson of Charles and Alice Treffry, July 1942, Toronto, Canada.

47. (*bottom left*) Edwin Treffry, fourth son of John and Hanna Treffry. He helped his father to build the log house in 1834.

48. (*bottom right*) Harvard and Harriet Froelich Smith, great granddaughter of Edwin Treffry at the celebration of their golden wedding, 1975.

bolted. The beams are all English oak. The panels and dividers, wainscot and all were sound'. (Quotation from Treffry's 'Memorandum Book'.)

The old floor of this room was of random planks, black oak two and three feet wide. Under it were two other oak floors resting on oak beams and girders of immense size, one cut with the bark on. In 1827 Joseph replaced these beams with beams from the *St Nicolas,* a Spanish 74-gun ship, which was taken in 'such gallant style by Lord Nelson and which lay many years in Caffa Mill Pill and was there broken up'. The supporting beams removed from the dining-room floor Joseph converted into the stairs of the main staircase. He replaced some principal beams supporting the roof, and converted the old ones into bannisters. He noted 'the beams being at least as old as the re-building of the house—1457'.

Over the mantel in the dining-room he added 'the present neat and ornamental shield to the arms of Treffry and Tresithney. I also designed the sideboards and had them built by the same man who did the staircases'. The arms of the Earl of Bedford he moved from another part of the house to the dining-room, and placed it on the wall opposite the fireplace.

In restoring the entry porch Joseph Treffry salvaged what he could from the old coats of arms cut in French stone that had been removed by his grandfather for cleaning, but had not been replaced, as his grandfather died soon after. Servants living at Place, not realising what the stones were, used some of them for scouring or cleaning the white hearth stones in the house. Joseph Treffry, using such stones as remained, added the rest from Pentewan: 'as three out of four of the corbels remained I obtained the lines from them of the former groins and filled them in with plain panels not knowing what coats of arms were lost or destroyed'. This display of heraldry can be seen on the stairway to the front door, and is illustrated in the plate section.

Joseph Treffry also made the sweeping driveway that begins at Place Road and continues around to the front of the house and to the above entry way. There is also a stairway down from this driveway to a gate that leads to St Fimbarrus churchyard, the church itself, and the town of Fowey.

Most of the restorative work on Place was completed by 1834, in spite of the disruptions caused by some incompetent and drunken workmen who seemingly took advantage of Joseph when he was off in London on business. In restoring Place he refitted all windows with stone window mountings. He also replaced some entire walls. He recorded that, 'Most of the old walls round the dining room and Bookroom remain. A part of the walls surrounding each staircase is also old as well as the sitting parlour chimney wall. All the others have been rebuilt within my recollection and mostly by myself'.

While remodelling, his stock of seasoned oak became exhausted 'and luckily, I made a large purchase of timber of the *Bellerophon.* The beams, amongst the rest, on which I myself saw Buonaparte and all his suite walking in Plymouth Sound. With this supply of timber I pannelled the bookroom, framed the Porphyry sideboard in the dining room, with carving Buonaparte and the Duke of Wellington in front of each leg, the Black Prince and Sir John Treffry with various other figures in other parts of the legs of same. With the same oak made almost all the oak doors in the house and the moulding round the breakfast room and Paradise chamber doors'. Paradise is the room above the bookroom. George Gauntlett did the carving.

In 1841 Joseph started to build Porphyry Hall and the tower on the south-west end of Place, both requiring the engineering ingenuity used to build his viaduct. Porphyry Hall is named from the Cornish granite porphyry used in the building of this room. The walls are of pinkish-red highly polished porphyry and the high arched ceiling is of grey granite. The floor and fireplace are also of porphyry and granite. The only wood used is in the doorways at each end of the room. It is a very cold room, even on a warm day.

The tower built from Joseph's own white granite rises to 105 feet. It is built in two halves joined at the top. Each block is bolted to the next, so there seems little chance of this ever falling down. Inside, the tower is supported by a 22-foot arch of solid porphyry, highly polished. There is an inside stairway to the top, where I found a fine lookout point to watch for an enemy coming either by sea, land or air—a spectacular view. Elizabeth Treffry Blair told me that in World War II the air-raid alarm was sounded from the top of this tower.

Joseph Treffry was a many faceted man as is shown in his depth of interests in the remodelling of Place. He was completely fascinated by the archaeological artefacts discovered around Place during the digging for the new tower foundation, and he wanted these findings preserved. He was greatly interested in the antiquity of the house, and was careful to preserve the stained glass windows in which family history and historical events had been recorded.

He was interested in the history of the Treffry family, and in its heraldic achievements being correctly depicted. In 1841 he corresponded with the College of Arms in London, adding to the earlier history of the Treffrys beyond what the College already had, and making corrections in some of their Treffry family records. He carried on a correspondence with the Lysons brothers as they were preparing their *History of Cornwall,* published in 1814.

Joseph Treffry was a conservationist. He planted over 1,000 trees, and scientifically farmed over 1,000 acres. Yet with all his many interests and activities he did not shun his responsibilities in public affairs. He was Sheriff of Cornwall in 1838. He was chairman of the Cornwall Railway Company. He chaired the meeting of the Devon and Cornwall Railway Company that considered Brunel's design for the Royal Albert Bridge over the Tamar. He was an active magistrate.

In December of 1842 Treffry's mother died, and he wrote, 'My beloved kind and good natured parent relieved from all her sufferings on Friday the 9th. December at about five minutes after nine o'clock in the morning. I shall no longer delay recording various local affairs connected principally with the neighbourhood of Fowey and the Treffry family, for with my dear departed mother the neighbourhood has lost a sort of register of the times during which she lived'.

Susanna Treffry Austin was in her 95th year at the time of her death. Her health with few exceptions had been remarkably good. Her appearance since the age of 70 had changed little. Her eyesight and hearing were good; she was able to read small print, and work with a small needle without glasses. There was not a wrinkle on her face. She was always an early riser; up by seven o'clock or earlier, and kept herself busy all the day. She seldom felt fatigue though on the move all the day. If they had company in the evening she would play whist sometimes as late as midnight. During the last summer of her life she would often go for hour-long walks. Mrs. Austin was very fond of company, being herself cheerful and entertaining. She kept up with all the fashions and the news by reading the papers daily. She rarely was out of spirits, and often said that she never knowingly did an ill-natured thing in her life, nor wronged anyone to the value of a pin. She generally had a good appetite. She liked the best meat, 'though not made dishes'. She ate fat with impunity, never drank with her dinner, but usually had two glasses of wine after, though at times she would drink none for weeks together. Unfortunately she did not live to see the tower completed, as only about two-thirds of the front wall and staircase were finished when she died.

Four years after Mrs. Austin's death Queen Victoria and the Prince Consort visited Place. Joseph Treffry recorded:

> About breakfast time the Royal party landed at Broadslip. As I was too ill to go myself, I sent Captain Davis in my carriage, in order to show the Queen anything which she might desire to see. Mr. Davis enquired if Her Majesty intended driving on to Par Consols mine, and returned to say that Her Majesty had not contemplated going to the mine; but the Prince Consort added 'had Mr. Treffry paid us the compliment of asking us to visit Place, we would have gone there'.

Captain Davis told them that Mr. Treffry was seriously ill, but was sure that he would be happy to show them Place. Between 1 and 2 o'clock Her Majesty, Prince Albert and suite arrived.

> I there with Captain Davis received them and conducted them into the drawing room. On entering the Hall, Her Majesty pointed out to the Prince the porphyry floor. From the drawing room they passed through the sitting parlour into the large breakfast room where there were paintings of Place and the Viaduct, the former of which the Queen appeared to view with much attention. From thence they passed into the Dining room into the Library, where stood a model of Restormel Castle which I offered to Her Majesty for the Duke of Cornwall, and which was graciously accepted. In returning through the dining room, the porphyry slab supported as a sideboard on a frame of oak taken from the beams of the *Bellerophon*, attracted the particular attention of Her Majesty and the Prince; when I offered to them a similar slab, and which was also graciously accepted. From thence we went to Porphyry Hall, and on entering which Her Majesty made a full stop opposite the great arch, and raising her hands to the arch exclaimed, 'That is magnificent!' The Prince, however, told her that he thought the Jasper stone on the Western side of the Hall was the prettiest stone that he ever saw, and the Queen agreed with him that it was very beautiful. From the Porphyry Hall I escorted them into the Church-yard, where I took my leave of them, with thanks for my attention, and under the hopes that I should not suffer from the excitement as they saw how very ill I was.

It is thought that there were about 5,000 people in Fowey that day to get a glimpse of their Queen.

Joseph Thomas Treffry died at Place on 29 January 1850 and was buried in the south chancel of St Fimbarrus church. It was estimated that many times the number of people who had come to Fowey to honour their Queen came to honour Joseph Treffry at his funeral services.

In ending this all-too brief biography of Joseph Treffry we may note the many ways his life and achievements were similar to those of Hugh Peter. Both were sons of Treffry daughters; both had lost a parent in infancy or young childhood; both had grown up in Fowey; both were university educated. Both were deeply interested in improving the economic conditions of those around them by utilising all the local natural resources. Both had great influence in the United States, Hugh Peter with his contribution to the Massachusetts Bay colony and the founding of Harvard; Joseph Treffry by the many advanced methods developed in his mines that were carried by Cornish miners to the United States, especially after the discovery of gold in California in 1849. The Cornish miners were widely recognised as the best and most skilled in the world.

A statement from the *Mining Journal* of 1850 honouring Joseph Treffry could have also been said of Hugh Peter, 'He was indeed a host in himself, and never did a man more deserve regard or more anxious was he to do good unto others as good should be done unto him'.

PART III

*

19th-CENTURY DESCENDANTS OF THOMAS TREFFRY

Chapter Eight

THE FAMILY OF EDWARD JOHN (WILCOCKS) TREFFRY (1809-1880)

JOSEPH THOMAS TREFFRY left the bulk of his estate to the Revd. Edward John Wilcocks, the son of his cousin, Jane Treffry Dormer Wilcocks. At the time of Treffry's death much of his property was mortgaged to raise funds for his many enterprises. However, his will directed that all work under way should be completed and probate be finalised within five years. A 'Treffry's Estate Act 1852' was passed to aid Chancery in establishing the trusts required by the will.

Before Revd. Wilcocks could take over the property there were additional mortgages and assignments, and some holdings sold to pay debts. Revd. Wilcocks was to inherit the Treffry estates provided he took the name of Treffry. He complied quickly, assuming by a royal licence dated May 1850, the arms and name of Treffry, thus becoming the 22nd of Place in the 24th generation and 27th in line of inheritance. This was the third time that the Treffry name was assumed by the son of a mother from the Treffry family: first Jane Treffry Toller, then Susanna Treffry Austin and Jane Treffry Dormer Wilcocks. Since 1850 the Treffry estates have descended through male heirs carrying the Treffry name. Joseph Treffry, who took great pride in his Treffry heritage, wanted his estate not only to provide for the maintenance of Place, but also to make it possible for the Treffrys to continue to live there carrying on the tradition of many centuries of Treffrys living at historic Place.

Revd. Edward John Treffry, who inherited the Treffry estates aged 40, was the eldest son of Revd. Edward Wilcocks and Jane Treffry Dormer Wilcocks, and was baptized on 8 May 1809 at Sidwell, Exeter. He matriculated at Exeter College, Oxford, on 23 April 1828 and left on 6 May 1830. He was a scholar of Lincoln College between 1830 and 1832, and received his B.A. degree on 26 June 1832; his M.A. degree on 18 May 1842; and his B.C.L. and D.C.L. in 1864. On 30 August 1835 Edward John Wilcocks married Anne, the only daughter of Charles Steele, Esq., R.N., St Mary's, Isles of Scilly, who was the Inspecting Commander of the Coast Guard. Anne was born in Harwich on 19 October 1815.

From 1835-1842 Revd. Wilcocks was a Clerk in the Holy Orders of the Church of England in the Isles of Scilly. In 1842 he became headmaster of the Great Berkhamsted Grammar School, serving until 1850 when his inheritance of the Treffry estates imposed on him great responsibilities which he never forgot or neglected.

* Chapter headpiece: baptismal font,
   St Fimbarrus's church

89

Thirteen years after inheriting Place and the other Treffry properties Revd. Edward John (Wilcocks) Treffry became the vicar of Fowey on 28 January 1863. He served until May of 1867 when he resigned and was followed by his son-in-law, Revd. Hanfield Noel Purcell, who was the husband of Anne Ellen Treffry, the eldest daughter. Revd. Treffry later served as rector of Lansallos, east of Fowey, in 1871–1872. He published a number of religious writings and sermons, including:

Family Prayers (1835); *two Assize sermons at Launceston and Bodmin* (1838); *A sermon preached at the anniversary of the Royal Cornwall Infirmary, Monday, August 12, 1861, at St Mary's, Truro,* which was published and circulated by the Governors. (Truro, Netherton, 1861); 'The Duty and Benefit of Seeking God', which appeared in the *Church of England Magazine,* vol. V, pp. 217–19, in 1838.

There was great excitement in 1865 when Place again received royal visitors. The Prince (later Edward VII) and Princess of Wales landed at Fowey in the royal yacht *Osborne,* and were entertained at Place. They visited the Par smelting works, Fowey Consoles mine, and Restormel.

St Fimbarrus's parish church

The Treffry family enjoyed a fine life at Place—yachting, boating, fishing and riding, with a large and happy family to share it all. Apparently the Revd. Treffry was interested in the arts as he allowed the portrait of Hugh Peter, painted in 1627, to be taken from Place to London to be exhibited in the National Portrait Collection Exhibition of 1868.

The great responsibilities of the fortune Revd. Treffry had inherited he took seriously: he entered into many varied business ventures. He had holdings in the South Cornwall Granite Company, the Phoenix and West Phoenix United Mines, various rental properties, and Liskeard District Bank. In May of 1861 he became a partner in the South Cornwall Bank, called Willyams, Treffry, West and Co. After Revd. Treffry's death, his son, Charles Ebenezer Treffry, was admitted as a partner in 1881. The name of the firm then became Willyams, Treffry and Co. A branch was opened in Fowey; it became Bolitho's in 1890 and Barclays in 1905.

Besides acquiring property Revd. Treffry sold some of his holdings. He received £103,500 from the Great Western Railroad Company for the Par Tramway, the Newquay Tramway and the Newquay quays in November 1887. In 1858 the Revd. Treffry held 64 shares in the brigantine *Concord* and in 1871 acquired 20 shares of the *Superior,* a 67-foot sailing ship. In 1853 he held interests in a number of hotels in Cornwall, Devon and London.

Revd. Treffry served as a magistrate for Cornwall and was considered firm and thoughtful, but never harsh. From his activities in church, school and various business enterprises it is evident that he was interested, involved and able in whatever he undertook; another example of an outstanding son of the distaff side of the Treffry family.

Revd. Edward John and Anne Steele Treffry were the parents of a very large family of 13 children.

The Revd. Edward Treffry died in Fowey on 10 July 1880, aged 71, and his wife died at Place on 22 March 1881, aged 65. In Revd. Treffry's will he provided for his wife in a trust held by their son, Joseph Thomas; son Charles Ebenezer succeeded his father as 23rd of Place. One of his daughters, Annie Ellen Purcell, preceded her father in death leaving seven children. His daughter Maria Stuart had an income settled on her, some other children being already provided for in whole or in part, or having drawn from him during his lifetime much more than others, 'I have taken these things into consideration, together with other things personal and relative which I do not care to specify –in making this my last will and testament'. All the furniture, plate, linen, china, pictures, wines, etc., were left to his 'dear wife'. His interests and shares in business enterprises were divided among the children and all were given various sums of money. The executors were his wife and his sons, Charles Ebenezer and Joseph Thomas.

15th-century porch entrance, St Fimbarrus parish church

His children were as follows:

1. *Edward Augustus* was born on 14 June 1836, but died in infancy.

2. *Edward* was born on 21 September 1838 and died on 21 September 1844. He is buried in St Mary's, Scilly Isles.

3. *Anne Ellen* was born in St Mary's on 16 April 1840, and died at Fowey vicarage on 5 March 1877. She married the Revd. Handfield Noel Purcell, on 24 July 1866, who became vicar of Fowey in 1886 and was also a canon of Truro Cathedral. He was educated at Exeter College, Oxford, gaining his B.A. degree in 1865 and his M.A. in 1866. They were the parents of four sons and three daughters.

4. *Charles Ebenezer* was born in St Mary's, Scilly Isles on 1 May 1842. He is the subject of the next chapter.

5. *George Steele* was born at Berkhamsted on 12 February 1844, and served as a lieutenant in the 63rd Foot and the 2nd West India Regiment. He married Jane Pott Stewart, and they had one son, John St George, who was killed in action on the Somme on 16 September 1916, whilst serving with the Canadian infantry. George Steele Treffry died in Plymouth on 16 June 1907 and was buried in Fowey.

6. *Reginald Heber* was born at Berkhamsted on 30 March 1846, and matriculated from Lincoln College, Oxford, in 1865, gaining his B.A. degree in 1870 and his M.A. in 1872. He was curate of Lydford from 1870 to 1872, and of Lansallos from 1872 to 1873. From 1873-9 he served as a naval chaplain aboard H.M. ships *Penelope, Encounter, Topaze* and *Belleisle,* and was awarded the Ashantee medal. He was rector of Endellion church from 17 February 1880 for many years, and Chaplain to the Sheriff of Cornwall in 1886. He married Blanch Keighley, and they were parents of two children. He died on 10 December 1927, and his wife on 1 March 1939.

The Family Tree of Reginald Heber and Blanch Treffry

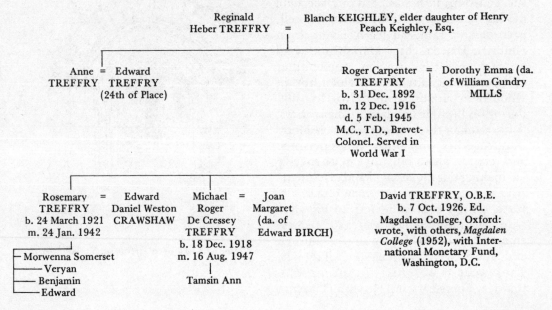

7. *Harry* was born at Berkhamsted on 8 March 1848 and served in the Royal Navy. He was awarded the New Zealand medal, and died in 1908.

8. *Zoe,* who was born at Berkhamsted on 11 December 1849, married Ernest Rüffer in November 1876. He was the eldest son of Baron Alphonse Rüffer, and was a Chevalier de la Legion d'Honneur, and a Chevalier de l'Ordre de Jesu Christe. They had three sons and four daughters. Zoe, Baroness Rüffer, died in 1934.

9. *Joseph Thomas,* born at Fowey on 29 December 1851, was educated at Somerset College, Bath and Sherborne, where he distinguished himself in the class-room and the playing fields. He married Ada, daughter of Colonel John Whitehead Peard, of Trenython, Cornwall, in 1874. Colonel Peard was known as 'Garibaldi's Englishman', because he had joined the latter in Italy and earned his affection and respect as a cool and brave soldier. Garibaldi later visited Colonel Peard at his home, just up-river from Fowey. Joseph Thomas Treffry and his wife lived in the parish of Alverdiscott in North Devon from 1877 to 1898, where he was chairman of the parish council and a member of the Highway Board for Torrington. He was a justice of the peace and sat on the Bideford bench. He was also Honorary Secretary to the Stevenson Hunt, but his greatest interest was yachting: he was a member of yacht clubs in Plymouth, Dartmouth and Fowey.

10. *Edward Lambert* was born at Place on 29 April 1854, and was educated at Magdalen College, Oxford, where he gained his B.A. in 1876. He was then ordained as a clerk in Holy Orders, and served as curate at St Buryan, Cornwall, from 1878 to 1880. He then became curate of Blankney in Lincolnshire in 1880, and subsequently rector of

Carved bench end with Treffry coat of arms, Fimbarrus parish church

Aswarby and vicar of Swarby in the same county. He married Evelyn, daughter of Thomas Henry Pares of Hopwell Hall, Derbyshire and Kirby, Frith in Leicestershire, on 29 April 1885, and they had four children. Edward Lambert Treffry died on 12 September 1925. His eldest son, Thomas Justin Treffry, studied agriculture at Cambridge, after which he managed an estate in Africa for several years before emigrating to Tasmania. Through the persuasions of his mother, the rest of the family joined him in 1914 and they lived together on a farm there for some years, later settling in Launceston in Northern Tasmania. Edward Lambert Treffry's younger son (John Edward Treffry) moved to Sydney, Australia, with his family in 1939, thus establishing one of the Treffry families of that country. Roger Treffry of Beer Barton—discussed later—has descendants in Australia through his son

Samuel, and there is also a family of 'Trefrys' descended from a Richard Trefry and his nephew George, emigrants from Cornwall. One of these Trefrys—David Trefry— is now a professor at Macquire University, New South Wales, but I have not been able to trace early records of this family.

The Family Tree of Edward Lambert and Evelyn Treffry

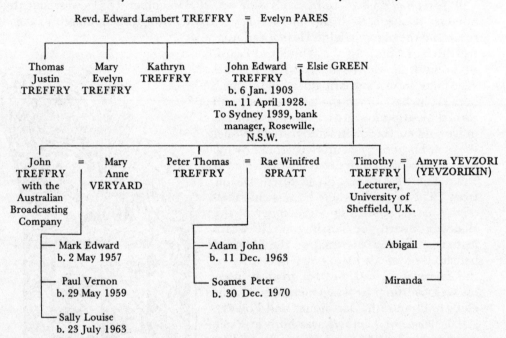

11. *Spencer Thornton* was born at Place on 14 December 1856, and was educated at Tavistock Grammar School and Canstadt, Wurtemburg. He became a captain in the Royal North Devon Hussars and the Yeomanry, and later served with the 3rd (King's Own) Hussars at Aldershot between September and October 1882. Between 1914-18 he was Commander of the Special Reserve Company of the City of London National Guard, and later Acting Adjutant of the School of Auxiliary Cavalry at Aldershot. He married Mary Emelin, sole daughter and heiress of Colonel George Washington Davis, on 16 July, 1893. Colonel Davis had left the United States when his daughter was two and settled in England. Mary Emelin Davis's mother was from the granite state of New Hampshire, where her family had mining interests. Spencer Thornton Treffry was associated with Alphonse Rüffer and Sons. merchant bankers, and he and his family lived in London. He was greatly interested in the family history, and used the Public Record Office and British Museum to help him in his researches, eventually producing his unpublished work 'The History of Fowey and the Treffry Family' in 1891, which has been of great help to the present author. Anne Treffry said that she had heard he spent so much time on research that it interfered with his business affairs. His six children were as follows:

(i) Stephanie Mary, who married Henry Haggard, Lieutenant Commander, Royal Navy in 1928. She was born on 23 November 1894.

(ii) Philip Spencer, born on 24 February 1896, died on 21 July of the same year.

(iii) Jessica Mae, born on 22 August 1898, who married John Douglas Spencer Dean on 22 April 1921.

(iv) Beryl Evelyn Blanch, born on 14 November 1901, who married John Edward Alfred Hoare, D.S.C., on 8 June 1942. She researched the Treffry family history and prepared genealogical charts with armorial illustrations.

(v) Sylvia Francesca was born on 18 May 1903 and married Major Henry Daniel Lysons, R.A., on 17 September 1938. He was the son of Colonel Henry Lysons and Vandah Louisa Bretton Treffry, daughter of Charles Ebenezer Treffry (*see* Chapter 9). Their son, Harry Lysons of New York, is interested in the family's history and sent me copies of his Aunt Beryl's records.

(vi) Bevil Courtenay was born on 26 July 1905.

12. *John De Cressy* was born on 3 April 1859 at Place. He joined the firm Moss, Treffry and Co., general merchants, as a partner, but the partnership was dissolved for Samuel Moss on 28 September 1881. John De Cressy Treffry married Lorina, daughter of Lieutenant-Colonel George Wilson of Hethel, Norfolk, in 1883; she died in 1897. His second wife was Mary Beatrice (C.B.E.), daughter of the Revd. R. H. Poole, rector of West Rainton. The family resided at Penarwyn. John De Cressy Treffry was a Justice of the Peace for Cornwall in 1901, and High Sheriff of Cornwall in 1921. He served with the British Expeditionary Force in France during World War I. For 42 years he was master of Fowey Harriers, and the Harriers presented him with his portrait (which hangs at Place today) as a token of appreciation. He died in 1927, on 14 December, and his second wife died in November 1942.

13. *Maria Stuart* was born at Place on 4 December 1860. She married Major William Robert Prickett, R.A., the fourth son of Thomas Prickett of Bridlington, on 4 July 1882. They had one son and one daughter. Maria Stuart Treffry Prickett died on 4 June 1935, outliving her husband, who died on 19 November 1917.

Chapter Nine

THE FAMILY OF CHARLES EBENEZER TREFFRY (from 1842)

CHARLES EBENEZER TREFFRY was the third son of Edward John and Ann Steele Treffry. The first son had died in infancy and the second aged six. Charles, born 1 May 1842 at St Mary's, Isles of Scilly, was eight years old when his father inherited the Treffry estates and the family with six children moved to Fowey. There he grew up in the same environment which Hugh Peter and Joseph Thomas Treffry had known. However, Place had been completely renovated and there were ample funds to maintain it from the extensive business conglomerate established by Joseph Treffry and preserved by the Revd. Edward Treffry. Charles was prepared in private schools for his entrance on 26 June 1859, aged 18, to Magdalene College, Cambridge. He served as a first lieutenant and later as a captain in the Royal Miners Artillery.

At the age of 38 in 1880 he inherited from his father the Treffry estates, thus becoming the 23rd of Place in the 25th generation, and the 28th in the line of inheritance. He then moved from Bagatelle House, Fowey, to Place. In 1881 Charles Treffry became a partner in Willyam, Treffry and Co., South Cornwall Bank. However, his interests were not so much directed toward business as Joseph Treffry's or his own father's had been.

Charles Treffry was known all over Cornwall as 'the Squire', a true Victorian gentleman, friendly and likeable. Being public-spirited and deeply concerned with the needs of the community, he gave the land in Fowey for the hospital which was opened in 1914. He served as Justice of the Peace, and became High Sheriff of Cornwall in 1887. He and Sir Arthur Quiller-Couch were the principal petitioners for the new Charter that was granted to the town of Fowey in 1913, the first since 1819. There was a great celebration on this occasion, beginning with the ringing of the church bells at 8 a.m. The proclamation was read from the town hall steps by the acting town clerk, followed by a service in the church of St Fimbarrus. There was then a procession from the church, including local dignitaries, other Cornish mayors, and many distinguished guests, to the beautiful gardens of Place where the Charter was presented by Sir Reginald Pole-Carew at 2.30 p.m. to Mr. Charles E. Treffry, first mayor under the new

Charter. This was followed by a public luncheon, afternoon sports for the children, and a carnival procession after tea. In the evening a fancy dress ball was held at the Armoury, to climax a very happy day in the history of Fowey.

For recreation Charles Treffry enjoyed yachting, hunting and shooting. On 5 February 1907 for the rent of £1, he made an agreement with Louise, wife of John Cosmo Rashleigh of Menabilly, Esq., for permission for himself, his friends, his gamekeepers and servants to enter Point Neptune plantation and St Catherine's, Fowey, to hunt, shoot, and enjoy similar sports. He agreed to keep down rabbits and prevent them from increasing and injuring the young crops. This added to lands available to him for hunting.

On 30 August 1866 Charles Treffry married Udney Maria Von Blakeley, elder daughter of Baron Joseph Von Bretton of Copenhagen, at St George's, Hanover Square, London. A collateral ancestor of hers, Captain Johnston Blakeley of North Carolina, brought to the family history an interesting historical event which had been a turning point in the early history of the infant United States of America. Captain Blakeley, commanding the sloop-of-war *Wasp*, helped considerably in saving America from its threatened reconquest by the dominant British forces at the most critical period of the War of 1812–1814. He was the commander of the second *Wasp*, 22 guns and 160 men, built at Newburyport, Massachusetts, in 1814. On 28 June 1814 in the English Channel, the *Wasp* captured the British sloop *Reindeer*, and then sailed to France for refitting. On 1 September 1814, the *Wasp* captured the British brig *Avon*, and on 9 October following, the *Wasp* met the Swedish brig *Adams* and picked up Lieutenant McKnight and a master's mate, who were from the U.S. *Essex* and were being taken from Brazil to England. The *Wasp* was never heard from again. Theodore Roosevelt in his *Naval War of 1812* stated that the *Wasp* 'both because of her signal daring and success, and because of the tragic mystery of her end, became one of the most famous [ships] in the annals of the American Navy'.

Captain Blakeley, who lost his life at the age of 33, left an infant daughter, Udney Maria Blakeley. Out of gratitude for his deeds the state of North Carolina educated her and presented her with a tea and coffee service. This historic collection of sterling silver was inherited by Colonel Edward Treffry, 24th of Place, the eldest surviving son of Squire Charles and Udney Blakeley Treffry. (Recently the silver service was returned to North Carolina to be added to its historical collection from the early days of the young nation.)

Udney Blakeley Treffry perhaps had an extra interest in the welfare of seamen because of the fate of Captain Johnston Blakeley. In 1883 she was one of four women who laid the four foundation stones for a building in Fowey which was built for a Sailor's Rest. She took a great interest in developing the grounds surrounding Place, laying out formal gardens and pathways and planting many varieties of shrubs and trees. There was a head gardener who lived on the premises, with a large staff to keep the grounds. On my first trip to Cornwall I was quite amazed to find palm trees growing at Place, and in other areas of Cornwall. The palm trees, the rhododendrons, the sea, all reminded me very much of my home area of northern California.

The children of Charles and Udney Blakeley Treffry were as follows:

1. *Blakeley Von Bretton,* born on 11 August 1867, lived in Fowey. He was a bright, lively and active youngster. One morning (23 August 1879), shortly after his 12th birthday he rode over to Par where his uncles were working, planning to return with them to Fowey. As they were busy in the Par office, while waiting for them he played about the Par harbour siding when three loaded horse-drawn trucks passed. He grabbed a rope hanging from a tarpaulin covering one of the trucks and pulled himself up to the grease box. Tragically he missed his footing and slipped between the wheels. Before the trucks could be stopped, he was badly crushed. He died at Par two hours later. The grief to the family must have been beyond description. A memorial to Blakeley Treffry was placed in the Treffry chapel of St Fimbarrus's church by his mother's younger sister, Alice Florence de Bretton, who was married to Charles, second Baron Garvagh.

2. *Edward,* born on 1 March 1869 at Newquay. The 24th of Place and the subject of Chapter 10.

3. *Florence,* born 5 March 1871. Married, firstly, Charles Perkins, late captain, Duke of Cornwall's Light Infantry, by whom she had one son and one daughter. She married, secondly, R. M. H. Tighe, who died in April 1935. She died on 15 October 1939.

4. *Vandah Louisa Bretton* married Captain Henry Lysons, V.C., son of Sir Daniel Lysons. Their son, Major Henry Daniel Lysons, R.A., married his cousin, Sylvia Francesca, daughter of Spencer Thornton Treffry. (q.v. Chapter 8 above.)

5. *Dormer Kierulff de Bretton,* born on 7 May 1877, was educated at Eton. He served as a second lieutenant in the Coldstream Guards in World War I, and was killed in action on the Somme on 15 September 1916. There is a memorial to him in St Fimbarrus's church.

Udney Blakeley Treffry died 5 April 1904. Charles married, secondly, on 30 March 1905, Henrietta, daughter of John Kingsley of Manchester. She died March of 1937. 'Squire' Charles Ebenezer Treffry died on 27 February 1924 and was followed by his second son, Colonel Edward Treffry, as 24th of Place.

Chapter Ten

THE FAMILY OF EDWARD AND ANNE TREFFRY (from 1869)

THE ANCIENT, quaint and historic village of Fowey had by 1950 recovered from World War II. In the harbour were sailboats dwarfed by ocean-going freighters carrying Cornwall's famous China clay in which the Treffrys from Joseph Thomas Treffry's time had held interests. The narrow, hilly shop-lined streets with pedestrians here and there had only an occasional motor car. This was before the 'jet age' which poured hordes of tourists into England, and as petrol was then rationed, few motorists ventured into this far corner of Great Britain.

Anne Treffry had invited me to tea and instructed me to come via the church-yard gate to Place. As I walked down the Esplanade the sun was bright, birds were singing, and flowers were spilling over ancient rock walls in great profusion. I was captivated forever by the jewel that is Fowey. No wonder the family had resided there for centuries. Through the churchyard gate, then made of wood, I mounted the stonewalled stairway leading up to the gravel driveway where I viewed for the first time the massive south front of Place with its turrets, battlements and family shields carved in stone. I also noted the heraldry in the entry way, with the many shields of the Cornish and Devon families who had married into the Treffry family over the past 800 years.

Anne Treffry greeted me at the door where we began an exciting tour of Place. The first room to the right was the drawing-room. On entering Anne said, 'The dust covers have been removed so you could see the matching arm-chairs and sofas'. They were of French design, but of English craftsmanship and were upholstered in petit-point, picking up the delicate colours of the rug. Rare porcelain filled glass-enclosed cabinets. The walls were of gold brocade with matching draperies. All this was in great contrast to the plaster ceiling, painted brown with a variety of heads carved in the cornices. Since the reconstruction of this room was done by Joseph Thomas Treffry, I noticed a bit of Celtic expression of design typical of early Celtic times when heads were used as art motifs. To confirm this thought were the animal heads carved in the massive stone supports of the window sills and the head designs carved at the top of the heavy double doors of the room. The Celtic expressions everywhere seemed to emerge so naturally, reflecting the early heritage of the Treffrys.

The next room was a small sitting-room facing east, with the portrait above the mantel of Anne's husband, the late, distinguished Colonel Edward Treffry,

24th of Place (*see* the plate section). From there we entered the breakfast room
or morning room that seemed almost as large as the drawing-room, with a large
bay window facing east. On the opposite wall was a cabinet filled with blue and
white porcelain, while a large table and chairs stood in the centre of the room.
Undoubtedly the table had held many delicious hunt breakfasts and other festive
meals for family gatherings. Anne told me that now many committee meetings
were held there, to discuss borough problems, land preservation, church affairs,
welfare causes, and other interests of great concern to her. It was a comfortable
and inviting room.

From there we walked down the granite-floored colonnade flanked with green
and flowering plants. The large windows looking into the courtyard were entirely
filled with fleur-de-lis patterned glass reflecting the Treffry's privilege of quartering the French fleur-de-lis in their coat of arms since the time of the battle of
Crécy. History was everywhere.

The library walls of dark stained wood from the *Bellerophon* were brightened
with colourful shields reflecting centuries of history of the ancient Treffry family.
The coat of arms of the Treffry family quartering France, dating from the time
of the Black Prince, was above the mantel, and the Treffry coat of arms above
that. Anne told me that she and her husband had had the shields prepared and
added to the room. One wall of the room was solid with books, many pertaining
to the early history of Cornwall with references to the Treffry family. From the
library we entered the dining-room, which was originally the great hall of the
oldest part of the house. This was the room where Joseph Thomas Treffry had
raised the sagging ceiling and put in a new floor, restoring the room to its present
beauty. On the walls were hanging many family portraits. In 1904 there was a
fire in this room, but Charles E. Treffry would not let the firemen use water to
stop it as he thought water would do more damage than the fire. In so doing,
Place lost its only Joshua Reynolds painting.

After tea we went up a circular staircase near the library and passed through 'Paradise', the room over the library, to Porphyry Hall. There I stood in the doorway where Queen Victoria and Prince Albert had exclaimed over the beauty of the scene. The light grey of the vaulted granite ceiling was supported artistically by the deeper pink-red colour of the polished porphyry walls. The colours alternated in squares on the floor. At the far end of the room, in the glass above the doors, were again to be found the brilliant colours of the family coat of arms. From this door we came out under the vast tower that Joseph Thomas Treffry had built.

Anne told me that her elder daughter, Elizabeth Morgan (now Blair), was living in China. Later Elizabeth made her home in the Porphyry Hall wing of Place with 'Paradise' as her living room. Anne's only other daughter, Pamela, was summering at Castle Ruins in Fowey with two of her three children, Fiona and James Crichton. The elder son, Angus, was off at school. Pamela invited me to dinner to meet some of her sailing friends. Sailing was a must for the young of heart who lived at Fowey and did great battle in many regattas.

On another day Anne Treffry took me through the extensive grounds surrounding Place. From many areas there were picturesque views of the village and the harbour below. Each day there were excursions to historic places of interest, Luxulyan Viaduct, St Mawes, St Ives, and to lunch at the *Tresanton Inn*. Anne was an excellent guide and fine navigator as we travelled the narrow, winding hedge-bound roads which meandered everywhere.

As the first week in Fowey drew to a close, I realised that in finding the charming village of Fowey, seeing ancient and historic Place, and travelling around Cornwall, I had found a treasured spot that I wanted always to be a part of, as my ancestors for centuries had been. Perhaps one of the reasons this visit had been so very special, was because Anne Treffry and her daughter Pamela had helped to make it so.

Anne Treffry was the only daughter of the Revd. Reginald Heber Treffry, and had resided as a child at Endellion where her father was the rector for many years. Endellion, not far from St Kew, was in the heart of the area long associated with King Arthur. Besides Anne's only brother, Roger, she had as companion for several summers a young cousin, Jessica Treffry, who had had polio and needed the fresh Cornish air. Anne as a young lady attended parties and balls in the great houses of Cornwall. Although she had a number of young Cornish admirers, she chose to marry her dashing and handsome older cousin, Colonel Edward Treffry, son of Charles E. Treffry, 23rd of Place, her father's older brother. After Colonel Edward and Anne Treffry's marriage on 15 January 1913, they lived in St Austell until 1924 when Colonel Treffry became the 24th of Place and they moved there with their young family of two sons and two daughters, John, Dormer, Elizabeth and Pamela. Shortly after moving to Place, Colonel Treffry gave five acres of Treffry property to the people of Fowey as a recreation field. It was to be called 'Squire's Field' in memory of his father, who was known all over Cornwall as the 'Squire'.

Colonel Edward Treffry had been educated at Eton and the University of Heidelburg. He served for many years with distinction in the military, receiving many awards, among them the C.M.G. (1915), the O.B.E. (1919), and the T.D. (1923). He was aide-de-camp to King George V from 1927 until 1936, dividing his time between Fowey, London and other places, as he represented the King at many functions as required. He was a Doctor of Law and served as Justice of the Peace for Cornwall in 1897 and High Sheriff in 1928, and as Deputy Lieutenant and Vice-Lieutenant from 1936 until his death. He was joint chairman of the Cornwall Quarter Sessions from 1923 until 1939. Colonel Treffry served in South Africa in 1900-1, winning the Queen's Medal with five clasps. He also served in the Uganda Protectorate as Assistant District Commissioner during 1905-1909, and served in the European war of 1914-1918. Before his death on 7 January 1942 he saw Fowey bombed in World War II, both of his sons serving in the army, and his younger son, Dormer, a prisoner-of-war in Germany. Colonel Treffry was a great sportsman, a good cricketer, a first-class shot, an enthusiastic fisherman, and a keen follower of hounds. He was Vice-Commodore of the Royal Fowey Yacht Club and a member of the Royal Yacht Squadron, Cowes.

During World War II, no part of England was untouched by the severity of the times. Fowey in the south-western coast of England, not far from Plymouth, was in a more dangerous situation than during the days of the great Armada. Every member of every family bore an active share of the burdens, privations and sufferings, the Treffrys outstanding among them. Lieutenant Dormer Treffry who served with the 51st Highland Division was taken prisoner at St Valerie on the north-west coast of France before Dunkirk. He was a prisoner-of-war in Germany for five years, during which time he could receive packages once a month containing soap, cigarettes, clothing, etc. Packages seemed to get through to him when posted from Lisbon. During this time Captain John Treffry was serving in the Duke of Cornwall's Light Infantry for which service he received the Territorial Decoration. He was injured in 1943.

The Treffry daughters, Elizabeth and Pamela, were also contributing to the war effort. Elizabeth started a canteen in Fowey which was open from 10 a.m. to 10 p.m. where pasties and tea were served to servicemen. The volunteers also helped with letter-writing and other chores to make the seamen's stay in Fowey

more comfortable. Elizabeth, who later served in the W.A.A.F., was two years at radar stations and two years at a training station in the Midlands.

In August of 1940, Polruan, across the harbour from Fowey, was bombed, demolishing the schoolhouse. Fortunately there was no loss of life. There were other raids in 1941. After many raids on Plymouth with great damage and loss of life, especially the lives of young children, Fowey was made an evacuation centre for the Plymouth children. Fowey with its strategic location on the English Channel was also a base for Air-Sea Rescue, submarines, and for torpedo boats manned by British and Polish crews.

Following the Pearl Harbour attack on 7 December 1941, many Treffry cousins on the other side of the Atlantic were joining in the struggle. My youngest brother, now Lieutenant-Colonel A. L. Rideout, U.S. Air Force, retired, was at Westover Field in Massachusetts only 10 days later helping to prepare the first advanced elements of the 8th Air Fighter Command to take off for England by mid-January 1942. Later, arriving in England, he was stationed at Ashford, Kent, between London and Dover, directly in the path of the first of the German buzz-bombs. One of my Hudson school classmates from Ohio, Jean Teas, worked on the development of the proximity fuse which was used in stopping the buzz-bombs. This device was considered second in importance to the atomic bomb in shortening the war.

In 1943, a U.S.A. Advanced Amphibious Training Force was established in Fowey. Anti-aircraft guns and balloon barrages defended the port and the south coast of Cornwall. From the jetties at Fowey, ammunition was loaded on to ships. A small fleet assembled with U.S.A. troops and left Fowey to take part in the D-Day landing on the coast of France on 6 June 1944. Place was a battle post with soldiers stationed in the house. The library served as the port post. Even with all this going on Anne shared Place and its treasured rations with tired servicemen on leave.

The years following World War I in England were a golden age compared to the years after World War II, when England was almost brought to her knees. In the 'twenties and 'thirties, fantastic sums were spent by those who had it, on horses, yachts, motor cars, entertainment and travel. During these years the titled and landed gentry of England enjoyed a life with plenty of servants, gardeners, chauffeurs and groomsmen. The whole of that life has gone forever. Many of the great houses now belong to the National Trust and are open at times to the public. Place, however, remains a private residence and has been the home of Anne Treffry for 60 years.

St Fimbarrus's church, adjacent, and just below Place, holds great interest for Treffry family members. Around 1500, Sir John Treffry and his brothers, William and Thomas, widened the south aisle of the church making a Treffry family chapel where most of the memorials to members of the family are. Some memorials are in the stained glass clerestory windows, some scratched in stone, and earlier ones recorded in brass are on the window sills. Heavily carved bench ends display many Treffry-related family shields. Early memorials to the Treffrys are the oldest in the church. Outside on the south side of the church porch rests the tombstone in memory of Thomas and Elizabeth Killigrew Treffry. Formerly it was inside the church.

St Fimbarrus's church has a very early history, as Celtic Christianity was well established in Cornwall before the missionaries arrived there from Rome in 597 A.D. It is thought that St. Goran or Duron's church preceded St Finn Barr's church in Fowey. St Finn Barr is thought to have been the first Bishop of Cork. He is said to have followed the early trade route from Ireland by sea to Padstow, overland to Fowey, and by sea to Brittany and on to Rome. On the way he built a little church in Fowey. Around 1150 A.D. a Norman church was built, of which only the font remains. A new church was built in 1328, which was partially destroyed when the French attacked in 1457. This was at the time that Elizabeth Colyn Treffry is credited with saving Place and much of Fowey by pouring molten lead on the heads of the invaders. Later her husband, Thomas, with the Earl of Warwick, rebuilt the church (*see* Chapter 3). The brasses in the church are of this Thomas and Elizabeth Colyn Treffry and of his father, Thomas, and mother, Amicia Michelstowe Treffry.

In 1947 the wooden reredos and panelling were given in memory of Colonel Edward Treffry and the Revd. Reginald H. Treffry. Anne Treffry took great interest in the affairs of the church and up until her late eighties was responsible for artistic flower arrangements for the altar. She also arranged fresh flowers every day for Place, which were gathered from the grounds or from the greenhouse. Flowers and birds are two of Anne's great interests.

Anne Treffry, devoted to her family, is fortunate in having her son, John, and daughters, Elizabeth and Pamela, living nearby. Dormer, who had three children (Sarah Jane and the twins, Dormer Blakeley and Dozmare Anne) lives in Devon. Grandchildren and great-children come and go. John's elder son, Jonathan, is in the U.S.A., following eight years in the army. Last summer he visited California when we explored the 'Mother Lode' mining area, where many Cornish miners had worked. John's son, William, is in Australia, and his daughter, Peregrine, in London. Pamela's daughter, Fiona, lives in Houston, and her son, James, serves in the British army.

Anne Treffry is, as her husband had been, public spirited and philanthropic, and has participated in many community activities in Fowey. In 1963 she and her family, and with her daughter, Elizabeth Treffry Morgan and her husband, Frederic F. L. Morgan, presented to the people of Fowey two maces made of Cornish tin. Mr. Morgan, distressed over the borough of Fowey being deprived of its maces, which had been presented by Sir Bevil Grenville in 1685, decided to see that they were replaced. He designed two maces of tin which were symbolic of its production and exportation since early Celtic days. As the exportation of China clay dated back to Cookworthy's days, replacing tin as an important export, a clay tip supported a globe, symbolic of the China clay being exported all over the world. The Treffry mace bore the Treffry crest, and an inscription denoted the connection over many years between the family and the borough since the first charter in 1685. The Morgan mace with the Morgan crest celebrated the fiftieth anniversary of the 1913 re-granting of Fowey's charter, under which Elizabeth Morgan's grandfather, Charles E. Treffry, was the first mayor.

The inscriptions are as follows on the Treffry mace: 'Presented to the Borough of Fowey by the Treffry family in A.D. 1963 to commemorate their associations since the first Charter in A.D. 1685', and on the Morgan mace: 'Presented to the Borough of Fowey in A.D. 1963 by Councillor Elizabeth and Frederic F. L. Morgan to mark the 50th Anniversary of the present Charter'. Following the presentation of the maces at Fowey town hall, the maces preceded the Mayor and Corporation to the St Fimbarrus church for a dedication service, followed by a trumpet fanfare.

Borough of Fowey

DEDICATION

of the

NEW MACES

and Commemoration of the

50th Anniversary

of the

Re-granting of the Charter

in

FOWEY PARISH CHURCH

on

THURSDAY, 7TH NOVEMBER, 1963 at 7.15 p.m.

Anne Treffry in 1967 brought a great and distinctive honour to the Treffry family when her name was added to the roll of 'Freemen of the Borough of Fowey'. The last person to receive such an honour was the distinguished Sir Arthur Quiller-Couch in 1937. No woman in Fowey had ever been given the honour, and it was the last time it would be given, as Fowey was soon to be amalgamated with nearby St Austell; but she is also the first in the new borough for the roll continues with the new authority.

Anne Treffry of Place was chosen because she had done so much over many years for the welfare of the town. Although it was a personal honour, the name of Treffry had been held in high esteem, in wartime and in peace, for centuries. A great tribute was given to Anne Treffry when the mayor said, 'The Treffry family has had a long and varied influence on the life of the community, but none has ever had the love and respect of the people more than has the present owner of Place'.

PART IV

*

THE FAMILY OF WILLIAM TREFFRY, SECOND SON OF MATHEW TREFFRY (from 1605)

Chapter Eleven

THE FAMILY OF WILLIAM TREFFRY (from 1605)

MATHEW TREFFRY, the third son of John and Emblen Tresithney Treffry, was born at Fowey, and christened in St Fimbarrus's church on 20 February 1566. He grew up in Fowey in the shadow of his two older and very prominent brothers, William, who became the friend of Carew and was Master of Ordnance under Sir Walter Raleigh, and Thomas, who became a Councillor of Law, in the exciting age of Elizabeth I and the Spanish Armada. Apparently Mathew lived in Fowey until about the time of Queen Elizabeth I's death in 1603, which was near the time of his marriage when he took up residence at the manor of Rooke in St Kew (q.v.) with his young bride, Elizabeth Sumaster. Their eldest son, Thomas, was born and baptized there on 21 October 1604, and on the death of his cousin, Colonel John Treffry of Place, Thomas inherited the Treffry estates as the next male heir (*see* Chapter 6).

In English records those of the heir-male and his immediate family are often kept for centuries, and can be found in the Visitations and later in Burke's publications and other similar works. The lineage of the Treffry family in the heir-male line is thus recorded. However, the records of the younger brothers or cadet lines are often lost track of over the years, and must be reconstituted by searching parish records, wills and family archives. Part IV of this book deals with the descendants of Mathew Treffry's second son, William, some of whom still carry the Treffry name through the male line of descent to date and therefore back to Mathew, and thus, as far back as records go.

From Mathew's will and the St Kew parish records we know there is no question concerning the order of birth of the sons or daughters. In the original parish records of St Kew kept in an ancient leather-bound book beginning in the 16th century, which I examined in June 1980, the christening dates of four of the five children are given. There is a William Treffry baptized in St Kew in 1606, but he is the son of 'Walteri', not Mathew as incorrectly given in the Latter-Day Saints' microfiche. Mathew's son, William, the subject of this chapter, was baptized in St Fimbarrus's church at Fowey on 20 March 1605.

Nothing being recorded of the childhood of Mathew's children, we can only assume that they had a happy life at Rooke with possible excursions to Tintagel and other nearby places of Arthurian lore, as well as holiday visits to Place. By Mathew's will we know that many and varied agricultural pursuits took place at Rooke, in which it is reasonable to believe that Mathew's sons, Thomas, William and John took part.

HUSBAND Mathew TREFFRY of Rooke, St. Kew, Cornwall Occupation   Gentleman

Born	Place	
Chr.	20 Feb 1566	Place Fowey, Cornwall, England
Marr.	Place	
Died	Place On Monument in St. Kew Church, "He dyed in the
Bur. 3 Nov 1626 St. Kew, Cornwall	Place Reigne of King James I"
Father John TREFFRY	Mother Emilyn TRESITHNEY
Other Wives		

WIFE   Elizabeth SUMASTER

Born	Place Peynsford, Devon, England
Chr.	Place	
Died	Place	
Bur. 19 Sep 1656	Place St. Kew, Cornwall, England
Father	Mother	
Other Husbands		

	Children	Sex	When Born-Chr. When Died	Where Born Where Died	Marriage Date & Place To Whom
1	Thomas	M	21 Oct 1604	St. Kew	28 Apr 1641 Fowey Jane, dau of John VIVIAN
2	William	M	20 Mar 1605	Fowey	21 Oct 1641 St. Minver Jane DIMANT
3	Elizabeth	F	18 Mar 1606	St. Kew	
4	Jane	F	14 Mar 1607	St. Kew	
5	John	M	1 Jun 1608	St. Kew	20 Jun 1634 Mary BOWDEN
6					
7					
8					
9					
10					
11					
12					
13					
14					
15					

Sources of Information	Other Marriages
Christening dates for #1 and #3, from LDS IGI. Other Christening dates from VISITATIONS OF CORNWALL. Mathew TREFFRY'S will is extant, Cornwall Record Office, Truro. It names only the five above children. Will adm. 1626/27.	

HUSBAND   William TREFFRY   Occupation   Gentleman

Born		Place	
Chr.	20 Mar 1605	Place	Fowey, Cornwall, England
Marr.	21 Oct 1641	Place	St. Minver, Cornwall, England
Died		Place	
Bur.	21 Feb 1684	Place	St. Minver, Cornwall, England
Father	Mathew TREFFRY of Fowey	Mother	Elizabeth SUMASTER
Other Wives			

WIFE   Jane DIMANT

Born		Place	
Chr.		Place	
Died		Place	
Bur.	25 Dec 1676	Place	St. Minver, Cornwall, England
Father		Mother	
Other Husbands			

	Children	Sex	When Born-Chr. / When Died	Where Born / Where Died	Marriage Date & Place / To Whom
1	Mathew	M	23 Nov 1641	St. Minver	
2	Elizabeth	F	24 Mar 1643	St. Minver	
3			1645)	)	
4			1647)	) No record of births in this period. See text.	
5			1649)	)	
3 -	Richard	M	10 Feb 1651 / 1 Jul 1736	St. Minver / St. Minver	
4 -	William	M	1 Jun 1653 / 10 Jun 1709	St. Minver / St. Minver	5 Feb 1682, St. Breock / Thomazin CEELEY
5 -	Johan	F	4 Jun 1655	St. Minver	
6 -	Thomas	M	2 Sep 1656	St. Minver	
10					
11					
12					
13					
14					
15					

Sources of Information	Other Marriages
Marriage of William and Jane, LDS IGI.	
Christening dates from LDS IGI.	
Christening dates from St. Minver Parish Register, from	
Baptisms and Burials 1558 - 1812, transcribed by	
Reginald M. Glencross 942.37/S9 V26 S.	
Burial dates from Glencross.	

HUSBAND	Richard TREFFRY			Occupation	Gentleman		

Born		Place				
Chr.	10 Feb 1650/51	Place	St. Minver, Cornwall, England			
Marr.	1 Jan 1691	Place	St. Minver, Cornwall, England			
Died		Place				
Bur.	1 Jul 1736	Place	St. Minver, Cornwall, England			
Father	William TREFFRY		Mother	Jane DIMANT		
Other Wives	Honor TOM, m 12 Jun 1700, St. Minver, (two daughters only)					

WIFE	Constance GRAY				
Born		Place			
Chr.		Place			
Died		Place			
Bur.	9 Mar 1698/99	Place	St. Minver, Cornwall, England		
Father			Mother		
Other Husbands					

Children	Sex	When Born-Chr. / When Died	Where Born / Where Died	Marriage Date & Place / To Whom
1 William	M	5 Dec 1692	St. Minver	
2 Richard	M	3 Dec 1694	St. Minver	25 Apr 1726, Padstow / Alice BOUND
3 Henry	M	16 Nov 1697	St. Minver	
4				
5				
6				
7				
8				
9				
10				
11				
12				
13				
14				
15				

Sources of Information	Other Marriages
Original St. Minver, Cornwall, Parish Register, Truro, Cornwall Record Office.	

At the age of 36, Mathew's second son, William, married Jane Dimant on 21 October 1641 in St Minver (about five miles due west of St Kew), after which they resided there. Their four sons and two daughters were christened there and appear in that parish's register (*see* the above charts).

Burke's *Landed Gentry* of 1894 gives a son by the name of Robert to Mathew's son William. From the chart we find no children recorded from March of 1643 until February 1651, and no Robert, so I surmised that perhaps a Robert fell in this period. Many births during that time were not recorded, due to the disruption caused by the Civil War which was raging then. Perhaps William was participating. His cousin, Colonel John Treffry of Place, was serving his King, while his cousin, Hugh Peter, was on the side of Parliament. I have found no record of these war years for William, so I do not know what side he was on.

Hypothetically following Burke's lineage of William Treffry's supposed son named Robert, who could possibly have been born in the missing years 1643–1651, we can see that he would have been 63 to 71 years old at the time of his son Samuel's birth in 1714. If Robert was born after the last child recorded, he would then have been in his late fifties when Samuel was born. As I am quite certain that the Robert of this history died in 1755 in St Budeaux, Devon, it is most unlikely that he would have been born either before or after the last recorded child of William in 1656. It is reasonable then to believe that a generation is missing. As William had a son named William born in 1653, I believe that he must be the *father* of Robert, as it seems impossible for the first William to be Robert's father. On close scrutiny of Vivian's *Visitation* it is noted that the place for Robert's father's first name is left blank, indicating that Robert most definitely is not the son of William born in 1605, but a generation later, and that possibly a disruption occurred in the line of descent. This then sent me on searches in other directions.

In St Fimbarrus's church in Fowey I found the following epitaph:

> Here lieth ye Body of John Treffry, Esqr who married ye Daughter of Philip Champernowne of Modbury, by whom, having no issue, gave his Estate to Thomas Treffry of Rook, from his own Sister for ye Support of his name & family; who left it to John Treffry, Esq., his Eldest son, who, having no issue, has Setled it on Willm Toller, his Sister's Son and ye heirs male of ye Said Willm Toller for ye same intent & Purpose, & incerted it here to Prevent *all future disputes or cavills* & yt mine Ancestors & my intent may allways be fulfilled
>
> FOWEY

'Disputes or cavills' being so prominently mentioned led me to bèlieve that there had been law suits over the heir-male rights to the Treffry estates when they descended through Jane Treffry Toller to her son William Toller, brought by a descendant of Mathew Treffry's second son, William. Up to this time the Treffry estates had descended from father to son or brother to brother until Mathew's son, Thomas, had inherited the estates from his cousin. The precedent of a male heir had been established over many centuries, but times were changing and as the Cornish were known for their litigiousness, the chances of finding the records of a legal battle were within the realm of possibility. As there could be no claim to the Treffry estates unless descent from Mathew could be proved, I should then find the genealogical records that I was seeking.

When David Treffry, nephew of Anne Treffry of Place, came to visit me in California on his way to the Far East in 1982, I asked him where I should search if there had been such a suit. He said that it would be in the records of the Court of Chancery in London. A few days later I was in London where David's niece, Tamsin Treffry, accompanied me to the Record Office. I told her that I was going on a 'fishing expedition' where perhaps I would get something or perhaps not. We discovered six listings of law suits in the mid 1700s Treffry versus (Toller) Treffry. As Tamsin Treffry and I could each sign out three documents, that covered the lot. The first one (dated 1732) that we read was definitely of a suit over the heir-male rights to the Treffry estates brought by Richard Treffry, second son of William Treffry of St Minver and grandson of Mathew of Rooke. As we read further we discovered that after the first Richard's death, his son, Richard, jr., carried on the suit. In his suit he stated that he was the only son and heir of Richard (*see* the charts). This indicated that his only two brothers were dead, and proved that there was not a Robert, son of Richard. There do not appear to be any suits carried on after the second Richard's death. I could find no children for the second Richard. This, then, would be when the line of descent fell into Mathew's grandson, William's line, as he is the older William's next-in-line son.

William's son William, I then assumed, must be Robert's father since both Burke's *Landed Gentry* and the *Visitations* bring the male Treffry line of descent down through Mathew's son William. I believe that Burke's is correct in saying Robert is the son of William, but the William christened in 1653 and not the William christened in 1605.

The chart below shows the descent from Mathew Treffry through William:

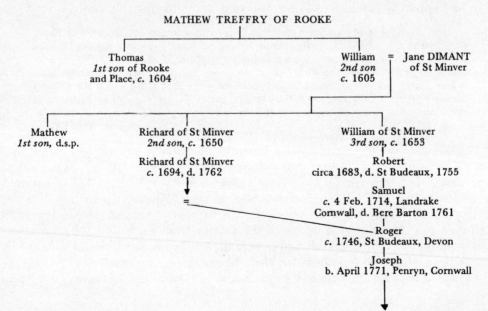

MATHEW TREFFRY OF ROOKE

Thomas
1st son of Rooke
and Place, *c.* 1604

William   =   Jane DIMANT
2nd son   of St Minver
c. 1605

Mathew
1st son, d.s.p.

Richard of St Minver
2nd son, c. 1650

Richard of St Minver
c. 1694, d. 1762

William of St Minver
3rd son, c. 1653

Robert
circa 1683, d. St Budeaux, 1755

Samuel
c. 4 Feb. 1714, Landrake
Cornwall, d. Bere Barton 1761

Roger
c. 1746, St Budeaux, Devon

Joseph
b. April 1771, Penryn, Cornwall

In the nearby parish of St Breock, a William Treffry married Thomazin Ceeley on 5 February 1682. If this, then, is Robert's father, William, we can assume that Robert was born between 1682–1692, thus being aged 22 to 32 when he became the father of Samuel in 1714 in Landrake, Cornwall. I have not been able to locate brothers or sisters of Robert. However, the records from then on are quite complete.

From the Harriet Smith Collection, an Elizabeth Roberts is given as Robert's wife. There was a prominent Roberts family living in Landrake at the time which had children named Elizabeth, Anne and Samuel. These were also the names Robert and Elizabeth gave to their children. Robert and Elizabeth Treffry's only son, Samuel, died in January 1761 at Bere Barton before his cousin, Richard, jr., died in 1762. The heir-male line then would have fallen to Samuel Treffry's eldest son, Roger of Bere Barton, who was only 16 at the time. There do not seem to be any records of any law suits pertaining to the heir-male line being carried on by Roger or any of his descendants.

The chart pertaining to Elizabeth and Robert Treffry is shown on the next page (116).

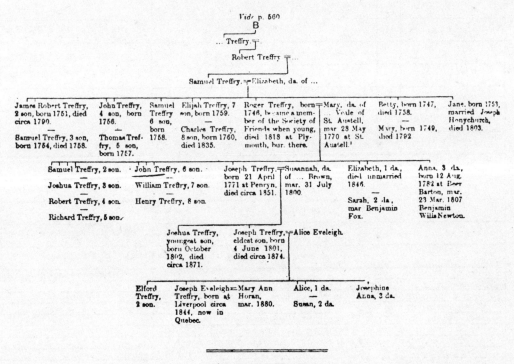

THE VISITATIONS OF THE COUNTY OF CORNWALL.

Robert TREFFRY line as shown from The Visitations of Cornwall, 1530, 1573 & 1620, *with additions by Lt.-Col. J.L. Vivian, 1887.*

HUSBAND	Robert TREFFRY		Occupation	Gentleman

Born	circa 1682/83	Place	
Chr.		Place	
Marr.	circa 1712/13	Place	
Died		Place	
Bur.	9 Feb 1755	Place	St. Budeaux, Devon, England
Father	William TREFFRY	Mother	Thomazin CEELEY
Other Wives			

WIFE	Elizabeth ROBERTS		
Born		Place	
Chr.	21 Dec 1680	Place	Landrake, Cornwall, England
Died		Place	
Bur.	20 Dec 1754	Place	St. Budeaux, Devon, England
Father	John ROBERTS, Gentleman	Mother	Jane
Other Husbands			

Children	Sex	When Born—Chr. When Died	Where Born Where Died	Marriage Date & Place To Whom
1 Samuel	M	4 Feb 1714 25 Jan 1761	Landrake Beer Barton, Bere Ferrers, Devon	5 Sep 1745, St. Issey, Cornwall Mrs. Elizabeth BETTY
2 - Ann	F	13 Apr 1718	Landrake	
3 - Ann	F	2 May 1720 3 May 1720	Landrake Landrake	
4 - Elizabeth	F	20 Jun 1723	Landrake	16 Dec 1746, St. Budeaux, Robert DAGGE Devon
6				
7				
8				
9				
10				
11				
12				
13				
14				
15				

Sources of Information	Other Marriages
Christenings LDS IGI and Landrake Parish Registers.	
Bishop's Transcripts of St. Budeaux, Devon, Parish Register	
gives burial dates.	
Samuel states he is from St. Budeaux 1745 when marrying in	
St. Issey. He is still living in St. Budeaux until 1757/58	
by birth dates of his children, so I am assuming that the	
Robert and Elizabeth TREFFRY burial dates above are for his parents.	
Elizabeth ROBERTS has a brother named Samuel and a sister named Anne,	
and these are the names of her children.	
Elizabeth ROBERTS was given as name of Robert's wife in Harriet	
Smith Collection (my Cousin). No source given.	

Chapter Twelve

THE FAMILY OF SAMUEL TREFFRY OF BERE BARTON

SAMUEL, THE ONLY SON of Robert and Elizabeth Roberts Treffry, was christened on 4 February 1714 in St Michael's church in Landrake, Cornwall, a parish in the union of St Germans, north-west of Saltash. He had two sisters named Ann, who died in infancy, and a third sister, Elizabeth. The sisters were also christened in St Michael's church which rests on a hilltop with its 100-ft. high tower visible for miles around. In 1980 Peregrine Treffry and I visited this church, where it is thought that the south side contains some Norman masonry. The chancel almost touches the village street, quite unusual in Cornish churches. The buildings on the main street of the charming village of Landrake range in date from the 16th century.

The manor of Landrake was considered by Tonkin to be the very best in the county. The Earl of Buckinghamshire gave it to his daughter when she married Lord Mount Edgcumbe in 1789. In the early 1800s the manor house was occupied by a farmer. I do not know where the Robert Treffry family lived while in Landrake. Apparently they were acquainted with the Earl of Buckinghamshire, as his name appears on a family indenture tripartite. Many records of the Lord Mount Edgcumbe family were lost in World War II when his manor house was completely demolished. Perhaps if these records still existed, there might be found legal documents and other references to this branch of the Treffry family.

By the birthdates of Samuel's sisters, we know his parents lived in Landrake through June of 1723. The next date that I found for Samuel Treffry was 5 September 1745, when he married Mrs. Elizabeth Betty in the parish of St Issey, Cornwall, which is in the King Arthur area south of the Camel River estuary on the road between Wadebridge and Padstow. In the mid 1700s, the abbreviation 'Mrs.' for mistress was used as a title of respect, and did not necessarily indicate that Elizabeth had been married before. On the marriage record Samuel is listed as Mr. Samuel Treffry; at the time 'Mr.' was also used as a title of respect. Later, on the Indenture Tripartite he is listed as 'gentleman'. Since this Indenture has John Betty's signature as of St Issey, and he was married on 6 February 1745 to a Mrs. Elizabeth Nankivel in St Issey, I believe that he was Elizabeth Betty's brother. We may note that his bride is also listed as 'Mrs.' in the same year as Elizabeth. There are memorials

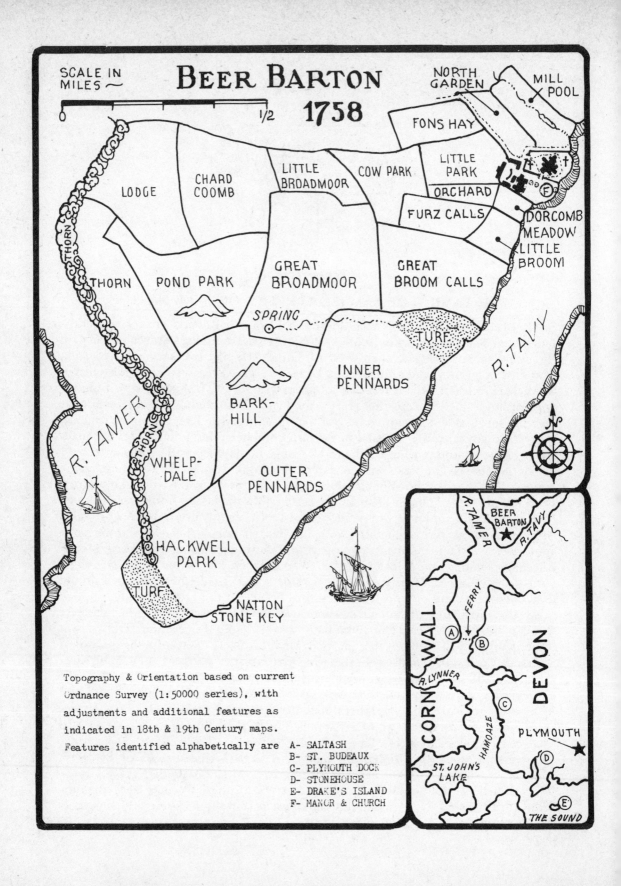

Beer Barton
1758

SCALE IN MILES ~

0   1/2

NORTH GARDEN   MILL POOL

FONS HAY

LITTLE BROADMOOR   COW PARK   LITTLE PARK

LODGE   CHARD COOMB

ORCHARD

FURZ CALLS

F

DORCOMB MEADOW

LITTLE BROOM

THORN

THORN

POND PARK

GREAT BROADMOOR

GREAT BROOM CALLS

SPRING

TURF

R. TAVY

INNER PENNARDS

R. TAMER

THORN

BARK-HILL

WHELP-DALE

OUTER PENNARDS

HACKWELL PARK

TURF

NATTON STONE KEY

Topography & Orientation based on current Ordnance Survey (1:50000 series), with adjustments and additional features as indicated in 18th & 19th Century maps.

Features identified alphabetically are

A- SALTASH
B- ST. BUDEAUX
C- PLYMOUTH DOCK
D- STONEHOUSE
E- DRAKE'S ISLAND
F- MANOR & CHURCH

CORNWALL

DEVON

R. TAMER

BEER BARTON

R. TAVY

FERRY

A

B

R. LYNNER

HAMOAZE

C

PLYMOUTH

D

ST. JOHN'S LAKE

E

THE SOUND

THE LONG BARNS

BEER BARTON MANOR
ON THE TAVY

Inset: an enlarged map of section F from opposite page, with drawings of the marked buildings

to the Betty family in the St Issey church, and many Bettys in the parish register. An Elizabeth Betty with an older brother, John Betty, are recorded there. (*See* Appendix.) The marriage record did, however, reveal that Samuel Treffry was not from St Issey, but from St Budeaux, Devon, at the time of his marriage. And from the St Budeaux parish records, we discover that is where Samuel took his bride to live.

St Budeaux was then just north of Plymouth, but is part of Plymouth today. It is near the Devon end of the Royal Albert Bridge that spans the Tamar, the river that separates Devon from Cornwall. The parish church there is named for a Celtic saint, St Budoc, who came from Brittany in A.D. 480. A very ancient Celtic cross was recently found in the churchyard. This I photographed in 1982 when visiting the church. Their church records date from 1538, but their present hilltop church of St. Budeaux dates from 1563. Sir Francis Drake and his wife were married in this church, and she is buried there. Samuel and Elizabeth Treffry's first eight children were baptized in this same church from June of 1746 to June of 1757. The Bishop's Transcripts of this parish show that on 16 December 1746 an Elizabeth Treffry married a Robert Dagge. I am assuming that she is Samuel's sister as she would be of marriageable age and marrying just a year after Samuel. Also, a Robert and Elizabeth Treffry were buried in this churchyard in 1754 and 1755. I believe that they are Samuel's parents, as he was of St Budeaux at that time.

The panoramic view from the church is described by C. W. Bracken in *A History of Plymouth and her Neighbours*. 'The picturesque old forts, the quiet wooded Tamerton Creek, with its ancient mill below, the Hamoaze, once teeming with our old "wooden walls" backed by the Cornish heights, Mount Edgcumbe, the Sound, and Straddon heights appear till we come full swing to Dartmoor in the northern mists. All these on the horizon's bounds; near at hand small woodland patches, valleys, farmsteads, and the carpet of civilization.'

Samuel Treffry's signature appears on an indenture of 1752 as being of St Budeaux and taking as an apprentice for household help a Mary Shears. This is the only signature that I have found for Samuel. He did leave a will that was proved in 1761, as I have in my possession an original indenture tripartite of 1768 with many references to this proved will. I have been unable to find this will, or a record that it existed, or was proved. His wife's signature appears on this indenture along with that of their eldest son, Roger Treffry. John Betty's signature is also on it.

Sometime between 1757 and early 1758, Samuel moved his family from St Budeaux to Bere Barton, Bere Ferrers, Devon, just up-river from Plymouth. I had heard my great-aunts speak of Bere Barton, but I had no idea where it was, or even if it still existed. Since it was mentioned all through the indenture of 1768, I decided to try to find it on my exploratory trip of 1980. Peregrine Treffry and I arrived in Bere Ferrers on a May afternoon. She asked a passerby where Bere Barton was, and the answer was, 'Park by the church and walk down the cobble stone lane there'. We left the car by the lych gate to the churchyard adjacent to which were old mounting steps. We strolled down the lane with the church on the left side and ancient buildings on the right to discover a beautiful old ivy-covered stone house in a magnificent setting facing the Tavy

HUSBAND Samuel TREFFRY   Occupation Gentleman

Born	Place
Chr. 4 Feb 1714	Place Landrake, Cornwall, England
Marr. 5 Sep 1745	Place St. Issey, Cornwall, England
Died	Place
Bur. 25 Jan 1761	Place Bere Ferrers, Devon, England
Father Robert TREFFRY	Mother Elizabeth ROBERTS?
Other Wives None	

WIFE Mrs. Elizabeth BETTY

Born	Place
Chr.	Place
Died	Place
Bur. 8 Sep 1783	Place Bere Ferrers, Devon, England
Father	Mother
Other Husbands	Bapt.

Children	Sex	When Born / When Died	Where Born / Where Died	Marriage Date & Place / To Whom
1 Roger	M	13 Jun 1746 / 24 Nov 1818	St. Budeaux, Devon / Plymouth, Devon	28 May St. Austell Corn Mary VEALE
2 Betty	F	29 Dec 1747 / bur 1 May 1758	St. Budeaux, Devon / Bere Ferrers, Devon	--
3 Mary	F	29 Nov 1749 / 1792	St. Budeaux, Devon	Richard FURZEMA ?
4 James Robert	M	22 Nov 1751 / Circa 1790	St. Budeaux, Devon / at sea	18 Aug 1776 Penryn Cor Ann Mitchell
5 Jane	F	25 Mar 1753	St. Budeaux, Devon	1 Feb 1788 Penryn Corn Joseph HONYCHURCH
6 Samuel	M	20 Sep 1754 / bur 2 Apr 1758	St. Budeaux, Devon / Bere Ferrers, Dev	
7 John	M	11 Apr 1756	St. Budeaux, Devon	
8 Thomas	M	11 Jun 1757 / 5 Jul 1823	St. Budeaux, Devon / Luxulian Par. Corn.	Not married
9 Samuel		29 June 1758	Bere Ferrers, Devon	20 Aug 1781 St Leonard Shoreditch Mary MORRIS
10 Elijah	M	26 Aug 1759	Bere Ferrers, Devon	
11 Charles	M	25 Feb 1761	Bere Ferrers, Devon	8 Apr 1787 St. Charles Susanna ROWE Plymou
12				
13				
14				
15				

Sources of Information	Other Marriages
1. St. Issey Par. Reg. for marriage, Samuel Treffry and Mrs. Elizabeth Betty	
2. Bishop's Transcripts of St. Budeaux Par. Reg.	
3. Bere Ferrers Par. Reg.	
4. Indenture Tripartite, Eliz. Treffry, John Betty(probably her brother) and Roger Treffry, 1768 referring to Sam.Treffry's will of 1761. All above children living 1768 named. Many ref. to Beer Barton.	
5. Records of deaths of Soc. of Friends Quarterly Meetings, Cornwall for Thomas #8 above	
6. Mabel Lossing Jones records for #9 Samuel and #10 Elijah stated they had careers at sea.	

The signature of Samuel Treffry

River. At the rear there was a courtyard surrounded by very old stone barns, stables and small buildings. The Tavy flows down the eastern boundary of Bere Barton and joins the Tamar River that flows on the western side of Bere Barton holding Bere Barton in the tip of the peninsula. In America where houses come and go in the name of progress until declared of historical interest, it seemed miraculous to me to find the real, the ancient, the historical Bere Barton where three generations of my branch of the Treffry family had lived from the mid–1700s.

Mr. and Mrs. George Dawe, who owned the house in 1980, graciously offered to show us through. As I stood in the large square entry hall with a stairway dividing at the landing, I thought of my fourth great-grandfather, Samuel Treffry, who had moved his family of eight children there from St Budeaux, and how shortly after, within one month, two of his young children died and were buried in the adjacent churchyard. Those must have been very sad days for this family.

I turned to cheerier thoughts as I entered the living room at the left of the hall with its spectacular view of the Tavy from the tall windows flanked by solid shutters of light wood. The blue and white decorative tiles surrounding the fireplace, I noted, had pictures of people's faces with names written underneath. Hoping that I might find some family history recorded there, I inspected the tiles closely. I discovered the pictures were all of King Arthur characters. I wondered if this fireplace mantel had been where Samuel's children hung their Christmas stockings. Did that family deck this room with holly, ivy and mistletoe at Christmas time? Did that fireplace hold the yule log that burnt for days? In this room did this Treffry family celebrate with neighbours and other friends by singing madrigals and Christmas carols?

Across the hall was an L-shaped room with windows facing the Tavy, and with a very ancient stone-backed fireplace. This was certainly their dining-room where at Christmas and other festive occasions the family would have enjoyed pigeon pie, boar's head, mincemeat pies, plum 'porridge', saddles of mutton, beer and wine. Perhaps the adjacent hall was used for dancing.

Samuel's eldest son, Roger Treffry, who was my third great-grandfather, was brought here to live when he was 11 or 12 years old. Roger Treffry, when a married man, brought his family here to live, including my second great-grandfather, John Treffry, when he was only two years old. (He is the John Treffry who emigrated to Canada, *see* Part IV, Chapter 14). To see the actual home and beautiful setting so little changed where three generations of my family had lived took me back over 220 years in history and brought these ancestors back to life for me.

On my second visit to Bere Barton two years later, I discovered a great deal more about this historic place. Ownership had changed and in extensive renovating much old history was revealed that led me to do additional research. This spit of land, one and a half miles across, known as Bere Barton, was listed as 'Birlinda' in the Domesday Book. Bir or Beer of Celtic origin means peninsula. With the Celts travelling by sea from the Continent and accustomed to following waterways, the land now called Bere Barton in Bere Ferrers bordered by two rivers would certainly have been a choice place for a settlement. At the time of the Domesday Survey the lord of the manor was Rainald, who farmed the 40-acre 'barton'. Under him were 16 peasant farmers who farmed 120 acres. These peasants had to grind corn, carry water, and perform many other services for their lord. The land was ploughed by eight oxen with six ploughs. There were pack horses for travel. In Norman times salt was produced for salting pork and fish, and there was also silver mining in the nearby area.

Henry II gave Bere Manor between the Tavy and the Tamar to Lord de Ferrers. Some time in dim past history a de Ferrers built a castle there, the lower half and back of which still remain. Except for the adjacent church, Bere Barton manor house is the oldest building in the parish. There is an ancient stone wall and gate between the Barton and the churchyard.

In 1337, Edward III, father of the Black Prince, gave permission for the manor house at Bere Barton to be castellated and fortified, no doubt for protection against the French enemy. Part of the original keep still stands at the back of the manor house. Old granite window casements and a very ancient doorway are still in use and can be seen at the rear of the house (*see* the plate section). In 1696 a window tax was imposed by Parliament to replace the hearth tax that had been levied from 1662 until 1689. In order to reduce taxes, several windows at Bere Barton were permanently blocked with stonework. The window tax was not abolished until 1851. Since most large castles and manors had hearths in almost every room and many windows, it is difficult to determine which tax was more of a burden. (The present owners opened two blocked windows in the front hall facing the Tavy.)

In the *Western Independent,* 7 December 1958, I discovered a story headed 'R. Treffry' that told of a leather-bound book on chronology 4in. by 2in. and about one inch thick, being found, with the name 'R. Treffry' pencilled in two places. This newspaper story states, 'No Richard or Robert Treffry appears in Vivian's *Visitations'.* This, however, is incorrect, for on page 562 in Chart B, at the top of the page, it shows Robert as the father of the Samuel of Bere Barton. Apparently, Samuel took his late father's book with him when he moved from St Budeaux to Bere Barton in 1758. As Robert died in 1755, this book with its last entry for 1747, was his without a doubt. At the same time that the little book was found a heavy-bladed single-edged cutlass-type sword with a brass hand guard and pommel was discovered. It had a naval arrow just below the hilt. The sword was in a leather scabbard with a brass end cap. Two rusty reaping hooks were also found. All these relics were found in a wall on the upstairs landing of the house when a workman was replacing old plaster. If these relics were hidden by Samuel, it would have been between 1757/58 when he moved to Bere Barton and his death in 1761.

The present owners of Bere Barton, Mr. and Mrs. Nigel Faulks, also made discoveries pertaining to the antiquity of the building when renovating was being done to install a piping system through the wall of the old coal cellar. The workman's hammer disappeared when it went through the wall and fell six feet. More of the wall was removed in order for Mr. Faulks to go down a ladder to explore. There he discovered a four-feet high man-made channel complete with arches. When I visited Bere Barton in 1982, Mrs. Faulks showed me an opening they had found in a small bedroom on the second floor landing that revealed the upper part of this shaft. She called it a 'garderobe' for carrying away effluent. In A. H. Gardener's *Outline of English Architecture* (third edition, 1949) he states, 'In the larger castle privies were planned in the thickness of the walls, the best examples having shafts which delivered into the moat below water level'. Gardener says, 'Where no running water was available great pits were dug'. The Faulks believe that the channel under their house, which was used to carry away the waste, could be more than 80 feet long, leading from a spring in the courtyard. Since the garderobe is in the old part of the house it could be of 13th- or early 14th-century construction when the tower for the fortification of the house was added. The Faulks believe that their house at one time had a third floor. The 'new' part of the house, they think, was added to the remains of the old castle in the early 1700s. This part of the house then would have been quite new when the Samuel Treffry family moved to Bere Barton in 1758.

Mrs. Faulks kindly showed me through the house. There were two large bedrooms in the new part facing the river. The dressing room off the master bedroom, complete with fireplace, had been converted into a bathroom. The bedroom, also, had a fireplace as did most of the rooms. Both of these large bedrooms had had oversized high doors off the large square second floor hall. One door had been reduced to normal size, while the other remained quite an oddity. The older part of the second floor contained a number of small bedrooms.

It is thought that huge old beams in the older part of the house date to Elizabethan times. When the Dawes lived in the house, old meat-hanging equipment was still suspended from the kitchen ceiling. The Mountjoy family owned Bere Barton in the 16th and 17th centuries. It was a Mountjoy, the Earl of Newport, who entertained his famous neighbours from Buckland Monachorum, the ancient home of Sir Francis Drake, just up-river from Bere Barton. The Earl of Newport lent his house to Lady Elizabeth Drake, widow of the nephew of Sir Francis Drake for her second marriage in 1639. There is a story that in 1664 the fourth Sir Francis Drake rowed across the Tavy to elope with his cousin, Dorothy Bampfield, from Bere Barton, escaping through the garden gate to the churchyard. He was 22 and she nineteen.

St Andrew's church in the parish of Bere Ferrers on the bank of the river Tavy holds many memories of three generations of Treffrys. The church dates from the 13th century and the church bells from 1775. Three generations of my family would have heard these same bells ring. A transept in this church was known as the Barton aisle until around 1950, reserved for the Barton squire and his family. This, then, is where the family of Samuel Treffry worshipped in the last half of the 1700s. The ancient Norman font in St Andrew's church was used to baptize the last three children of Samuel and Elizabeth Betty Treffry (*see* chart).

During some of the time that the Treffrys occupied Bere Barton, the Earl of Buckinghamshire was patron of the living of St Andrews. Certainly he was known to the Treffry family. (If his papers could be searched one might find reference to the Treffry family there, as the earl had holdings in Landrake and his name appears on the indenture tripartite.) In 1783 the earl added a gallery for the musicians in St Andrew's church. The musical instruments used at the services then were viol, cello, bass viol, tenor viol and oboe.

Barely three years after moving to Bere Barton, Samuel, aged 47, died and was buried on 25 January 1761 in St Andrew's churchyard. A month to the day later on 25 February 1761, Charles, the last of Samuel's children was christened. Since he is mentioned in the indenture referring to Samuel's will, he must have been born and named before his father's death.

Elizabeth Betty Treffry was left to raise nine children, all minors. As Samuel's will has not been located, the indenture triparite has to be used as a substitute. Briefly, the estate was left in trust to Elizabeth Treffry and John Betty, who I am assuming was her brother, for the benefit of all the children. The estate was to be divided between the two older brothers when they both became of age, and they then were to provide for the younger children. Roger was the eldest brother, and James Robert was the second son. When Roger came of age, apparently he did not wish to carry out the responsibilities required of him by his father's will. In 1768 he asked to be released from these responsibilities, and asked for his equity in the estate to be paid to him in cash by his mother. However, she advised Roger that the estate was burdened by a debt of £1,000, and managed to give him only £400, at a time when about £20 was the average yearly income.

Roger, the subject of the next chapter, left home to marry soon after receiving his inheritance. However, he returned with his family to live at Bere Barton before his mother's death.

Elizabeth Betty Treffry, widow of Samuel, was able to stay on at Bere Barton raising her young family there until her death in 1783, 22 years after that of her husband. Her burial at St Andrew's, in the parish of Bere Ferrers on 8 September 1783 was the last entry in that parish register of the Samuel Treffry family.

I am including the indenture triparite here as it shows that Elizabeth Treffry, Samuel's widow, was a well-educated and capable woman who was able to take on the responsibilities of raising a fine family along with running this very large barton.

1   THIS INDENTURE TRIPARTITE made the seventeenth day of October in the
     eighth year of the reign of our sovereign Lord George the third by the
2   grace of God of Great Britain, France & Ireland king, defender of the
     faith & so forth & in the year of our Lord one thousand seven hundred
     & sixty eight   BETWEEN Roger Treffry, late of Beerferris in the county
3   of Devon, but now of St Austle in the county of Cornwall, malster, of
     the first part; John Betty, of St Issey in the said county of Cornwall,
     yeoman, of the second part; & Elizabeth Treffry of the parish of Beer-
4   ferris aforesaid, widow, of the third part.   WHEREAS Samuel Treffry of

the parish of Beerferris aforesaid, gent[leman], late deceased husband
of the said Elizabeth Treffry & father of the said Roger Treffry, did

5   duly make & publish ,his last will & testament in writing, bearing date
on or about the twenty second day of January, which was in the year of

6   our Lord one thousand seven hundred & sixtyone & did thereby give &
bequeath unto the said Elizabeth Treffry & John Betty & the survivor of
them & the executors & administrators of such survivor   ALL   that his

7   barton, farm & lands called Beer Barton, situate within the parish of
Beerferris aforesaid, which he held by lease and all his right & title
thereto, & all his stock, goods & chattels & personal estate whatsoever

8   IN   TRUST to & for such ends & purposes as are therein & hereafter
mentioned (that is to say): that his said trustees did & should as soon as
conveniently might be after his decease cause an inventory to be taken

9   of all his stock, goods, chattels & personal estate; & take upon them the
management of the said barton & effects & make the best advantage thereof,

10   as they in their discretion from time to time think fit, until his sons,
the said Roger Treffry & James Robert Treffry, should both have attained
their respective ages of twenty one years, in trust to & for his sons &
daughters, the said Roger Treffry, Mary Treffry, the said James Robert

11   Treffry, Jane, John, Thomas, Samuel, Elijah & Charles Treffry; & did &
should by the profits arising from his said barton & effects maintain &
provide for all his said children untill they should severally become
fit to be bound out apprentices to some trade; & that his said trustees

12   should pay any sum with each of them not exceeding twenty pounds to be
allowed again in their accounts; & that on such the said Roger & James
Robert Treffry attaining their respective ages of twentyone years his

13   will was that an equal division of such of his land, stock & goods &
chattels & the produce thereof & of his said barton should be made by his
s[ai]d trustees between all his s[aid]d children or such of them as
should be then living; & that his said trustees should then after put

14   out at interest the share of the said children untill they should attain
their age of twenty one years or be marryed; & his will further was that
on his said sons, Roger Treffry & James Robert Treffry, attaining both
their ages of twenty one years, then legally bequeathed one moiety or

15   halfendeale of all that his said barton & prem[is]es unto his said son,
Roger Treffry, & the other moiety or halfendeale thereof unto his
son, James Robert Treffry, their ex[ecut]ors, adm[inistrat]ors or
assigns, during all his right term of years & interests therein & which

16   should be then to come & unexpired, they maintaining at their joint and
equal expence all such of his said children as should not be bound out
apprentices, untill they should be thought fit by his said trustees to

17   be bound out to some trade, they & each of them paying with every & each
of them which should be so bound out the sum of ten pounds apiece in
consideration of their having the said barton, which he charged with the
payment & raising thereof; & if both his s[ai]d sons should happen to die

18   before they attain twenty one years, that then all his said other
children should be equally entitled [un]to his s[ai]d barton or the moiety
of such of them so dying, & made, nominated, constituted & appointed his
said wife Elizabeth Treffry & John Betty whole & sole ex[ecut]ors of his

19   said will IN TRUST as aforesaid & afterwards died without revoking the
same, since whose death the said Elizabeth Treffry alone hath proved the
said will & taken upon herself the burthen & execution thereof & managed

20   the said barton & effects & maintained & provided for all her said children
of whom the said Roger Treffry alone hath attained his age of twenty one

years; and he having been, at his own request, brought up in the business
of a maltster; & the said barton having been mortgaged for a very consider-
21   able sum, of which upwards of one thousand pounds remains still due &
unpaid; & the estate & effects of the said Samuel Treffry being charged &
incumbered with the payment of several other debts at the time of his
death; & the said Roger Treffry having been made thoroughly acquainted
22   & perfectly understanding the nature, circumstances & present situation
of his said affairs & being well satisfyed with the conduct & management
of the said Elizabeth Treffry under the said will; & being desirous of
23   not taking upon himself any share in the execution of the said will, hath
requested the said Elizabeth Treffry to purchase his the said Roger
Treffry's moiety or halfendeale of the said barton & prem[is]es & his share
of the said stock, goods, chattels & effects & all other his estate, claim,
24   interest, property & demand whatsoever of, in or to any of the goods,
chattels & effects whatsoever of the s[ai]d Samuel Treffry deceased & to
take upon herself the payment & discharge of all the debts now due & owing
on account of the estate of the s[ai]d Samuel Treffry deceased or of the
25   said trust & to maintain & provide for his said brothers & sisters as
directed by the said will & generally to do & execute all & whatsoever he
could or might be charged with under the said will so that he may not at
26   any   time or times hereafter be sued, prosecuted or molested on account
thereof or on any other account whatsoever relative thereto AND WHEREAS
on a treaty had of & concerning the same & after a full & mature deliber
27   -ation of the prem[is]es & due consideration of everything relating to or
in any wise concerning the estate & effects of the said Samuel Treffry
deceased, they, the said Roger Treffry & Elizabeth Treffry, have concluded
& agreed to & with each other in manner following (that is to say): that
28   in consideration of the sum of four hundred pounds of lawfull money of
Great Britain to be paid to him by the said Elizabeth Treffry as hereinafter
mentioned & of the said Elizabeth Treffry's undertaking to pay & discharge
all the debts, legacies & other incumbrances affecting the said barton,
29   estate & prem[is]es; & to maintain & provide for his said brothers &
sisters; & generally to do & execute all & whatsoever could or might have
been charged or chargeable on him by virtue of or under his said father's
will; & freeing, indemnifying, discharging & keeping harmless him the
30   s[ai]d Roger Treffry, his heirs, ex[ecut]ors & adm[inistrat]ors, & his
& their lands & tenements, goods & chattels of, from & against the same &
all actions, claims & demands whatsoever on account thereof, he the said
Roger Treffry shall & will assign, transfer & sett over unto the said
31   Elizabeth Treffry all that his moiety or halfendeale of the said barton
& prem[is]es & all his share & claim, interest, property & demand whatsoever in or to the stock, goods, chattels & effects of the said Samuel
Treffry deceased or which he, the said Roger Treffry, is, could, or
32   might be entitled unto in any wise howsoever under the will of the said
Samuel Treffry. NOW THIS INDENTURE WITNESSETH that for carrying the
aforesaid agreement into execution & for & in consideration of the sum
of four hundred pounds of lawfull money of Great Britain to him, the said
33   Roger Treffry, in hand paid by the said Elizabeth Treffry, at & before the
sealing & delivery hereof, the receipt of which s[ai]d sum he, the said
Roger Treffry, doth hereby acknowledge & thereof & of every part thereof,
doth hereby exonerate, acquit & for ever discharge the s[ai]d Elizabeth
34   Treffry, her ex[ecut]ors, adm[inistrat]ors & assigns, & of the sum of
five shillings of like lawfull money of the s[ai]d John Betty in hand
also paid by the s[ai]d Elizabeth Treffry at & before the sealing &

35 delivery of these presents, the receipt whereof is hereby acknowledged, he the [sai]d John Betty, at the request & by the direction & appointment of the [sai]d Roger Treffry (testified by his being a party to & his executing of these presents) HATH assigned, transferred & sett over & in & by these presents DOTH (as far as he lawfully may or can) assign,

36 transfer & sett over & the s[ai]d Roger Treffry HATH granted, bargained, sold, assigned, transferred & sett over & in by these presents DOTH fully & absolutely grant, bargain, sell, assign, transfer & sett over unto the s[ai]d Elizabeth Treffry, her ex[ecut]ors, adm[inistrat]ors & assigns ALL that his the s[ai]d Roger Treffry's moiety or halfendeale

37 of all that the afores[ai]d barton, farm & lands called Beer Barton, situate within the parish of Beerferris aforesaid & now in the possession of the s[ai]d Elizabeth Treffry, together with all houses, edifices, buildings, barns, stables, orchards, gardens, lands, meadows, pastures, feedings,

38 hays, paths, passages, waters, watercourses, easements, profits, commodities, advantages, heredit[ament]s & appurt[enace]s to the s[ai]d moiety of the same prem[is]es belonging or in any wise appertaining (except nevertheless as in the original indenture of lease thereof formerly granted to the s[ai]d Samuel Treffry deceased by the right honourable John, earl of

39 Buckinghamshire, is mentioned to be excepted) & all the estate, right, title, interest, term & terms of years, use, trust, property, benefit, share, claim & demand whatsoever of him the s[ai]d Roger Treffry of, in & unto the same & every part thereof AND ALSO of, in & unto all &

40 singular the stock, goods, chattels, personal estate & effects whatsoever of the s[ai]d Samuel Treffry deceased & every part & parcell thereof which he, the s[ai]d Roger Treffry, now hath or is entitled unto or which he could or might claim by virtue of or under the s[ai]d will of the s[ai]d

41 Samuel Treffry or otherwise howsoever TO HAVE AND TO HOLD the s[ai]d moiety or halfendeale of the s[ai]d barton, farm & lands hereby assigned or meant, mentioned or intended so to be with their & every of their appurt[enance]s (except before excepted) unto the s[ai]d Elizabeth Treffry, her ex[ecut]ors, adm[inistrat]ors & assigns from henceforth

42 for & during all the residue & remainder of the term of years therein granted by the s[ai]d hereinbefore mentioned indenture of lease & which is now determinable on the deaths of the s[ai]d Elizabeth Treffry, Roger Treffry & James Rob[er]t Treffry, subject nevertheless to the rent,

43 herriotts, exceptions & covenants in the s[ai]d original indenture of lease resolved & contained, & which from & after the day of the date of these presents on the tenant & lessees' parts shall be to be paid, done, performed AND ALSO TO HAVE AND TO HOLD all his the s[ai]d Roger

44 Treffry's share, property, interest, claim & demand whatsoever of, in & to the s[ai]d goods, chattels & personal estate of the s[ai]d Samuel Treffry deceased & every part & parcell thereof unto the s[ai]d Elizabeth Treffry, her ex[ecut]ors, adm[inistrat]ors & assigns, to her & their own

45 proper use & behoof for ever AND the s[ai]d Roger Treffry for the considerations afores[ai]d doth hereby release, acquit & for ever discharge the s[ai]d Elizabeth Treffry, her ex[ecut]ors, adm[inistrat]ors & assigns of, from & against all & every action & actions whatsoever for & relating

46 to the estate & effects of the s[ai]d Samuel Treffry deceased or the trust in her by the same reposed, & of & from all manner of [action] & actions, suits, troubles & [prosecutions] whatsoever on account of the s[ai]d trust [es?] or any part thereof [   ] the s[ai]d Roger Treffry doth hereby for himself, his heirs, [executors & administrators,

47 consent, promise, grant & agree to & with the s[ai]d Elizabeth Treffry,

her ex[ecut]ors, adm[inistrat]ors & assigns, that she, the s[ai]d Elizabeth Treffry, her ex[ecut]ors, adm[inistrat]ors & assigns, shall & may for the consideration afores[ai]d peacably & quietly have, hold, use, occupy, possess & enjoy all & singular the s[ai]d moiety of the s[ai]d barton [&
48   premises?] hereby assigned or intended so to be with their & every of their appurt[enance]s during the residue & remainder of the term of years therein yet to come and unexpired, and all his the s[ai]d Roger Treffry's share of the s[ai]d goods, chattels & personal estate of the s[ai]d
49   Samuel Treffry deceased without the lett, suit, trouble, eviction, ejection, molestation, intervention, claim, hindrance or denyal of him, the s[ai]d Roger Treffry, his ex[ecut]ors or adm[inistrat]ors or any person or persons lawfully claiming or to claim by, from or under him, them, or any of them or the s[ai]d Samuel Treffry deceased   AND   the s[ai]d
50   Elizabeth Treffry doth hereby for herself, her heirs, ex[ecut]ors, & adm[inistrat]ors and every of them, covenant, promise, agree to & with the s[ai]d Roger Treffry, his ex[ecut]ors & adm[inistrat]ors that she, the s[ai]d Elizabeth Treffry, her ex[ecut]ors, adm[inistrat]ors or assigns
51   shall & will pay off & discharge all & singular the debts, legacies, payments & other incumbrances charged by the will of the s[ai]d Samuel Treffry or due from him at the time of his death or in any wise affecting the s[ai]d prem[is]es hereby assigned, & maintain & provide for all the
52   s[ai]d Roger Treffry's s[ai]d brothers & sisters in the manner & as directed by the s[ai]d will & generally do, execute & perform all & whatsoever now is or can or may at any time hereafter be charged or chargeable on him, the s[ai]d Roger Treffry, his ex[ecut]ors or adm[inistrat]ors, or to which
53   he is or may be subject or lyable by virtue of or under the s[ai]d will; AND ALSO shall & will at all time & times hereafter free, save harmless & keep indemnifyed the s[aid] Roger Treffry, his heirs, ex[ecut]ors & administrators, & his & their lands, tenements, goods & chattels of, from
54   & against all & all manner of action & actions, suits, troubles & pro- secutions whatsoever to be brought, sued or prosecuted by his s[ai]d brothers & sisters or any or either of them, their any or either of their ex[ecut]ors or adm[inistrat]ors or any other person or persons
55   whatsoever claiming under the s[ai]d Samuel Treffry deceased on account of the s[ai]d barton, farm, lands, stock, goods, chattels & personal estate whatsoever of the s[ai]d Samuel Treffry deceased or on any other account whatsoever relative to the s[ai]d will & trusts therein contained   AND
56   for the true & faithfull performance of all & singular the articles, covenants, agreements & things herein contained on each of their parts & behalfs to be respectively done, performed, observed & kept, they, the
57   s[ai]d Roger Treffry & Elizabeth Treffry do hereby bind themselves, their heirs, ex[ecut]ors & adm[inistrat]ors each to the other of them in the penal sum of eight hundred pounds of lawfull money of Great Britain, firmly by these presents   IN WITNESS   whereof, the parties afores[ai]d to these
58   presents engrossed or written on parchment (being first duly stampt) their hands & seals interchangeably have sett the day & year first above written

[signed]   ROGER TREFFRY   [signed]   ELIZ[ABETH] TREFFRY

OLD GARDEN GATE BEER BARTON

Chapter Thirteen

THE FAMILY OF ROGER TREFFRY OF BERE BARTON (1746–1818)

ROGER TREFFRY, the oldest son and first child of Elizabeth Betty Treffry and Samuel Treffry, was born on 20 May 1746, according to records in the Harriet Smith Collection. He was christened on 13 June 1746 at the St Budeaux parish church, St Budeaux, Devon. This christening date appears in the Bishops' Transcripts at the Devon Record Office, Exeter (examined June 1980). As far

June 13th: 1746 was Baptized Roger the Son of Samuel Treffry and Elizabeth his wife.

as I can ascertain, he was the first of this branch of the Treffry family to be born outside of Cornwall. This may explain why his exact birthdate or christening date had not been found. I have not been able to locate his home in St Budeaux, or the home where his father was born in Landrake. At the age of 12 Roger moved to Bere Barton with his parents and his brothers and sisters; there he grew up in the beautiful old stone house by the Tavy River adjacent to St Andrew's church which he attended.

The Plymouth he knew in his first 12 years while living in St Budeaux, and later while nearby at Bere Barton, would have been a hilly seaport town of narrow and winding streets; a community which lived largely by shipping, fisheries, sail-cloth making, rope works, manufacturing of wool, soap, candles and starch. Other industries included sugar refining, paper mills, and potteries.

When Roger was just two years old, William Cookworthy, the Plymouth chemist found the excellent China-clay deposits in Cornwall in 1748. He was the first person in England to discover the process of making true porcelain. He was also the first to manufacture it in his own factory at Coxside, Plymouth.

In 1769 James Watt took out his first patent on the steam engine bringing about vast changes in production of all kinds of products. It was very clear that the Industrial Revolution was under way. The last half of the 18th century was the period of change from the old way of life which had endured for centuries

HUSBAND	Roger TREFFRY		Occupation	Malster, Gentleman Farmer Author, Business
Born	20 May 1746	Place		
Chr.	13 June 1746	Place St. Budeaux, Devon, England		
Marr.	28 May 1770	Place St. Austell, Cornwall, England		
Died	24 Nov 1818	Place Plymouth, Devon, England		
Bur.	29 Nov 1818	Place Friends Burial Ground, Plymouth, Devon, England		
Father	Samuel TREFFRY, Gentleman		Mother	Mrs. Elizabeth BETTY
Other Wives	None			

WIFE	Mary VEALE			
Born	14 March 1749	Place St. Austell, Cornwall, England		
Chr.		Place		
Died	22 June 1830	Place Plymouth, Devon, England		
Bur.	27 June 1830	Place Friends Burial Ground, Plymouth, Devon		
Father	Joseph VEALE		Mother	Elizabeth HINGSTON
Other Husbands				

	Children	Sex	When Born - When Died	Where Born - Where Died	Marriage Date & Place - To Whom
1	Joseph	M	21 Apr 1771 - 9 Nov 1851	Penryn, Cornwall - Plymouth, Devon	31 Jul 1800 - Susannah BROWNE
2	Robert	M	22 Jul 1772 -	Penryn, Cornwall - Plymouth, Devon	30 Oct 1822, Tideford - Sarah BAWDEN
3	Samuel	M	16 Dec 1773 - 25 Nov 1850	Penryn, Cornwall - Exeter, Devon	30 Oct 1799, St. Austell - Ann DUNSFORD
4	William	M	29 Jun 1775 - 30 Apr 1852	Penryn, Cornwall - London	Blanchette STILES
5	Elizabeth	F	24 Mar 1777 - 21 Sep 1846	Penryn, Cornwall -	
6	John	M	3 Nov 1778 - 27 Sep 1849	Penryn, Cornwall - Norwich, Ontario, Canada	14 May 1810, Stoke DAM - Hannah HAYWARD
7	Sarah	F	1 Jun 1780 - 1 Oct 1856	Penryn, Cornwall -	10 Apr 1800, Kingsbridge, Dev - Benjamin FOX
8	Anna	F	12 Sep 1782 - 8 Jun 1877	Beer Barton, Beer Ferris -	23 Mar 1807, Lostwithiel - Benjamin Wills NEWTON
9	Henry	M	22 Jul 1784 - Mar 1846	Beer Barton, Beer Ferris -	1838 - Emily LUCKEY B.BLOOM
10	Richard	M	29 Mar 1786 - 17 Nov 1838	Beer Barton, Beer Ferris - London Rd., Manchester	12 Jun 1816, St.Peters, Lvrpl - Rachel WATERHOUSE
11	Joshua	M	30 Mar 1788 - 5 Apr 1788	Beer Barton, Beer Ferris - Beer Ferris	
12			Bur. 8 Apr 1788 -		
13					
14					
15					

Sources of Information	Other Marriages
1. Indenture Tripartite 1768-Roger TREFFRY, his Mother & John BETTY. Original in possession Eugene W. RIDEOUT.	
2. Visitations of the County of Cornwall - TREFRY of TREFRY & place comprising Heralds Visitations 1530-1573-1620 with additions by Lt.Col. J.L. VIVIAN 1887.	
3. Table showing the members of several branches of the family of Roger TREFFRY of Plymouth, Devon 1878, prepared by John DAWSON of Exeter. In possession Dr. Charles TREFFRY, Canada.	
4. Personal Diary of Joseph TREFFRY 25 June 1830, Plymouth.	
5. Harriet Froelich SMITH Collection, Kenosha, Wis.	
6. Society of Friends-West Div.of Cornwall Re FRG 6/1218 Reg.Book #5 Penryn & Falmouth- Births, Marriages, Burials from 1654-1788. LDS Film 814847, Salt Lake	13-2

to a period of rapid, violent and revolutionary change in industrial life in England. During this time there was an increase in population as babies were living longer because of better sanitary conditions and improved medical knowledge. There was a great expansion of British trade in new markets at home and abroad.

Changes were also going on in agriculture between 1750–1780. Hundreds of Enclosure Acts were passed, developing England into a countryside of hedges, fields and scattered farms, thus making each farmer independent of his neighbours. In this way the farmers could introduce improvements in crops and breeding without fear of his efforts being wasted. Owners of rich and large estates were willing to try new experiments to improve their agricultural output. Thus we come to Roger and his part in the increase in production of disease-free grains.

Anyone involved in the development and progress of the industrial and agricultural revolution had to have a certain degree of education. Unfortunately, I do not know where Roger Treffry was educated, but from his letters and publications it is apparent that he had a very fine education, beginning in the St Budeaux area, and continuing after the age of 12 at Bere Ferrers. According to the Indenture he was trained at his own request as a maltster, a maker of malt used in the production of beer and other products.

At the age of 15 when Roger lost his father, I imagine many responsibilities fell on his young shoulders in helping his mother carry on at Bere Barton. According to the Indenture, when he became of age he elected not to accept the responsibilities required of him by his father's will. Undoubtedly, it was then that he trained as a maltster and worked in that field for a while. Perhaps this was where he learned the necessity of having a good, clean, disease-free grain for marketing. In 1780 he returned to Bere Barton, where he began to study and experiment in the growth of healthy grain. This led him to research in most counties of England over the next 10 or 12 years. In September of 1792 he prepared an advertisement for a scientific process that he had developed showing the cause and proving the cure of smut-balls on various grains. An original copy of this advertisement is in the University of London's Goldsmith Library, and a microfilm copy is in the main library of Stanford University, Stanford, California. High praise for the results of Roger's research is printed on the advertisement. These excellent references came from Lord Eliot of Port Eliot, Edmund Hambly of Menheniot, and John Browne of Landrake, all from eastern Cornwall, not far from Plymouth; in Devon from Richard Hawkins of High-House, J. Pearse of Easton—both near Kingsbridge—and from Edmund Andrews of Modbury. Roger Treffry was undoubtedly well known to all these people.

Roger Treffry's scientific study was published in 1793 under the title of *A Dissertation on Smut-balls Amongst Wheat and Other Grain*. It is listed in the Library of Congress, Washington, D.C., under 'Agriculture', and under 'General'. Another copy is in the Society of Friends' Library, Euston Road, London. The book must have been in demand as more than one edition was published.

A sentence from one of Roger's letters pertaining to the diseased grain problem, shows several things about him; that he was very well educated, that he had a creative and scientific mind, and, thirdly, that he was concerned with

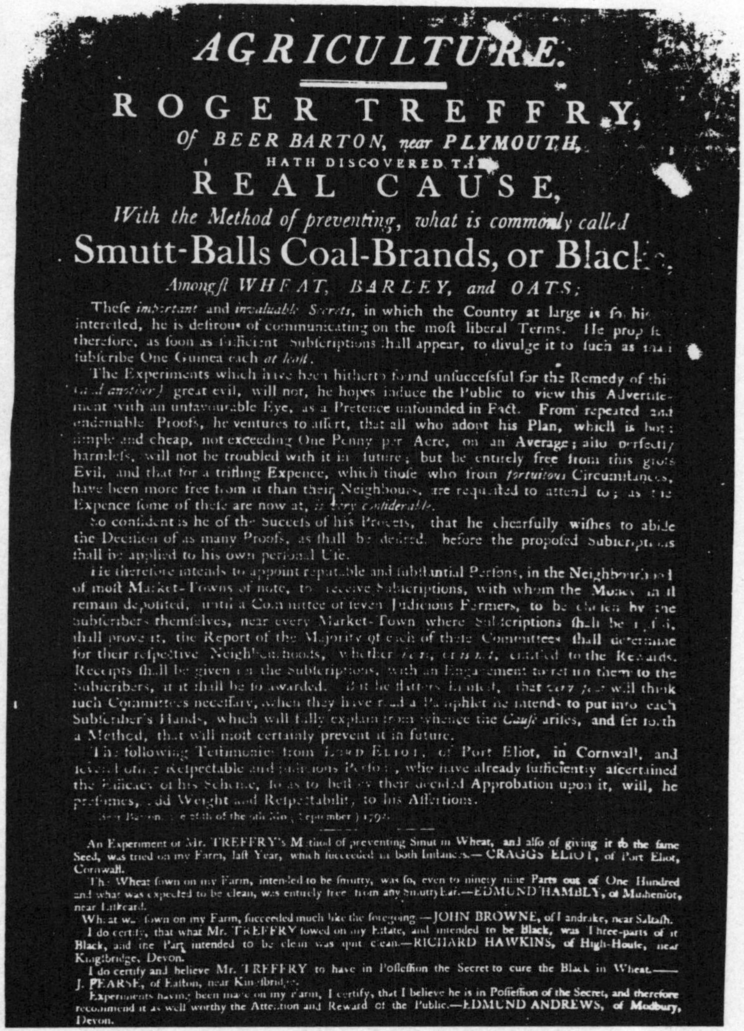

AGRICULTURE.

ROGER TREFFRY,

Of BEER BARTON, near PLYMOUTH,

HATH DISCOVERED THE

REAL CAUSE,

With the Method of preventing, what is commonly called

Smutt-Balls Coal-Brands, or Blacks,

Amongst WHEAT, BARLEY, and OATS;

These *important* and *invaluable Secrets*, in which the Country at large is so highly interested, he is desirous of communicating on the most liberal Terms. He proposes therefore, as soon as sufficient Subscriptions shall appear, to divulge it to such as shall subscribe One Guinea each *at least*.

The Experiments which have been hitherto found unsuccessful for the Remedy of this *(and another)* great evil, will not, he hopes induce the Public to view this Advertisement with an unfavourable Eye, as a Pretence unfounded in Fact. From repeated and undeniable Proofs, he ventures to assert, that all who adopt his Plan, which is both simple and cheap, not exceeding One Penny per Acre, on an Average; also perfectly harmless, will not be troubled with it in future; but be entirely free from this gross Evil, and that for a trifling Expence, which those who from *fortuitous* Circumstances, have been more free from it than their Neighbours, are requested to attend to; as the Expence some of these are now at, *is very considerable*.

So confident is he of the Success of his Process, that he chearfully wishes to abide the Decision of as many Proofs, as shall be desired, before the proposed Subscriptions shall be applied to his own personal Use.

He therefore intends to appoint reputable and substantial Persons, in the Neighbourhood of most Market-Towns of note, to receive Subscriptions, with whom the Money shall remain deposited, until a Committee of seven Judicious Farmers, to be chosen by the Subscribers themselves, near every Market-Town where Subscriptions shall be [illegible], shall prove it, the Report of the Majority of each of these Committees shall determine for their respective Neighbourhoods, whether *he is, or is not*, entitled to the Rewards. Receipts shall be given for the Subscriptions, with an Engagement to return them to the Subscribers, if it shall be so awarded. But he flatters himself, that *very few* will think such Committees necessary, when they have read a Pamphlet he intends to put into each Subscriber's Hands, which will fully explain from whence the *Cause* arises, and set forth a Method, that will most certainly prevent it in future.

The following Testimonies from LORD ELIOT, of Port Eliot, in Cornwall, and several other Respectable and Judicious Persons, who have already sufficiently ascertained the Efficacy of his Scheme, so as to bestow their decided Approbation upon it, will, he presumes, add Weight and Respectability to his Assertions.

Beer Barton, the 26th of the 9th Mo. (September) 179[illegible]

An Experiment of Mr. TREFFRY's Method of preventing Smut in Wheat, and also of giving it to the same Seed, was tried on my Farm, last Year, which succeeded in both Instances.—CRAGGS ELIOT, of Port Eliot, Cornwall.

The Wheat sown on my Farm, intended to be smutty, was so, even to ninety nine Parts out of One Hundred and what was expected to be clean, was entirely free from any Smutty Ear.—EDMUND HAMBLY, of Menheniot, near Liskeard.

Wheat was sown on my Farm, succeeded much like the foregoing.—JOHN BROWNE, of Landrake, near Saltash.

I do certify, that what Mr. TREFFRY sowed on my Estate, and intended to be Black, was Three-parts of it Black, and the Part intended to be clean was quite clean.—RICHARD HAWKINS, of High-House, near Kingsbridge, Devon.

I do certify and believe Mr. TREFFRY to have in Possession the Secret to cure the Black in Wheat.—J. PEARSE, of Easton, near Kingsbridge.

Experiments having been made on my Farm, I certify, that I believe he is in Possession of the Secret, and therefore recommend it as well worthy the Attention and Reward of the Public.—EDMUND ANDREWS, of Modbury, Devon.

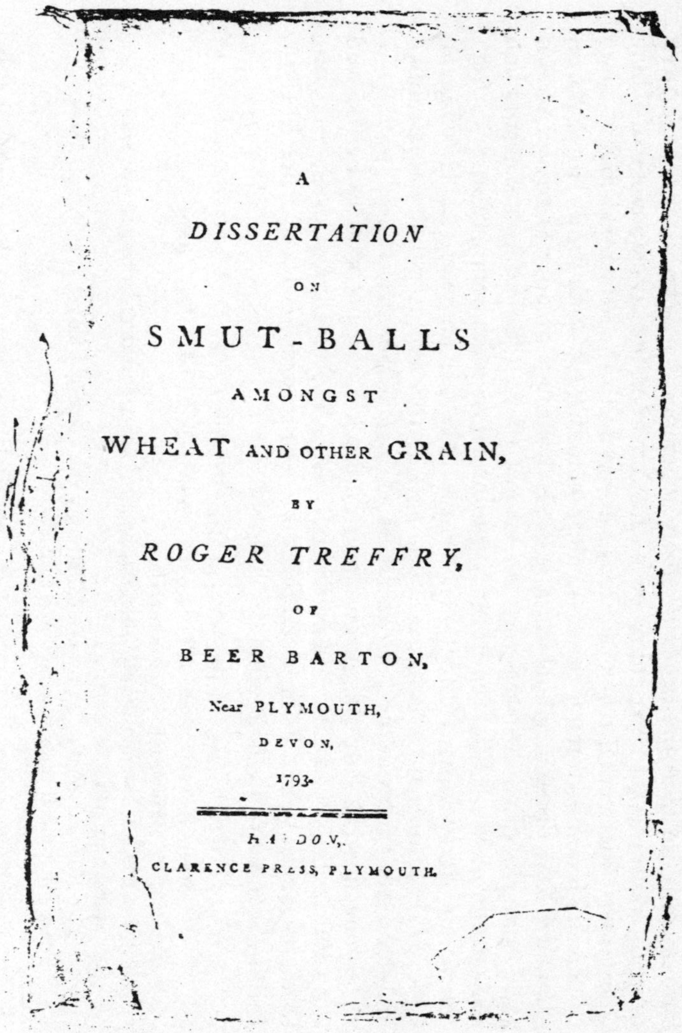

A

DISSERTATION

ON

SMUT-BALLS

AMONGST

WHEAT AND OTHER GRAIN,

BY

ROGER TREFFRY,

OF

BEER BARTON,

Near PLYMOUTH,

DEVON,

1793.

HAYDON,

CLARENCE PRESS, PLYMOUTH.

The title page and an advertisement for Roger Treffry's book on smut-balls in wheat and other grains

others: 'I was long endeavouring to ascertain the true cause of Smut-balls which hath so long puzzled the heads of many ingenious Farmers; diverse have been the conjectures and various have been the remedies prescribed: most of which have proved ineffectual *when the cause did exist* to the very great loss at times to the farmers and through them in degree to the Community at large'. Roger estimated that diseased grain was a loss of thousands of pounds to the nation each year. His discovery was of great benefit to all the people of England and also further afield. A brief report on his published research appeared in A. Young's *Annals of Agriculture,* vol. 19 (1793), pp. 259–61, and vol. 21 (1793), pp. 410–33. He also wrote a description of a new harrow and drag that was published in *Letters and Papers of the Bath and West of England Society,* vol. 4, pp. 330–33.

Turning now to Roger's personal and family life, two years after he received the £400 spelled out in the Indenture, he was in St Austell, Cornwall, preparing to marry Mary Veale. From Society of Friends records on L.D.S. film 814845, for St Austell, Cornwall, I found the following:

Roger TREFFRY and Mary VEALE 1770

The 18th day of April 1770 Roger Treffry and Mary Veale proposed their intention of taking each other in marriage.

The 23rd of the 5th month above appearing declared their continued intention of taking each other in marriage.

The 28th day of the 5th month called May the aforesaid Roger Treffry and Mary Veale solemnized their marriage in Veale Town.

Mary Veale was the daughter of Elizabeth Hingston Veale and Joseph Veale. Her mother was from the Hingston family of Holbeton, Devon, not far from Plymouth. The Hingstons were a very early and prominent Quaker family. In the Rogers' collection at the Society of Genealogists in London I found the records of the Hingston family traced back into the 1550s at Holbeton. In Cornwall, just over the border from Devon, there is a place called Hingston Down where a great battle was fought in the year 838, showing that Hingston was a very early name in that region. As people often took names from places, this very well may be where the Hingston family came from. The name is not Celtic. I have not been able to trace Joseph Veale's parentage. Veale is an old Celtic name, a shortened version of TRE+VEALE, meaning farm settlement of Michael's or M'ael's, a shortened version of Michael.

Mary Veale was one of two daughters and eight sons. The Veales were active Quakers in St Austell, Cornwall, in the 1700 and 1800s. They were a prominent, influential and widely-known merchant family manufacturing wool blankets and cloth for great coats. For miles around, they bought wool from the farmers and supplied small shops in the villages with finished goods. Some of Mary's Veale relatives owned a very successful grocery shop. The older Veales made moderate fortunes and built homes for themselves outside the town in order to let the younger Veales take over their businesses. After retiring, the older ones would visit Quaker meetings around the county and hold meetings. Their theme was love and mercy of God. They visited the sick, afflicted and aged and were greatly beloved by those who knew them.

With Roger Treffry's marriage to Mary Veale, he soon joined the Society of Friends, undoubtedly influenced by the Veale and Hingston families. From 1770, when Roger married Mary Veale, many of their descendants have remained in the Society of Friends. Many members of the Veale and Hingston families were buried at Tregangeeves, which was less than a mile west of St Austell on the main road to Truro. Unfortunately, this Quaker burial ground is no more.

At the time of Roger Treffry's marriage, St Austell was a quiet place in a tin-mining area. Clay needed for Mr. Cookworthy's porcelain was being produced in the region. This is the area that Joseph Thomas (Austin) Treffry later developed with his many mining enterprises.

Roger and Mary Treffry lived in Penryn, three miles up-river from Falmouth, for the first 10 years of their marriage. Their first seven children were born there, including my second great-grandfather, John Treffry. I do not know where they lived, or for certain what Roger's occupation was. Since he was trained as a maltster he may have been employed in one of the Penryn breweries. Sometime in the latter half of 1780 Roger Treffry with his family returned to make his home at Bere Barton, where his mother was still living. His last four children were born at Bere Barton.

While living at Penryn Roger and Mary Treffry were members of the Society of Friends there. After returning to Bere Barton they became members of the Plymouth Society of Friends. Being a Quaker family with only a stone wall to separate their Barton from the adjacent Anglican churchyard caused many great sufferings for Roger because of church tithes. Tithes were based on the appropriation system, whereby 10 per cent. of the main produce of the land, stock and labour could be appropriated by the rector. Roger Treffry vehemently fought the system by refusing to pay, as he felt that the local rector was levying 'pretended' taxes. When Roger refused to pay, seizure of some of his livestock would take place—sometimes with a warrant, but many times without. These seizures were called 'sufferings' by the Quakers in their *Great Book of Sufferings*. When the Anglican churchmen became aware of the detailed records being kept, they became a bit less aggressive in their seizures.

By 1784, 1785 and 1786 the rector of Bere Ferrers was demanding £30 a year from Roger in tithes, which he refused to pay. For the average family, £20 was at that time the annual income. The amount of tithes sought from Roger indicate clearly that he was a very prosperous gentleman farmer. In 1784, 30 ewes and one fat heifer were seized from him; in 1786 he was threatened with prosecution in the ecclesiastical court for refusal to pay church rate. Also in 1786 a hog, a cow, and 26 sheep were taken from him. Later in the year 100 sheep, valued at £80, were taken, and £50 was returned. These seizures for tithes from Roger continued into the 1790s.

From the feuding over tithes with the rector, we can ascertain to some degree not only the size of the operation at Bere Barton, but also the kind of animals and produce raised. Besides cattle, sheep and hogs, I found mention of geese and honey. In Roger's writings he mentions 'my horses eating all kinds of chaff', and 'last autumn the potatoes being taken up, the land was sown with wheat'. He was experimenting on other grains, so we can assume he raised barley and oats. Since the climate in the Plymouth area was conducive to raising most kinds of vegetables and fruit, Roger undoubtedly produced many varieties of both.

It is quite apparent that Roger was running Bere Barton as a large agri-business with a great deal of help, or he would not have been able to travel about England and be away as much as he was. In 1787 an indenture with Roger's signature shows him to be of Bere Ferrers, taking William Popplestone, a poor child, as an apprentice to be taught and instructed in good husbandry until he was 21 years of age. Probably many more apprenticeship indentures exist as Roger, according to his own statement in his *Dissertation* said, 'For not withstanding I have discovered the cause, and appear certain of the Remedy, having many servants, I forbode to apply it'.

whereof, the Parties abovesaid to these present Indentures,

WE whose Names are subscribed, Justices of the Peace Country ——— aforesaid, (

The signature of Roger Treffry, 1787

Roger Treffry, besides running profitably a large barton and travelling over most of England in his scientific agricultural research, found time to attend Quaker meetings and to accept Quaker responsibilities. In July of 1781 he was appointed a Trustee of the Plymouth Meeting House along with 'James Fox, John Fox, Jr., Philip Cookworthy, Wm. Clark, Wm. Gillett, Joseph Cookworthy, Wm. Soady, Rich^d and Andrew Hingston, James Hingston, Wm. Prideaux, Jr., George Prideaux and John Hingston'. In 1784–1785 Roger Treffry was attending Quaker meetings in Plymouth concerned with the negro slave trade. It was agreed that no Quaker was to hold slaves or trade in slaves; this was over 75 years before the great Civil War over slavery in the United States!

Besides attending Quaker meetings in Plymouth, Roger was appointed to attend the yearly Friends meeting in London in 1785. On 1 November 1785 Roger advised the Plymouth meeting that because of the distance from Bere Barton to Plymouth and the largeness of his family he had been holding meetings in his own home. They approved and suggested his applying for a license to the Quaker Sessions.

I do not know when Roger and Mary left Bere Barton; however, I found a land agreement document in the Cornwall Record Office dated July of 1811 between Samuel Nicholls of the parish of St Austell in the County of Cornwall, gentleman of the first part. Roger Treffry of the Borough of Lostwithiel in the same county, gentleman, of the second part with others. It names Richard Veale, maltster, brother of Mary Veale Treffry. Her brothers, John and James, were also named. Since Richard is named as a maltster, I am wondering if Roger met his wife through Richard or perhaps one of the other brothers working in this same field.

After this date of 1811 I found no further information recorded about Roger until his death on 24 November 1818 in Plymouth. He was buried in the Friends' burial ground there. Mrs. Francis Lawson, a present member of the Plymouth meeting, showed me where the burial ground had been. It was in the centre of the area that was so totally and devastatingly bombed in World War II. A wide highway runs through there now in the busy centre of new Plymouth, just as the highway runs through Tregangeeves in Cornwall.

Excerpts follow from Roger Treffry's will (dated September 1815 and proved on 24 April 1819 in London). Roger Treffry's sons, Joseph and Robert, and his friend, William Collier, were appointed executors to manage trust funds or to provide annuities of £200 a year for his 'beloved widow Mary Treffry'; £55 per year was bequeathed to his daughter, Elizabeth, and £20 per year to his widowed daughter, Anna Newton.

Roger bequeathed to his wife 'all my household Furniture, Plate, China and Books to have the use thereof during her life. If my Daughter Elizabeth Treffry, remains unmarried, and my Daughter Anna Newton remains a widow at the time of my decease, my desire is, that they will both continue to live with their mother dutifully bearing with the infirmatives incident to age; taking proper care of her, and that they will not leave her on any other account, but that of marriage'. In consideration of this 'I give them or such of them as has taken proper care of their mother the use of all the aforesaid Household Furniture, Plate, China and Books during the time they may live together after Mary's decease. When they separate to be divided between them share and share alike'.

Roger was concerned about his brother Thomas needing assistance and support 'in the declining of life'. Roger provided for this a sum 'not to exceed in any one year £20'. 'And whereas my old and faithful servant Mary Julyan is at the time maintained at my expense', Roger provided funds for her not to exceed £20 per year. 'And whereas I have a sum of money in the hands of my son Joseph Treffry and whereas there have been sundry sums of money advanced by me to my Sons Henry and Richard Treffry in addition to what I gave them when they first engaged in business on their own account, I direct that all accounts between me and my said sons Joseph, Henry and Richard, may be settled as they stand in my books . . . and that the Executors deduct aforesaid debts from any Legacy that may become due to either of my said three sons.'

After Mary Treffry's decease, withholding in trust the funds to pay annuities to daughters Elizabeth and Anna Newton, brother Thomas Treffry and servant Mary Julyan, the estate was to be shared in the following proportions, 'To my Son Joseph, his heirs etc., the sum of £250. To my Sons Robert, Samuel, William, John, Henry and Richard and to my daughters Elizabeth Treffry, Sarah Fox and Anna Newton, the sum of £100 pounds each'. In case of the death of any of Roger's children, leaving a child or children, they would receive their parent's share.

Roger left £50 to his grandson, Benjamin Wills Newton, 'on his attaining the age of twenty-one'. He directed 'whatsoever and whensoever any sum or sums are divided between his children, either more or less than £1,200 at a time, they are to be divided in the aforesaid proportions'. Any disputes were to be settled by the executors, who were not to be answerable for failure of any security in the trust. Roger Treffry's estate was valued at £6,000, and consisted of 'Ready Money, Policies of Insurance, Rents, Arrears of Rents, Debts and other property of whatsoever nature in kind'.

Mary Veale Treffry, Roger's widow, lived in Plymouth until her death in 1830. After Roger and Mary left Beer Barton, I found no record of any of the Treffry family residing there. Their two oldest sons remained in Plymouth. All of their other children settled in various places in England, as far as I have been able to ascertain, except John, the fifth son, who emigrated to Canada. His family is covered in the next chapter. Information about the other children follows.

First, I think it would be appropriate to make reference to the longevity of Roger and Mary's children. Except for the youngest of the 11 children, who died a few days after birth, seven of the remaining children lived past seventy. One of them reached 80, and a daughter reached 95—all remarkable ages for those days! One great-grand-daughter reached 98, and several other great-grandchildren lived into their late 80s and 90s, and one reached 100 years.

Descendants of Roger and Mary Veale Treffry

Joseph Treffry, the eldest of Roger and Mary Veale Treffry's children, left Beer Barton in 1797 to work in Plymouth as a corn factor until 1800. By 1801 he was a corn merchant in Liverpool. Later he returned to Plymouth where he engaged in business as a corn and flour merchant, and wholesale grocer.

In the Devon Record Office, Plymouth, I found a lease and release of a warehouse consisting of a 'cellar on the ground floor, three lofts over same, in Foxhole St. on east, Stillman St. or Seven Stars Lane on north, *Prince George Inn* on south, to Joseph Treffry of Plymouth, grocer for consideration of £1,200,

The signature of Joseph Treffry, 1812

10 and 11 October 1817'. Another document showed the conveyance of this property from Joseph Treffry of Plymouth, gentleman, to John Burnell of Plymouth, merchant, 5 February 1850, indicating Joseph's retirement from business.

Joseph Treffry belonged to the Society of Friends in Plymouth, Devon. He laboured for the repeal of capital punishment. He and his wife were Elders of the Society.

In 1836 Joseph Treffry wrote *Strictures,* a rebutal of a late publication titled *A Remonstrance to the Society of Friends,* written by Benjamin Wills Newton, his nephew. The *Remonstrance* peremptorily denied the grounds of the doctrines held by the Society of Friends. In *Strictures* Joseph refuted B. W. Newton's writings which he felt were inaccurate and unfairly critical. The first paragraph of the *Strictures* shows Joseph to be well educated, deeply religious and of strong Quaker faith.

> When any writer, but particularly one of high religious pretensions, undertakes to sit in judgment on the religious principles of a Society, claiming to be Christian as well as himself, he should not suffer his mind to be biassed by prejudices—he should refrain, not only from direct misrepresentation, but also from giving a false colouring to the subjects of his criticism: he should recollect that he himself is not infallible. His own interpretation of Scripture differing in some points from that of many other Christian professors, should induce him to judge with caution and charity; and to remember one point of doctrine, in which we should all agree, namely,—to do to others as we would wish them to do to us.

In November 1843 Joseph sent a letter to George Crosfield, author of *Memoir to Samuel Fothergill* in which he suggested that a good *Biographical Dictionary* of Society members should be compiled. Joseph had suggested this idea for the past 10 years to members of Friends and suggested that Mr. Crosfield was capable of doing it.

Apparently Joseph kept a diary or journal as on 25 June 1830 he recorded the birthdates of Roger and Mary's children and his brother John and Hannah Hayward Treffry's children. A copy of his records was given to me by John's grand-daughters, my great-aunts.

In 1850 Joseph suffered 'a spasm of the stomach'. He died on 9 November 1851 at Portland Villa, Plymouth, aged eighty-one.

Joseph Treffry married Susannah Browne, daughter of John Browne, farmer of Landrake, Cornwall, from a Quaker family. Among the witnesses at the wedding were William Fry of Plymouth, mercer; John Wadge of Liskeard, grocer; and Samuel Treffry, woollen manufacturer of Par, Cornwall, brother.

As the male line of descent of the Treffry family came through Joseph, it is included overleaf in chart form:

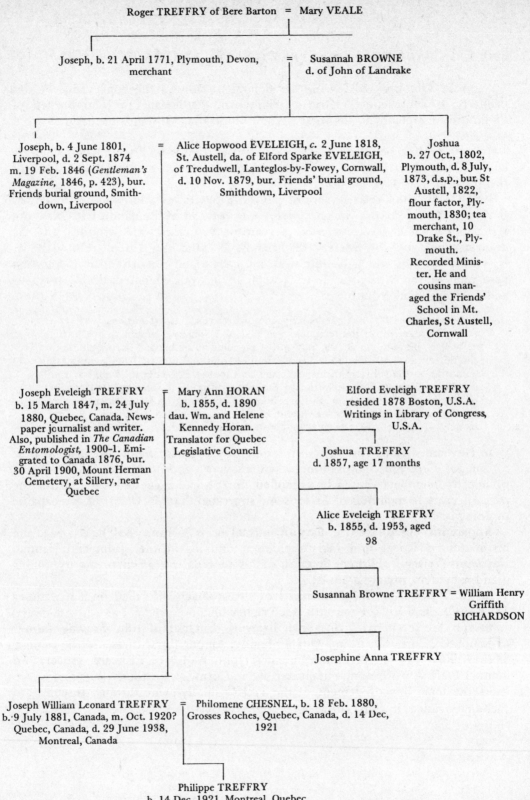

Roger TREFFRY of Bere Barton = Mary VEALE

Joseph, b. 21 April 1771, Plymouth, Devon, = Susannah BROWNE
merchant   d. of John of Landrake

Joseph, b. 4 June 1801, = Alice Hopwood EVELEIGH, *c.* 2 June 1818,   Joshua
Liverpool, d. 2 Sept. 1874   St. Austell, da. of Elford Sparke EVELEIGH,   b. 27 Oct., 1802,
m. 19 Feb. 1846 (*Gentleman's*   of Tredudwell, Lanteglos-by-Fowey, Cornwall,   Plymouth, d. 8 July,
Magazine, 1846, p. 423), bur.   d. 10 Nov. 1879, bur. Friends' burial ground,   1873, d.s.p., bur. St
Friends burial ground, Smith-   Smithdown, Liverpool   Austell, 1822,
down, Liverpool   flour factor, Ply-
    mouth, 1830; tea
    merchant, 10
    Drake St., Ply-
    mouth.
    Recorded Minis-
    ter. He and
    cousins man-
    aged the Friends'
    School in Mt.
    Charles, St Austell,
    Cornwall

Joseph Eveleigh TREFFRY = Mary Ann HORAN   Elford Eveleigh TREFFRY
b. 15 March 1847, m. 24 July   b. 1855, d. 1890   resided 1878 Boston, U.S.A.
1880, Quebec, Canada. News-   dau. Wm. and Helene   Writings in Library of Congress,
paper journalist and writer.   Kennedy Horan.   U.S.A.
Also, published in *The Canadian*   Translator for Quebec
Entomologist, 1900–1. Emi-   Legislative Council
grated to Canada 1876, bur.   Joshua TREFFRY
30 April 1900, Mount Herman   d. 1857, age 17 months
Cemetery, at Sillery, near
Quebec

    Alice Eveleigh TREFFRY
    b. 1855, d. 1953, aged
    98

    Susannah Browne TREFFRY = William Henry
    Griffith
    RICHARDSON

    Josephine Anna TREFFRY

Joseph William Leonard TREFFRY = Philomene CHESNEL, b. 18 Feb. 1880,
b. 9 July 1881, Canada, m. Oct. 1920?   Grosses Roches, Quebec, Canada, d. 14 Dec,
Quebec, Canada, d. 29 June 1938,   1921
Montreal, Canada

Philippe TREFFRY
b. 14 Dec. 1921, Montreal, Quebec,
Canada. Librarian, Provincial Museum,
Quebec

Robert, the second son of Roger and Mary Veale Treffry, was a wine merchant residing in Plymouth Dock at the time of his marriage to Sarah Bawden, the daughter of Jonathan and Anne Bawden of East Looe. No children of this marriage are recorded. Sarah died on 13 November 1836. She was a sister of Esther Bawden, who married Philip Cookworthy Prideaux (1776-1842) in 1799. In the Prideaux pedigree of 1889, Esther is said to be co-heiress of Jonathan and Anne Tuckett Bowden of East Looe.

Samuel, the third son of Roger and Mary Veale Treffry, was sent at the age of 12 to John Benwell's school at Sidcot, after which he returned to assist his father at Bere Barton. From the age of 18, Samuel was in the ministry of the Society of Friends, and wrote several published articles: 'Publicans and Sinners Friends' (1838); 'Expostulatory Remarks on the Use of Water Baptism' (reprinted 1847, 1850, 1856, 1857).

Samuel Treffry married Ann Dunsford, daughter of Ann and Stephenson Dunsford of Bideford, Devon. Witnesses at the wedding were Joseph Treffry, his brother, Jane Honeychurch, his aunt, and Eliphaz Jackson. Samuel and Anne were parents of Mary, born on 19 September 1800; Anna, born on 28 November 1802; Robert, born on 31 May 1805; Samuel, born in 1807; Thomas Towill, born about 1809; Henry, born in 1811, who died aged 20 in 1831.

The Samuel Treffry family settled in Bath in 1813 for about 25 years, then moved to Exeter in 1838. In 1841-49 he was holding public meetings. He died 25 November 1850, and was buried at the Friends' burial ground, Exeter.

As far as I have been able to ascertain, Samuel and Ann Treffry's son, Robert, was the first descendant of Roger and Mary to emigrate to Canada in 1821, 13 years before his uncle, John Treffry. Robert was educated at Sidcot school, Winscombe, Somerset. Arriving in Canada at the age of 16 he took up the study of medicine at Kingston, Ontario, and was a practicing physician for many years in Canada. He married, first, Sarah Law, who died childless.

Robert married, secondly, Fleety Brooksbank on 5 November 1832. They were the parents of seven sons and four daughters. There are many of their descendants with the Treffry name in Canada and the United States. Dr. Robert Treffry died on 27 February 1890.

Samuel and Ann Dunsford Treffry besides having a son in Canada had a grandson named Robert Samuel Treffry, son of their son Samuel, who emigrated there about 1845. He married Mary Anne Johnstone and they were the parents of one son and eight daughters. The one son had seven sons and five daughters, so the Treffry name is carried on in this line in Canada and Australia.

Roger and Mary Treffry's son, *William,* married Blanchette Stiles who lived to be a hundred. They were the parents of William Henry Treffy who married Elizabeth Jane Prideaux on 2 June 1834 at St John the Baptist, Shoreditch, London; Henry William, who was living in Dublin in 1877; Jane, who married George W. Pound; Mary Jane; and Eliza Fanny. The family resided in London.

Roger and Mary Treffry's daughter, *Elizabeth,* died a spinster.

Roger and Mary Treffry's son, *John,* was, I believe, their only child to emigrate (*see* Chapter 14).

Roger and Mary Treffry's daughter, *Sarah,* married Benjamin Fox of the St Germans Fox family, which is of Plantagenet descent. They were the parents of three sons and three daughters, and were active in the Society of Friends. Their grandson, Cornelius Benjamin Fox, was a doctor and is mentioned in George Treffry's will of 1880 (q.v.).

Roger and Mary Treffry's daughter, *Anna,* married Benjamin Wills Newton of Devonport, gentleman, who left her a widow before 1815. She lived to the age of ninety-five. They were parents of one son, Benjamin Wills Newton, who entered Exeter College, Oxford, in 1824 at the age of sixteen. He was a member to 1832, and received his B.A. in 1829. A distinguished theologian, he was one of the early Plymouth Brethren. He was author of numerous publications. One was *The Judgment of the Court of Arches, and of the Judicial Committee of the Privy Council, in the case of Rowland Williams, D.D., considered by Benjamin Wills Newton* (1866). I found this book in the Stanford University Law Library.

In the printed memoirs of Frederick Prideaux (1817–1891) he states, 'more fruitful intellectually was the time spent with Mr. Benjamin Wills Newton, at Exeter College, Oxford, as a private pupil. He was a man of high Christian character, as well as a ripe scholar, and as a tutor did his utmost to draw out and inform the minds of the few young men who read with him'. He lived to the age of 92, dividing his time between Oxford and Plymouth. Here again we find a distinguished son of a Treffry mother.

Roger and Mary Treffry's son, *Henry,* married twice, but I have no record of children. He was a tea dealer in Exeter, Devon.

Roger and Mary Treffry's son, *Richard,* married Rachel Waterhouse and were the parents of Hannah, who married John Thomas Coudray on 23 March 1853 and were the parents of three children. Richard's son, Robert Waterhouse Treffry, and his daughter, Sarah Waterhouse Treffry, died without children. Richard, snr., was a chemist living in Manchester, and was credited with improvements in the method of preserving animal and vegetable substances from decay and in the apparatus for and mode of impregnating substances to be preserved. Richard died in Manchester in 1838 and his widow died on 23 March 1853 in Jersey.

Chapter Fourteen

THE FAMILY OF JOHN TREFFRY (1778–1849); EMIGRANTS TO CANADA

JOHN TREFFRY, born on 3 November 1778, in Penryn, Cornwall, was the fifth son of Roger and Mary Veale Treffry. (Vivian's *Visitations of the County of Cornwall* lists him incorrectly as the sixth son.) Several years of Quaker birth records are missing from the Penryn area, 1778 being one of these. However, records from three of his late grand-daughters verify this date, as does his own diary, which states on 3 November 1834 'my birthday 56 years of age'.

John Treffry was taken to Bere Barton, Bere Ferrers, when he was about two years of age, along with his four older brothers and two sisters, the third generation of this branch of the Treffrys to live in this beautiful and historic spot between the Tavy and the Tamar Rivers. He probably romped and played on the large grounds, picking wild flowers, playing with the animals and climbing the trees. As he grew older he undoubtedly went swimming and fishing in the Tavy and helped on the large farm. He may have accompanied his father on trips to Plymouth and further afield. With Bere Barton on the rivers leading to Plymouth he would have seen the tall ships that plied the oceans as Hugh Peter did in his childhood days in Fowey. Perhaps John hoped someday to sail to far-away places.

John was brought up in the Quaker faith of both his parents. He attended meetings in his own home conducted by his father, as Bere Ferrers was quite a distance from the Plymouth meeting house. However, when he married Hannah Hayward, who was not of a Quaker family, they married in Stoke Damerel parish. In that parish register (vol. 13, 'Marriages 1808–1810') their marriage was listed as no. 1085. The entry reads: 'John Treffry of East Stonehouse Manufacturer of Tessara. a Bachelor and Hannah Hayward, spinster. were married in this church By License: 14 May 1810. Witnesses, W. Hayward, Sarah Treffry, Hannah Hayward'.

Hannah Hayward was the daughter of William and Ann Galley Hayward of Plymouth Dock (now Devonport). I am assuming that the witness 'W. Hayward' is her father; Hannah Hayward, her mother; and Sarah Treffry, John's sister (all were alive at the time). A great-grandson of John Treffry, Dr. Charles Treffry, has in his possession original miniature portraits of both William and Ann Galley Hayward. In the original portrait Ann is wearing a light brown dress with a bright blue shawl. The white gimp matches her white bonnet.

* Chapter headpiece : Ann Galley Hayward's dress

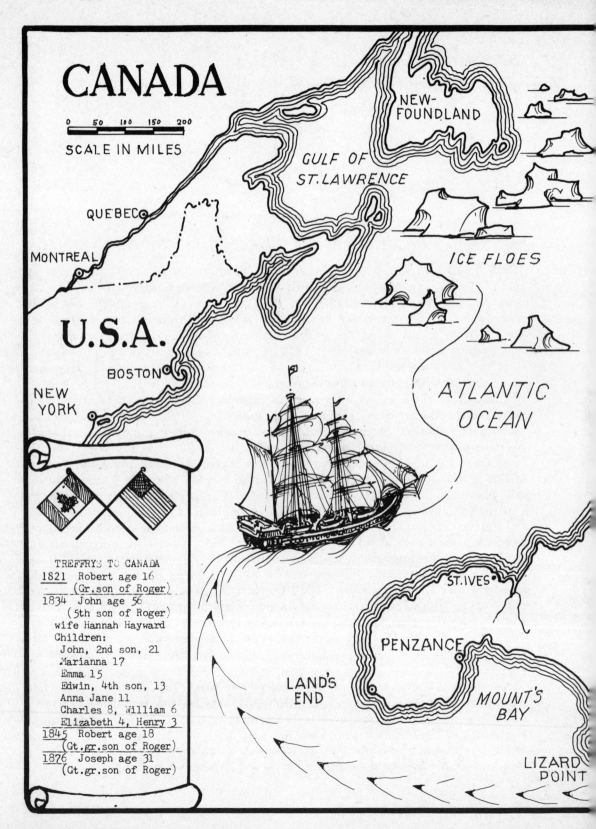

CANADA

0   50   100   150   200
SCALE IN MILES

NEW-
FOUNDLAND

GULF OF
ST. LAWRENCE

ICE FLOES

QUEBEC

MONTREAL

U.S.A.

ATLANTIC
OCEAN

BOSTON

NEW
YORK

ST. IVES

TREFFRYS TO CANADA
1821 Robert age 16
      (Gr.son of Roger)
1834 John age 56
      (5th son of Roger)
wife Hannah Hayward
Children:
John, 2nd son, 21
Marianna 17
Emma 15
Edwin, 4th son, 13
Anna Jane 11
Charles 8, William 6
Elizabeth 4, Henry 3
1845 Robert age 18
      (Gt.gr.son of Roger)
1876 Joseph age 31
      (Gt.gr.son of Roger)

PENZANCE

LAND'S
END

MOUNT'S
BAY

LIZARD
POINT

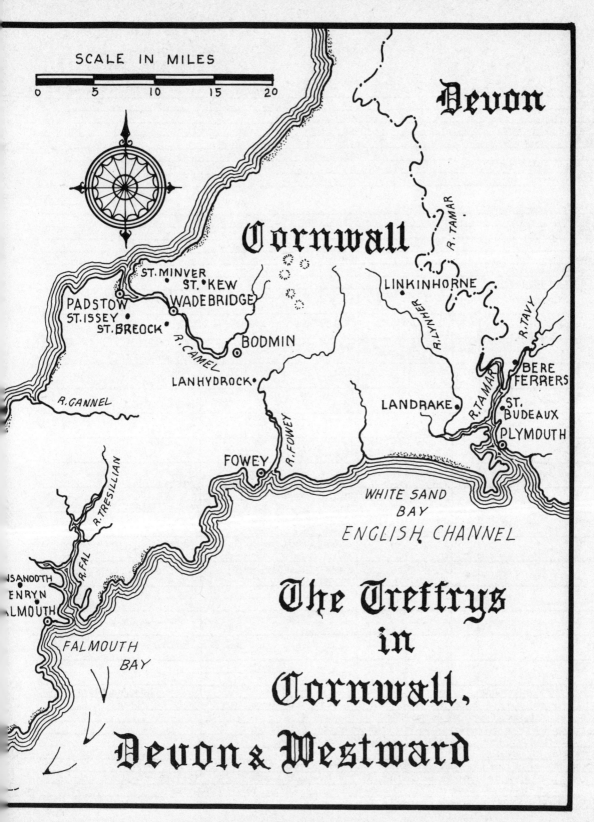

SCALE IN MILES

Devon

Cornwall

The Treffrys in Cornwall, Devon & Westward

Manufacturer of Tessara,
E.Stonehouse, Devon, Eng.
Corn & flour factor, general & com-

HUSBAND John TREFFRY   **Occupation** mission agent, Penryn, Cornwall

Born	3 Nov 1778	Place	Penryn, Cornwall, England
Chr.		Place	
Marr.	14 May 1810	Place	Stoke Damerel, Devon, England
Died	27 Sept 1849	Place	Norwich, Ontario, Canada
Bur.		Place	Ontario, Canada
Father	Roger TREFFRY		Mother	Mary VEALE
Other Wives	none			

WIFE Hannah HAYWARD

Born	6 Jan 1788	Place	Plymouth Dock, Devon, England
Chr.	2 Feb 1788	Place	Plymouth Dock, Morrice St.
Died	16 Feb 1879	Place	Hawtry, Ontario, Canada
Bur.		Place	Ontario, Canada
Father	William HAYWARD		Mother	Ann GALLEY
Other Husbands				

Children	Sex	When Born / When Died	Where Born / Where Died	Marriage Date & Place / To Whom
1 Robert John	M	18 Apr 1811 / 11 Sept 1879	Mill Bay par., E.Stonehouse, Devon / Colombia, S.A.	Colombia, S.A. / Joanna Manuella MONROY
2 John	M	1 Jan 1813 / 16 June 1850	par. St.Andrews, Exeter, Devon	1835 Norwich, Ontario, Canada / Mary Ann SOUTHWICK
3 George	M	18 Oct 1814 / 21 June 1880	par. Charles, Plymouth, Devon / Exeter, Devon, Eng.	unmarried
4 Marianna	F	15 July 1816 / 22 July 1842	par. Charles, Plymouth, Devon / USA	Henry WILSON
5 Emma	F	12 Aug 1818 / 22 Sept 1860	Penryn, Cornwall, Eng.	c.1844 / John LOSSING
6 Edwin	M	12 July 1820 / 1 Oct 1904	Penryn, Cornwall, Eng. / Froelich, Iowa, USA	22 Jan 1846 Canada / Maria KINGSFORD
7 Anna Jane	F	30 Dec 1822 / 30 May 1909	Penryn, Cornwall, Eng. / Dunkerton, Blackhawk, Iowa	4 Jan 1855 / Andrew B. McINTOSH
8 Charles John	M	11 Sept 1825 / 12 June 1908	Penryn, Cornwall, Eng. / Hawtry, Ontario, Canada	11 Oct 1854 / Alice CORLESS
9 William HAYWARD	M	3 Sept 1827 / 5 Sept 1910	Ponsanooth, Cornwall, Eng. / Hawtry, Ontario, Canada	unmarried
10 Elizabeth	F	17 July 1829 / 10 Oct 1912	Cosawes, Barton, Ponsanooth, Corn. / Whittier, Calif., USA	18 Feb 1852, Norwich, Canada / Dr. Asa SNYDER
11 Henry John	M	18 Dec 1830 / 24 Apr 1835	Ponsanooth, Cornwall, Eng. / Norwich, Ontario, Canada	unmarried
12				
13				
14				
15				

Sources of Information	Other Marriages
(1) Personal diary of Joseph Treffry, 25 June 1830, of Plymouth, Devon; copy in possession of Marianna Treffry 1948, Toronto, Canada.	none
(2) Table showing the members of several branches of the family of Roger Treffry of Plymouth, Jan 1878, by John Dawson, Exeter, Devon.	
(3) LDS, IGI (1981).	
(4) Obituary of Anna Jane Treffry McIntosh. (5) Death certificate, Elizabeth Treffry Snyder.	
(6) Arthur Garrat Dorland, History of the Society of Friends in Canada (1927).	(7) Copy of will & codicil of
George Treffry (#3 above). (8) Stoke Damerel parish register, vol.13 (1808-1810).	
(9) Records, Society of Friends, Euston Rd., London.	

A beautiful long red brocade dress lined with rough linen that belonged to Ann Galley Hayward is in the possession of Alice Treffry Parsons, Dr. Charles Treffry's sister. It is in excellent condition. Several members of the family, including myself, have, over many years, had pictures taken in this dress. I would judge by the size of the dress that Ann Galley Hayward was about five feet tall and weighed a bit over 100 pounds. There is a family legend that Ann Galley Hayward had two more dresses similar to the red brocade—one of green and one of purple. One of them was used to upholster a small loveseat. These dresses would date somewhere in the period 1778-1788 and would seem to indicate that the Haywards were quite active in the social life of the Stoke Damerel–Plymouth Dock area; other than this I know very little about them.

Another legend is that some member or members of the family had portraits sketched and painted by Joshua Reynolds. This I have been unable to verify. However, in reviewing the life of Joshua Reynolds, I found that he did spend several years in Plymouth Dock in the early part of his painting career. Plymouth Dock was adjacent to St Budeaux, so it is within the realm of possibility that there is some truth to this legend. In the midsummer of 1743 Reynolds settled in Plymouth Dock where he concentrated on portrait painting until the December of 1744 when he returned to London for a year. In 1745 when his father died Reynolds returned to Plymouth Dock to take a house with his two youngest unmarried sisters. There for the next two years he continued his portrait painting. From 1747-1749 Reynolds was chiefly in London with trips to Plymouth Dock.

From 1745 or before, Robert Treffry and his wife, Elizabeth, were living in St Budeaux with their only children, Samuel and Elizabeth. In the fall of 1745 Samuel, then 31 years of age, brought his bride, Elizabeth Betty, from St Issey, Cornwall, where they had just been married, to live in St Budeaux. Three children were born to them there before 1749. There is, then, the possibility that during this period Joshua Reynolds may have sketched one or more of the members of three generations of this Treffry family who were in the Plymouth Dock area when he, too, was there. Whether any of the Haywards or Galleys were in the area at this time I do not know, but it is possible. Hannah Hayward was born in 1788 in Plymouth Dock. Thus it is within the realm of possibility that Joshua Reynolds knew the Treffrys, Haywards, and Galleys, as they were all in the Plymouth Dock area at some time during his painting years. Whether he sketched or painted one or any one of them, I have no proof—only the legend.

After their marriage John and Hannah Treffry lived in East Stonehouse, Devon, where their first child, Robert John, was born. East Stonehouse, today a part of Plymouth, was at that time a village of about 1,500 families, with narrow, unpaved and unlighted streets, muddy in winter and dusty in summer. The town had no industry or commerce, only a post office and the Royal Naval hospital.

John and Hannah's second child, John, was born in Exeter, where the family may have been residing at the time, or staying with Treffry relatives. In the *Bibliotheca Cornubiensis*, George, the third child, is listed as having been born in a cottage in Gibbon's Field, Charles parish, Plymouth. The fourth child, Marianna, was christened in the same parish. The birth dates of the last two children definitely place John and Hannah Treffry in Plymouth when the *Bellerophon* arrived there in 1815 with the defeated Napoleon aboard. They doubtless saw him, as did also John's parents, Roger and Mary Veale Treffry. John's two older brothers, Joseph and Robert, also were living in Plymouth at the time. Joseph's two sons, Joseph, 14, and Joshua, 13, would have been old enough to remember the event. No resident of Plymouth missed the great spectacle of the British ship *Bellerophon* anchored in the harbour with Napoleon strolling on deck. We can be sure that three generations of the Roger Treffry family, all living in Plymouth, saw the defeated Emperor of France.

After the war ended there was great economic distress as inflated prices dropped to their normal level. European countries devastated by the war were not importing goods and materials from England. The demobilised military, now unemployed, flooded the country. With the labour-saving machinery that began with the Industrial Revolution there was little or no opportunity in industry. During this period of widespread distress everyone suffered. John Treffry, aged 37, with four young children, may have been affected by the depressed economic conditions of the time.

Sometime between July 1816 and August 1818 John Treffry moved his family to Penryn, Cornwall, where his next four children were born. Penryn, a village of 3,000 persons, located at the head of an inlet two miles north-west of Falmouth harbour, consisted principally of one long hilly street with smaller streets crossing it. The town had a considerable trade in the shipping of tin, granite, arsenic, leather, and paper. It imported flour, corn, coal, timber and saltpetre. On the quay there were warehouses for flour and grain brought from Ireland, Hampshire, and the Isle of Wight, as Penryn was the granary for the nearby mineral fields. Manufacturing of paper, woollen cloth, arsenic and gunpowder was carried on. In the area there were tanneries, breweries and corn mills.

In Pigot's *Commercial Directory* for 1824 for Penryn, John Treffry is listed under 'Merchants and Traders' as a corn and flour factor, general and commission agent, Broad Street, Penryn. John was probably well known to the other people listed in the directory. It is interesting to note other occupations and professions listed, as they tell us a bit about the times. There were three attorneys and three surgeons, five brewers and maltsters, two boot and shoe makers, two tanners, two fire insurance agents, one miller, three saddlers, one paint and colour manufacturer, two flour dealers, three general merchants, three drapers and grocers, one printer in 'Gluvais', two carpenters, one watch and clock maker, one druggist and tallow chandler, bookseller and stationer, one smith, 14 taverns and public houses; one currier, one ship agent, two earthenware dealers; and there was one ladies' boarding school, run by S. and M. Tilly. From this list it appears that the general needs of a family could easily be met within the immediate area. However, I found no cabinet-maker on the list; perhaps the single carpenter made furniture.

Information written on the back of the portrait of my great-grandmother, who was John Treffry's youngest daughter, stated that she was 'Elizabeth Treffry, born 17 July 1829, Cosawes Breda Farm, Ponsanooth, near Penryn, Cornwall'. This helpful information sent me on the search for Cosawes. The earliest history I could find was in the Domesday Book of Cornwall of 1086. This account shows that Cosawes existed before 1066. In 1086 it consisted of 15 villagers and 20 smallholders; woodland and pasture with 20 unbroken mares, 17 cattle, 13 pigs, and 240 lambs. Another reference to Cosawes was in the time of Henry VIII in 1522, from the *Henderson Calendars*: 'Eggembr Kt. Lord of the Manor of Cosawes to Stephen Gyn Leese of a plot in Cossawys Barton on the U side of the wood between the bridge called Pons on Oeth & the hegge of the wood on which to build a new mill house for the knockyng, stampying & crasyng of Tyn'.

In 1593, the 35th year of Elizabeth I's reign, a stamping mill called Ponsonwoth Mills in the manor of Cosawes is mentioned as part of the parish of Gluvais. In 1675 there was a dispute over high rents between Thomas Petytt (Petit), Thomas Treffry (of Place and Rooke), and John Cavell, owners of tinworks called Whelean Parke & Whelean Margh in Cosawes (*see* L.D.S. film 231-937, p. 291). Lysons, writing in 1814, tells us that 'the manor of Cosawes belonging to the Bodrugans was given by Henry VII to Sir Richard Edgcumbe whose descendant Lord Mount-Edgcumbe has lately sold it to Sir William Lemon, Bart. The Barton of Cosawes was formerly a seat of Carveths, as lessees under the Edgcumbe family, and the birthplace of Captain Carveth, a distinguished Naval officer in the reign of Charles II. On the death of the last heir-male of this family, the Barton passed to the Levertons. Cosawes is now a farm-house'. At Cosawes formerly there was a chapel dedicated to St Magdalen, thought to have been a chantry chapel connected with the ancient Glasney College of Penryn. There was a gunpowder mill in Cosawes Wood.

On my last trip to Cornwall I found in the Record Office in Truro the lease of Cosawes, dated 5 October 1826, between Sir Charles Lemon, Bart., of Carclew in Cornwall, and John Treffry of the borough of Penryn, yeoman, and John West of Plymouth, Devon, ironmonger, of the other part, concerning two messuages and tenements called Cosawes Broda in the parish of Gluvais, a parcel of the manor of Cosawes, excepting all tin, lead, copper, copper ore and all mines, metals, minerals, quarries of stone, granite, moonstone, clay and marble. Also excepted from the lease were all woods, trees and saplings. Sir Charles Lemon also reserved the liberty of diverting water courses flowing on the premises. He reserved for himself, servants, agents and friends the privilege to hawk, fish and fowl on the premises. If Sir Charles Lemon decided to build on the meadow he would have to compensate John Treffry and John West £3 per statute acre. The lease ran from 29 September 1826 for 14 years with a yearly rent of £100 to be paid on the feast days of the year—Christmas, Lady Day, Midsummer Day and Michaelmas—in quarterly payments. Also, Treffry and West were to pay land tax, rate tax assessments, whether parliamentary or parochial and share of any court suit pertaining to Cosawes. In the lease they agreed to keep the premises in good condition including houses, walls, roofs and hedges. On the acres they wished to till they had to put good salt sea sand or 80 bushels of well-burnt lime mixed with dung and earth according to the rules of good husbandry. They had to rotate crops, manage the farm and manure the premises. They were not to cut trees or underlet the property without permission of Sir Charles Lemon. Four months before leaving they were to allow the owner to sow wheat. The John West on this agreement was the husband of Hannah Hayward Treffry's older sister, Mary Anne. John and Hannah Treffry, however, occupied Cosawes Barton less than 14 years. Perhaps the conditions of the contract were too stringent and the economic rewards too small.

Cosawes Manor covers many acres, but the Cosawes Barton house rests on the top of the hill that winds upward from the Ponsanooth post office. It is a beautiful two-storey house in well-kept grounds with magnificent trees and flowers, and a spectacular view of the entire countryside. Conditions must have been bad for John and Hannah Treffry to leave beautiful Cosawes Barton before their lease expired.

By the early 1830s John Treffry's family consisted of seven sons and four daughters. John and Hannah realised that it would be difficult to place so many sons in profitable work in the years ahead. They saw their first two sons leave for South America, Robert John to New Granada, now Colombia, and John for Brazil, as book-keepers for English mining companies. The third son, George Treffry, at the age of 12 was sent to Exeter, Devon, to be with his uncle, Henry Treffry, to learn the tea business in which his uncle was engaged. George eventually took over the business and remained in Exeter for the rest of his life.

There were four more sons to place in positions when the second son, John Treffry, jr., returned from Brazil and persuaded his father to emigrate to Canada, as it was thought there would be better opportunities there.

In March 1834, before leaving Cornwall, portraits were made of John and Hannah Hayward Treffry and their children. I have in my possession originals of the three youngest children and photographs of portraits of the next six older ones. The only missing ones are of the two oldest sons. There may have been no portrait of the oldest son as he had left for Colombia several years earlier. These portraits appear in the plate section. On the reverse side of one of the photographs of a portrait was written 'painting by Emma Jane Tollman'. However, as I found the name 'Cousin Amy Jane Toulmin' in John Treffry's diary in several places, I believe her to be the artist. To substantiate this there is a later portrait of George Treffry, one of the children, signed A. J. Toulmin. I found that John Treffry's Aunt Jane Treffry, who had married Joseph Honychurch on 1 February 1788 in Falmouth, had a daughter Amy, who married John Butler Toulmin on 31 October 1812 in Falmouth. Amy is therefore John Treffry's first cousin, and her husband is the John or J. B. Toulmin mentioned so often in John Treffry's diary. Various records indicate that J. B. Toulmin was involved in some type of business related to shipping or importing/exporting where he was associated with some members of the Treffry family. Letters, records and passenger lists indicate that several members of the Treffry and Toulmin families were criss-crossing the Atlantic. Amy Toulmin, wife, aged 30, with four children arrived in New York in 1820. Later, the will of her spinster daughter, Amy Jane Treffry Toulmin, stated that she owned 20 acres of land near Mobile, Alabama, and that her brother, Morton Toulmin, lived in Baltimore, Maryland. On 3 October 1895, probate of Amy's will was granted to her cousin, Benjamin Wills Newton, of the Isle of Wight.

Shortly after the portraits were finished John and Hannah Treffry, with five of their seven sons and four daughters, set sail from Falmouth, Cornwall, on 4 April 1834 on a timber ship, the barque *Bragila,* along with two brigs and two other barques, all bound for Quebec, Canada.

John Treffry in the diary he kept from the time they left Cornwall wrote 'Friday at 3 p.m. weighed and made sail—at 8 off the Lizard Light—midnight

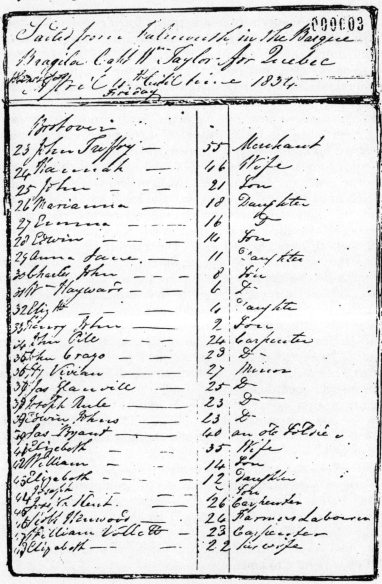

A page from John Treffry's diary, 1834

Scilly'. Almost 150 years later, I took an excursion ship from Penzance to the Scilly Isles, knowing that at some spot I would be crossing the very area their ship sailed when last they saw the hilly coast of their native Cornwall and Lands' End. Unfortunately, John does not write what thoughts and feelings he had as he left a son, brothers, sisters, cousins, friends and business associates and the ancient homeland of his ancestors, never to see them again. Perhaps his emotions were too deep and private to share. At the age of 55 this major move and complete change in lifestyle could not have been easy for him. This was a great sacrifice that he made to give better opportunities to his children in a new land.

John Treffry and family had an apartment for themselves aboard the *Bragila*, with access to the captain's cabin. John was permitted to copy records of weather, latitude, longtitude and course from the captain's log book. He also copied the list of passengers, ages, and occupations. Among the fellow passengers there were 17 miners, seven carpenters, three shoemakers, one cabinet-maker, one farm labourer, one merchant (himself), one old soldier, and one doctor. The rest of the passengers were women and children. Apart from mentioning passengers recovering from being seasick shortly after leaving Cornwall, practically nothing is written about his family or fellow passengers for the five-week trip.

On 19 April John noted seeing an 'Ice Berg to leward and a great quantity of Birds'. By the notes on weather the passage of five weeks was fairly uneventful until the first of May when the ships met the ice floes 'toward noon'. On Friday the second, the ships were 'amongst streams of ice, at 2 observed the ice open to the westward'. Needless to say, there was great anxiety while the ships were passing through this treacherous area. The capable and conscientious captain remained on the crosstrees, with a mate on either side at the foot of the ladders repeating the orders to the man at the helm. During this dangerous period no one on deck was allowed to speak. The route to Canada via Quebec was the most apt to be disastrous because of fog, high winds, and ice.

There was very little amusement for the passengers during the long five weeks other than watching the sailors perform their tasks. When the weather was good, sailors were allowed to play games on deck with the passengers. My great-grandmother, Elizabeth Treffry, only four at the time, vaguely remembered the ocean voyage, according to her daughters and son, George. The children became quite restless and bored, and the sailors tried to entertain them. One sailor wore beaded moccasins and often he would cut a thread that held a string of beads and let them roll. This gave the children the fun of hunting for beads on the rough deck.

After five weeks and a day, on Saturday evening, 10 May, the *Bragila* arrived at Grosse Island quarantine where the doctor complimented it on being 'the cleanest ship he had boarded in all the fleet'. John notes on 13 May, 'arrived at Quebec & John Jr., Dr. Quick, myself landed with Capt. Taylor'. Later the captain gave the Treffry family a nice tea at the home of a personal friend, where they had 'thin bread and butter' with marmalade, a great contrast to the ship's fare with hard biscuits.

The Treffry family left Quebec for Montreal on a steamer, the *John Bull*. (Steamers were not yet crossing the Atlantic.) John noted 'boat filled with filthy and lousey immigrants. Cabin passengers had to make own beds. Bad management this'. However, he was happy the next day when the steamer stopped for fuel, for John wrote, 'Had some good malt liquor. Great treat'. They landed on 18 May at Montreal at 6 a.m., where they went to an inn on the wharf for breakfast, but finding it dirty moved on to Mrs. Bellamy's hotel, where they stayed for $1.00 per day for adults. They left the next day along with Dr. Quick for Kingston via Lachine and Bytown (now Ottawa) and the Rideau Canal. The fare was £27 for the Treffry family, Dr. Quick and all their luggage. On 21 May they arrived at Lachine at 8 p.m. and had to go by coach to Greenfell over very rough roads, arriving there at midnight. Leaving there by a ship that ran aground on a ridge of rocks, they were delayed three hours. That evening they reached Bytown. At 7 a.m. the next morning they entered the locks that were many feet above the river, taking an hour and 40 minutes to go through. They were now on the steamer *Enterprise,* operated by Captain Richards. The ship sprang a leak flooding the cabin floor with six inches of water. The captain got a pump from a barge in tow to pump out the water. John shows a bit of humour in the diary when he wrote, 'only person to leave the boat through fear was a Methodist parson—his boots being filled with water'. On 25 May the boat reached Jones's locks, when both cranks of the rods broke; the flange of the pipe that connected the cylinder with the steam boiler also parted. If this had not happened, the boiler might have burst. John helped to put the pump in order by using a piece of leather cut from the captain's breeches!

Due to the delays, provisions were short. Because of this the captain, after consulting with the cabin passengers, left for Kingston for supplies. To have something to eat while the captain was away some passengers 'went a fishing and caught a plenty'. Some went deer hunting, without luck. The cook, unhappy over having nothing to cook except fish, got drunk and mutinied. The passengers made him a prisoner and put Mr. Chamber's serving man in the galley to cook. On 27 May the captain returned from Kingston with plenty of provisions, including wine and ale. Food was cooked for the passengers, including some to take away with them.

The ship arrived at Kingston on 28 May, too late for the Toronto boat. On 30 May they left for Toronto for £1 per head. Arriving in Toronto on 31 May at 2 p.m., the Treffry family had time to take tea before boarding the smack for Hamilton where they arrived the next day at noon. John settled the family at the *Commercial Hotel,* then took off with John, jr., and two others for Waterloo. They spent the night at *Groff's Inn* which was filled with all kinds of immigrants and had only one bed for three of the men. John noted 'Our driver slept in the stable with his horse and fared the best of us'. On 2 June they drove to Waterloo to Dr. Robert Treffry's, to breakfast at his house in the midst of pine woods. (Dr. Robert was the son of Samuel Treffry, an older brother of John Treffry.) Arriving there at 7.30 they found breakfast was over; John was most frustrated at having to wait two hours for breakfast and entered in his diary, 'appetites gone & patience exhausted'. They returned to Hamilton that night. On 3 June John attended a sale of government lands to a party of Dutchmen.

Travel conditions in undeveloped areas were very difficult and inconvenient. At times no feed could be obtained for the horses. Inns were crowded, and private rooms impossible to obtain. One night John and Dr. Quick were able to get only two beds in 'the end of a large room filled with men, women and children spread on the floor so that we could scarcely get to ours without stepping on them'. Another time they were comfortably resting on two sofas in a crowded room when they were asked to give them up to two ladies who had arrived by steamer. They picked up their clothes and moved to another room.

As John travelled about looking for land he talked to the natives, and commented they 'were profuse in praising the country and climate: of course they are like the company agents and Book Writers interested by puffing'. Evidently what he was finding was not up to what his expectations had been. Perhaps he was exhausted from the hard travel conditions and maybe a bit homesick for the milder climate he had left behind in Falmouth.

On 15 June, John was invited to attend a Friends' meeting and he wrote, 'very warm, several came to Meeting without their coats or shoes'. By 16 June, through a Quaker family, the Benson Lossings, John found property he thought suitable for settling his family. It was Lot 2 in the 10th Concession (Norwich), Oxford County, Ontario, a clergy reserve abandoned by a black man. To secure it, it meant a trip back to Toronto beginning with a seven-mile walk in the hot sun before they could hire a wagon for the next 28 miles. After reaching Hamilton they took a steamer to Toronto where they went to the Land Office to see about the property they had selected. John bought the land for $3.00 per acre.

The Lossing family were able to place the Treffry family in a vacant school house while they were building, and for a time they stayed with the Southwick family. John Treffry, jr., was sent to bring a load of goods brought with them from Cornwall. Then began many months of hard work clearing the land of trees, building a log house to have ready before the cold weather set in, and planting wheat and vegetables. There was help from local labour to cut the trees and their oxen teams to drag the logs. Hired men were paid $6.50 per acre to cut trees, but they had to provide their own board and lodging. Some workers were paid $1.00 per day, including the loan of their oxen.

Many acres had to be cleared for pasture and planting. The logs were required for building the house and making rail fences. Others were sent to the lumber mill to be quartered for the roof and cut into boards for flooring. John assisted a helper with sawing shingles and hewing logs and beams. Firewood needed to be cut and stacked. Before winter set in a barn and stable had to be built for the livestock.

The foundation of the house was not laid until 15 September, and on 19 September John had a house-raising with the assistance of his son John, 18 adult men and several lads. One man brought his black boy and another brought a team of oxen. They finished the raising by six in the evening and celebrated at supper. By 22 September the roof was going on, with sons John, jr., and Edwin helping along with two men. By 9 October two helpers were sifting lime and plastering. (A year later in August 1835 Edwin was still plastering and whitewashing.)

John hired a man with oxen to bring stones for the chimney and paid two others $20 for gathering stones and laying the hearth. Henry Southwick brought lime and 152 bricks for the oven, which was not finished until 21 November. On 20 October Henry Southwick with two hired employees brought the household goods and the Treffry family moved into their house, not yet finished. The floors were not laid until 16 December. With winter weather setting in, the family suffered much from the cold.

Some of their furniture was made by John, jr., from timber bought at the mill. Among the items listed were bedsteads, table of cherry wood, sideboard, bench, chairs with seats of ash, white maple or basswood. Other items made were washtrays, washtubs, wheelbarrow, harrow, sleigh, and a small sleigh for the children. Items purchased were tin pails, a 12-gallon keg, casks with lids at $3 a pair, $1.50 for a churn; also a tray, a griddle, and a small 'Irish' kettle. They had a tin oven for baking shortbread on the hearth.

John wasted no time in establishing a productive farm. He purchased apple, pear, cherry and plum trees to be planted in the spring. He bought wheat wherever he could get it, for sowing and to grind for flour. He planted every variety of vegetables that would grow in the area. He had undoubtedly been well trained in farming by his father at Bere Barton. On John's property there were over 100 maple trees, which were tapped. A sugar-house was built to boil the sap into maple syrup in the spring of 1835.

John bought a black mare for $70, and promised to pay $5 more if she had a colt. A horse-collar was $2.00, He paid $6 for a sow, $16 for a heifer, $2 to $4 for sheep. By 21 January 1835, the first eggs were gathered. The white sow had 10 young pigs, the heifer had a calf, and his mare had a colt! He bought one yoke of oxen for $70.00 and another called Buck and Brandy for $50. Their dog was called Nero. For food, besides their home-grown vegetables, the family had to have wheat ground into flour in Otterville. John noted in his diary buying a hind quarter of pork for $16.00. Occasionally, there was venison, pigeons and other wild game, and fish. However, on one trip to Otterville, John noted buying $120 of goods, $7 change and $23 in a promissory note out of a $150 cheque! Among items purchased were tea, soap, and writing paper.

Very little is mentioned in the diary about clothing, but note is made of making shoes, mending shoes, tapping and cobbling shoes. Young Edwin at one time was sent to Otterville with measurements of everyone's feet to have shoes made out of upper and sole leather which he took with him. At various times mention is made of shoes and boots being purchased in Otterville. Straw hats were made of rye.

The health of the family was generally good. In the two and a half year period after the family arrived in Canada a doctor was called for Edwin for two visits at $2 each. Various home remedies were used at other times. John recorded that he weighed 154lbs. before he left England, but five months later he weighed only 125lbs. However, John noted that his heath was better than when in England, 'all my complaints have left me, and I am stronger and healthier than I have been for several years past'. Other than digestive ailments, John mentioned only a bit of rheumatism in his right arm in December.

I do not know how the children were educated. One note on 18 November 1835 records that 'B. Lossing came to speak about a school master', and on 4 February John notes that he was teaching the children. Some member of the family was interested in painting, as artists' paints were listed in the diary. Marianna must have been qualified to teach, as she offered to teach the Sherwood daughters.

John and his family attended Quaker meetings; his wife not being a Quaker attended meetings but never joined. Various members of the family attended Methodist as well as Quaker meetings. Sundays were days for visiting friends for dinner and tea, or having visits from friends and writing letters. The social life for the women consisted of joining friends for sewing bees and quilting bees, and tea. Because of distances and inclement weather, visits often meant overnight stays. In winter travel was by sleigh using a horse shod so it could walk on ice. Snow was often six feet deep or more.

Letter-writing was a very important part of their lives in keeping in touch with sons Robert in South America and George in Exeter. Letters then took three months from England to Norwich, Canada. John noted writing to his brothers, Joseph in Plymouth, and Henry in Exeter, and Samuel and William, and his sister, Anna Newton, the widow of Benjamin Wills Newton. There were also quite a few letters coming and going between John and his cousins Amy Jane Toulmin and J. B. Toulmin.

On 6 April 1835 John, jr., married Mary Ann Southwick and moved to her home to live. Shortly after John, jr.'s, marriage a great tragedy befell the Treffry family in the death of their youngest son. My great-aunt Emma Treffry Snyder had this precious child's portrait which she often showed me with tears in her eyes saying he was lost in a fire. That is all that was said. So I never knew how it happened until I found a printed account in a book in the Stanford Library, taken from John's diary. Later I copied from his diary:

> An ever memorable day our darling little Henry caught his clothes on fire by a log heap and burnt in such a state about 4 o'clock in the afternoon & about midnight he breathed his last. His clothes were literally consumed on him. We washed him in sweet oil & then dusted him all over w/rice flour and gave him six drops of laudamun which appeared to kill the pain so that he did not appear to suffer much pain & was wonderfully patient and departed in the most quiet manner possible as tho he fell into a sweet sleep. The trial to us his Parents & Brothers and Sisters is very great yet we have abundant cause to be thankful to the almighty for his mercy in removing him so easy & so soon, had he lived until the following day his distressed condition would in all probability been beyond description. Therefore we say the Lord be praised and his will be done on earth as in heaven.

Neighbours and friends came 'to sympathize with us on the melancholy event that took place in the past night'. The next day a neighbour brought a coffin 'and we laid our dear child in it'. The following day John wrote, 'Took our dear child's remains to Friends Burial Grounds in the Upper Settlement and interred him there'. Neighbours had come with their wagons to assist. John noted 'All was done in the most quiet and peaceable manner. Mrs. Benson Lossing prepared refreshments for us and then we returned home'. Although the grief was deep and the sorrow great, life went on much as it had.

John was approached to subscribe to cutting a road, but he declined. Later a railroad did come through the property taking their log house, so the log house is no more.

John ordered a law book shortly after arriving in Canada and apparently made good use of it. In the spring of 1838, Solomon Lossing, a Friend, was being tried in Hamilton for high treason during the Canadian rebellion of 1837–38. On 31 March 1838, John records that he was at the courthouse most of the day hearing the trial of prisoners for high treason and 'attended on Mr. Strachan, the solicitor, with witness in behalf of Solomon Lossing'. The next day he notes, 'Self writing and preparing brief for counsel most of the day'. When some witnesses did not show up John pleaded with the judge and was granted delays. The trial lasted most of the day. The jury retired and returned in about three and a half minutes with a verdict of 'not guilty'. The others on trial were declared guilty and sentenced to be hanged, but were later pardoned.

On 4 April 1838 John wrote, 'This day 4 years, we left dear old England'. Life in Cornwall for him as a merchant certainly had been easier than the primitive conditions he encountered in the newly-settled area of Canada where he carved a homestead from a virgin forest. He and his family experienced many deprivations unknown to them in Cornwall. Being unaccustomed to the extremes of sub-zero weather in the winter, and sometimes over 100deg. in the summer, the family suffered greatly.

John worked and lived on his farm at Norwich until his death in September 1849, less than a week before his 71st birthday. Hannah outlived him by nearly 30 years, reaching the age of ninety-one. As John Treffry left records in his diaries of the early life of his pioneer family in Canada, his widow Hannah later added much to the history of the family in her letters to her youngest daughter, Elizabeth. Fortunately, Elizabeth passed the letters on to her daughters, my great-aunts, and eventually they came into my collection. Twenty years after the family settled in Norwich, Hannah wrote in 1854, 'We shall have to build somewhere this summer as the intended railroad takes the corner of our house, comes right through the orchard, takes 2 or 3 cherry trees, two large pear trees, all our quince and I don't know how many apple trees'. This would have been a sad sight for John had he lived to see his log house demolished and part of the orchard gone when it was in its prime.

On 1 July 1855 Hannah noted in one of her letters that their new house was raised that week, but that they did not expect to be in it until the end of September. This new and more modern house was built in Hawtry and named

'Tree Lawn'. There Hannah spent the rest of her days. Her life was filled with sewing and quilting and helping with grandchildren. She made 'a very pretty Basket pattern quilt' for Charles, and advised Elizabeth that she would patch one for her. In England, as a young girl in boarding school, Hannah had stitched two beautiful pictures that she later gave to her son George, showing her to be quite artistic, colour conscious, and good with the needle. She mentions making work shirts for Charles to use when out assessing.

The signature of Hannah Treffry, 1850s

Hannah attended Quaker meetings, but always remained a Methodist. One of her sisters had been baptized by John Wesley, who considered his followers to be a part of the Established Church of England. The Methodists became independent from the Anglican Church four years after John Wesley's death.

Descendants of John and Hannah Hayward Treffry

John and Hannah Treffry's first child, *Robert John,* who settled in Colombia, South America, about 1830, was sent there as a book-keeper by Poroles Bros. & Co. of London, a mining company. He was accompanied by 50 Cornish miners. The records indicate that the company was involved in the mining of gold. However, by 1857 Robert John had formed a business partnership with a Mr. Kingdon, whose father was an eminent consulting surgeon in London with many relatives in Exeter, who it was thought could be of help to them in their business. From the careers of later generations, it may be that this business partnership was involved in the manufacturing of jewellery.

Robert John Treffry married a Spanish lady, Joana Manuella Monroy, thus establishing the Treffry family of Colombia, South America. Settling first in Mariquita, a gold mining area, and later at Honda, the family record shows a son, Edwino (probably named after Robert's brother, Edwin). The records I have are of Edwino's children: Sara (unmarried); Enrique (Henry); and Guillermo (William). By the second generation the family was acquiring the Spanish version of the English names. Thus, Robert John had become Roberto Juan. Allyne Snyder, Elizabeth Treffry Snyder's great-granddaughter told me that she recalled her grandfather writing to Colombian cousins named Jaime, Fernando and Bernardo. As I do not have complete family records of Robert's descendants, I do not know where these three belong in his family. However, there are many descendants of Robert's son, Edwino, through his son Guillermo. Guillermo and his son, also Guillermo, were both expert technicians in the production of fine jewellery. The second Guillermo's brother, Ernesto, has a son, Jaime Treffry, also a specialist in jewellery, who lives in California. His cousin, Luz Angela Ampara of Calli, Colombia, sent the records of this branch of the Treffry family to my brother, Eugene Rideout, written in Spanish for him to translate into English.

Most of the descendants of Robert John Treffry are Spanish speaking. My brother Eugene made a number of business trips to South America for W. R. Grace & Co., so he had to be fluent in Spanish. On several of these trips, he visited the Colombian Treffrys, where he had no problems conversing in Spanish with them. Except for Jaime Treffry, who is the father of four daughters, all my records of the present generation of descendants of Robert John Treffry are of females. Most of whom are married to professional men. Some of the women have established professional careers of their own; one is an attorney and another an optometrist.

Robert John Treffry and a number of his descendants, besides being involved in various careers, also maintained small farms. Robert no doubt had had some training in farming from his father when the family lived at Cosawes Barton. There are indications in my records that Robert John Treffry visited his mother, Hannah Hayward Treffry, and brothers and sisters in Canada, and from there returned to visit England. This would have been before 1879, for that is the year of his death.

John, jr., the second son of John and Hannah Treffry, is mentioned throughout his father's diary as being of great help to him in establishing their homestead. John, jr. was married to Mary Ann, daughter of George Southwick, on 6 April 1835 in the Southwick home, where they lived after their marriage. They were the parents of six children: George, born 1839; Hannah, born 1841; Marianna, born 1843; John, born 1845; Alice, born 1847; and Joshua, born 1849. Marianna married John Richard Harris on 21 October 1863 and they had four sons. I have no record of any descendants of John and Mary Ann Southwick Treffry with the Treffry name.

George, the third son, was educated at the Bellevue school in Penryn. In 1827 he went to Exeter to enter his uncle Henry Treffry's tea business, established in 1822. In 1846 George took over the business which dealt in tea, coffee, cocoa and spices. They also roasted coffee and cocoa and manufactured cocoa nibs and ground cocoa nibs. Their warehouse was at 169 Fore Street, Exeter (opposite what was then the Lower Market). This area was totally bombed out in World War II. My glider pilot brother, Captain Harold B. Rideout, of the U.S. Air Force, who was in Exeter during World World II, saw this damage and the damage to the beautiful Exeter Cathedral before continuing on to fly many missions over Italy, France and Germany.

George retired from business in 1875 and resided at 2 Ballair Place, Mount Radford, Exeter, until his death on 21 June 1880. He is buried at Budoc in Cornwall. He was unmarried. A letter to his mother telling of his life in Exeter and business frustrations follows. His will is given in an Appendix.

Exeter, Oct. 29th, 1852

My dear Mother,

The last letter I had the pleasure of receiving from you was dated the 21st. of May I believe I have written to you once at least since that, so that you are in my debt. I have not had any letter from Robert since January, but I have heard of him thro cousin Henry William Treffry who called at the office in London to enquire after him. Robert is still in the employ of POROLES Bro^S & Co. and they get stories from him as usual. Mr. Jones told Harry that Robert was well when they last heard from him that was some time last month. I will now try to tell you how our relatives have been roving about during the past summer. Uncle and Aunt Fox & cousin Anna left Stoke I think in June and spent a month in Lodgings on the banks of the far famed river Dart near Totnes where I paid them a visit it is only 30 miles from Exeter, so, I went down one day after breakfast & dined & took tea with them & returned again in the evening. After leaving Totnes they came to Exeter & spent several weeks here enjoyed themselves very much, and it was very pleasant to me to have such kind relatives so near. Soon after they left Aunt Newton came up and spent a few days with me on her way to Maidenhead in Berkshire where she is at present residing with B. W. Newton his mother-in-law having taken a cottage there for them in order that they may enjoy a little country air. Amy has been some time with her father in Manchester & he returns about this time to the Ut States & Amy & Aunt Newton, H. W. Treffry was at New Orleans, where in July last he had a severe attack of cholera. As soon as he was sufficiently recovered he started off North intending to pay you a visit but on arriving at the Falls of Niagra he found a letter from J. B. Toulmin requesting him to come over to England without delay so on the 17th August he left the U States by Steamer for Liverpool & is I suppose ere this, again in New Orleans. He spent a few days with me during his short stay in this country—he hopes to run up to see you during the New Orleans sickly season when most Europeans go North for a little holliday. Anna Fox is pretty well again now & all the rest of our relatives are I believe in usual health. Now I have told you pretty much about our doings & at home here I want to know what you are about over yonder. I want to know all you can tell me about Emma & Elizabeth & Wisconsin how people live there and what sort of a climate it is whether it is a good place for Trade and Commerce and what business is most profitable The competition in our line here is very great if I had not Thomas Treffry to maintain I could do very well but I fear I shall not save very much this year. The Farmers complain of the low prices of produce & spend but little in Tea & Coffee. I sometimes think that if times don't improve I may as well vegitate in Canada as here but I fear your winters are too long and too cold for me. When do you intend to move to the neighbour-hood of Woodstock, would Woodstock support a Tea Dealer My old friend Tom Corfield has lost his mother. She died last week and was buried in Penryn on the 22nd. Aunt Rachel and Franny have shifted their quarters again! They have removed to another house not far from their former abode in Jersey. How have your pansies thriven? My Alleghany Creeper bloomed very well I have now several young plants for next spring. The weather is getting rather windy & my flowers are getting scanty but I can still manage to get a nosegay. Chrysanthamums are beginning to look gay. I have 36 or 40 different sorts. I often wish I had been a gardener instead of a Tea Dealer. I should like even now to quit the counter & turn Farmer and if it was not for your cold winters with fever and ague etc. etc. I would soon be with you.
with love to you all I remain
My Dear Mother
Your affectionate Son
George Treffry

Marianna, the fourth child of John and Hannah Treffry, married 22 July 1842, Henry Wilson, and moved to the U.S.A. where she died at the age of twenty-six. They had one son.

Emma, the second daughter of John and Hannah Treffry, married John Lossing, whose son, Charles, was the father of Mabel Lossing, born 3 April 1878 in Clayton, Iowa. Mabel Lossing graduated from Upper Iowa University, and in 1904 became a missionary of the Women's Foreign Missionary Society of the Tremont Street church in Boston. On 11 February 1911 she married Dr. E. Stanley Jones, one of the best-known American missionaries and authors of the 20th century, spending over 40 years in India, as contemporaries of Mahatma Gandi. Among his many books was *The Christ of the Indian Road* which sold over 600,000 copies and was translated into 20 languages.

However, Mabel Lossing Jones was also distinguished and well known for her own accomplishments. She founded the Methodist Boys' School at Sitapur, India, managed and taught by women. Mrs. Jones was responsible for the support of the school, and was its guiding spirit for over 35 years. Under her direction the school prospered and grew to become a far-reaching influence on educational policies in Northern India.

Mabel and E. Stanley Jones had one daughter, Eunice Treffry Jones, who married Bishop James K. Mathews. Their children are Anne, Janice and James Stanley Jones.

Mabel Jones was greatly interested in the Treffry family history and spent much time in gathering information on the subject which she passed to Harriet Froelich Smith, great-granddaughter of Edwin, fourth son of John and Hannah Treffry. While I studied the archives and historical data in England, these two remarkable women, Mabel and Harriet, were, by much patient correspondence, gathering the stories of the Canadian and American branches of the Treffry family. The results of their efforts have been added to my files.

Mabel Jones lived about six weeks past her hundredth birthday, dying on 23 June 1978. Her daughter says of her, 'She was a gifted teacher and if she had been a man could have risen to a high executive office in business, finance or government. But she was no retiring woman; rather she was an able and aggressive administrator while not yielding one iota of femininity. Finally, she was a deeply committed Christian woman, a servant of God and all the people'.

Edwin, the fourth son of John and Hannah Treffry, married Maria, the daughter of William Kingsford of England on 22 January 1846. They had three children, Robert John, Mary Hannah and Maria Helen. Mary Hannah married Captain Norman Bull and their daughter, Nora, married Edwin Theodore Froelich who became the parents of Harriet Froelich. Harriet married Harvard Charles Smith on 2 January 1925, and they resided in Kenosha, Wisconsin, where they both taught at school and were active in the community and the Episcopal Church. They often took exchange students from many countries to live with them. One year they visited their students in Europe, and while there visited Fowey and Place. Harriet and Harvard, parents of two children, Carolyn Ann and Warren Blake, reached their golden wedding anniversary in

January 1975. Harriet died the following July. After Harvard's death, their son moved into the family home which I had visited many times. Harriet was a gifted and productive artist, selling many fine water colours.

One of Harriet's many cousins, Walford Nilsson, son of Otto and Margaret Bull Nilsson, added many records to my collection and to those of Harriet. From these records I found that Edwin's only son, Robert, had three sons, all of whom died at an early age, and two daughters. So Edwin left no descendants bearing the Treffry name when he died at the age of 84 on 7 October 1904.

Charles John, the fifth son of John and Hannah Treffry, married Alice Corless in 1854. They remained at Hawtry, making a home for Charles's mother as long as she lived. Many of the family records, diaries, and other treasured family possessions brought from Cornwall by John and Hannah Treffry were kept by Charles John and later by his daughter, Marianna Treffry.

Charles John Treffry carried on the business of a conveyancer in which he was highly regarded. He and his family were Quakers belonging to the Milldale meeting, of which he was an elder and also clerk of the business meeting. He and Alice were parents of nine children: George, Margaret, Emma, Morton (died young), Elizabeth, Marianna, William John, Hiram C., and Edwin (died young). There are a great many descendants through Margaret, who married Miles Pennington; Elizabeth, who married John Atkins; and Hiram, who married Lillian Harris, and had three daughters. William John married Louisa McGregor and they had two children, Charles J. and Alice H., who married G. Percival Parson. The John and Hannah Treffry family records came to them through their Aunt Marianna Treffry.

In 1948 Marianna Treffry permitted me to copy the family records, photograph the family portraits, and try on the red brocade dress. She was living in Toronto with her nieces Alice and Margaret Pennington at that time. Late in life Marianna lost her eyesight but continued to crochet and knit for various charities while listening to talking books. She was indeed a remarkable woman! She lived to be 96 years old, dying on 15 June 1962.

Marianna's nephew, Charles, son of William John and Louisa McGregor Treffry, graduated from the University of Toronto School of Medicine in 1939. He served in World War II as Surgeon Lieutenant Commander in the Royal Canadian Navy at the naval base hospital in Greenoch, Scotland, from 1942-1945, where he had some very close shaves as the district was bombed many times. On leave in December of 1943 Charles was able to visit Fowey and spend a week at Place as the guest of Anne Treffry, who showered him with the most gracious hospitality possible. It was quite a change from navy life to have breakfast served to him in bed. One evening during his stay Anne Treffry had to attend a committee meeting for a charitable cause, so she let Charles play host at dinner to which she had invited some young people and service men stationed in Fowey. They had a partridge dinner with all the trimmings. It was not easy to obtain the makings of a company dinner in war-time Britain. Before Charles left Place, Anne Treffry gave him a copy of Spencer Thornton Treffry's *History of the Treffry Family* and some old pictures.

After Dr. Charles Treffry returned to Canada, he entered into the practice of pediatrics with the leading pediatrician in Vancouver, British Columbia, Canada, from 1947 to 1973. He served several years on the teaching staff of the Faculty of Medicine of the University of British Columbia. He was highly regarded in his medical field. As he was not married, I believe that other than Dr. Charles Treffry the only descendants of John and Hannah Treffry who carry the Treffry name are the Colombian South American Treffrys, descendants of Robert John, the eldest son.

William, the sixth son of John and Hannah Treffry, remained in Hawtry, Canada, unmarried, until his death, aged eighty-three.

Elizabeth, youngest daughter of John and Hannah Treffry, married Dr. Asa Snyder on 18 February 1852, and settled in Chester, Dodge County, Winconsin, where Dr. Snyder began his medical practice. By June of 1852 he had a few patients even though most people in the town were generally healthy. Besides his medical practice, he raised vegetables on 13 acres. Strawberries and flowers grew wild all over the woods and fields. He fished in the streams and lakes, and hunted wild ducks and hens. Sometimes his fees were paid in sacks of potatoes or pieces of furniture.

However, in 1854 Hannah Treffry was writing to Elizabeth saying, 'I am sorry Asa has any thoughts of moving if he is doing so well where he is, why not be content? A rolling stone gathers no moss'. In mid-1855 Hannah wrote again to Elizabeth, 'I wish I could see you and Asa to have a little conversation about the wild scheme you have in your heads of going to Kansas whilst you are doing well why not be content? You will have nothing but hardships and privations for years and your dear children no education. I do not advise you where to go, *but don't go to Kansas*. I think sometimes I would rather hear you were buried than you should go to such a place to be killed by Indians'. Asa's mother didn't want them to go either. Later Hannah wrote, 'I have heard wretched accounts of Kansas. I must beg and entreat you to give up all thoughts of going there. Charles and William both think it is a wild scheme. Do write soon to ease my poor mind and say you won't go. It is a great trouble to me'. Elizabeth and Asa apparently decided to stay in Wisconsin where their seven children were born. However, before 1875 they moved to Farina, Fayette County, Illinois, where Dr. Snyder carried on a successful practice until his death in 1890.

Dr. Asa and Elizabeth Treffry Snyder's children

1. *William Treffry Snyder,* born 26 December 1852, died 1 January 1864.
2. *Frank H. Snyder,* born 14 August 1854, died 20 June 1932. He married Lucinda Elizabeth Barker, 3 February 1878, and they had 12 children. He engaged in the lumber business in Fresno, California.

    (a) Their daughter, *Cora Belle,* married Terry Elmo Stephonson and lived in Santa Anna, California.

    (b) Their son, *George Edwin Snyder,* married Rena Lilla Owen and had five children: Owen (died young), Georgia, Muriel, Corinne (died young), and Allyne. Allyne and Georgia added to the family records.

3. *Emma Treffry Snyder,* born 17 April 1856 (died August 1943), was a college graduate, a teacher, and a gifted artist both in oils and water colours. I knew her well as she lived in our home when we were young children. She told us stories that increased my interest in the Treffry family, Place, and Cornwall. She painted pictures for us, and made exquisite dolls clothes for my dolls. Her collection of Treffry records and some of her paintings came to me. Of all of Elizabeth and Asa's children, I knew her best. She was well and active up until a week before her death, aged eighty-eight.

4. *Lily Maria Snyder,* born June 1859 (died 30 April 1930). On 3 November 1881 at Farina, Illinois, she married Willis Burdick; they were parents of nine children: Guy, Stella (my mother), Rolland, Jennie, Nellie, Elva, Mildred, Laura, and Elizabeth. All had children except Elizabeth.

5. *Elva Belle Snyder,* born 12 July 1863 (died 17 December 1955, aged 92). She married W. A. Matzke on 5 October 1905, and had one child who died as an infant.

Hannah Hayward Treffry's letters and other records came into my collection from Elva.

6. *Elizabeth Jane Snyder,* born 18 September 1865, married John T. Peck and died young, childless.

7. *George Snyder,* born 22 September 1867, married Elizabeth North on 8 November 1893. He died in 1948. They had only one child—*Evalyth.* George was a grain dealer like his grandfather, John Treffry. Their daughter, Evalyth Miriam, married first Hugh Chester Danforth on 17 June 1929. He was president of First Dakota National Bank, Yankton, South Dakota. They were parents of two daughters, Sara and Betsy. After her first husband's death, Evalyth married Dr. Daniel Lee Hamilton, Dean of Monterey Language School, Monterey, California. Evalyth and family for many years divided their time between Yankton, South Dakota, and Laguna Beach, California.

After Dr. Asa Snyder's death, Elizabeth lived in Chicago, Illinois, for several years, but eventually followed her son, Frank, to California, where she lived until her death aged 83 on 10 October 1912. My mother, Stella Burdick Rideout, spent a great deal of time with her as a young child in Farina, Illinois, and then later lived with her while going to high school in Chicago, and later nearby as a young bride and mother. Stories told by her grandmother about the Treffry family came to me from my mother as well as from my great-aunt Emma Treffry Snyder and great-aunt Elva Snyder Matzke and many others. They were a family that kept in touch with each other and which kept family letters and records.

It is not surprising to find many of Dr. Asa and Elizabeth Snyder's descendants living in California, for each time I visit Cornwall I am more aware of the similarity of climate with parts of California. I know that when I leave rhododendrons blooming in my California garden and jet to England that I shall find rhododendrons blooming for Anne Treffry at Place.

In following the history of the descendants of Mathew Treffry, we find many still in England; from coast to coast, and north to south in the United States; from east to west in Canada; in Colombia, South America; and Australia.

Mabel Lossing Jones left her mark on India, and David Treffry, O.B.E., in his world-wide travel for the International Monetary Fund has added distinction to the name of a very ancient family. Many Treffry men and women served their country in time of war in many areas of the world. Many were in industry, finance, medicine, government, agriculture, religion, education, science, art, and other fields. Those who left descendants have been honoured by them.

Wherever in the world a person lives with a drop of Treffry blood, he knows his Cornish heritage. He knows of Place and Fowey. Many have found their way back to Place, the home of Anne Treffry for over the past 60 years. Anne Treffry has unselfishly and graciously shared Place and its history with all who came. She shared it as though she was the keeper of a trust that belonged a bit to everyone with the Treffry name. She has added distinction, honour and a new dimension to the Treffry family history.

APPENDIX

Will of George Treffry, 1880

THIS IS THE LAST WILL AND TESTAMENT of me GEORGE TREFFRY of Mount Radford in St. Leonard Exeter   I bequeath to Charles Samuel Pearse of the City of Exeter Linen Draper my Skeleton Timepiece and the sum of Twenty five pounds   I bequeath to my Cousin Cornelius Benjamin Fox Doctor of Medicine now residing at Chelmsford the Portrait of my Dog 'Tiny' and the sum of Twenty five pounds   I bequeath to my Brother Charles John Treffry of Summerville in the Township of Norwich, Ontario in the dominion of Canada the two Pictures in guilt frames which were worked by my Mother   I bequeath to Charlotte Stone (Wife of James Stone) my late Shop Assistant the sum of Fifty pounds free of duty   I bequeath to Mary Weeks such a sum as shall be sufficient to purchase an Annuity of Ten pounds for her life   I bequeath to my Servant Ann or Annie Staddon the sum of Nineteen pounds and nineteen shillings if she be living with me at the time of my decease   I bequeath to my Brother William Hayward Treffry of Summerville aforesaid my Gold Watch and Chain but in case he should not be living at my decease then I bequeath the same to my Nephew George Treffry Son of my Brother Charles John Treffy   I bequeath unto my two Brothers aforesaid the Debt (being about One thousand three hundred pounds or One thousand four hundred pounds now due to me from my friend Thomas John Tressider Corfield), and the securities for the same which are in my bron chest but with an expression of hope that they will not press for the payment hereof to his ruin but not to bind them   I give devise and bequeath all the rest residue and remainder of my property estate and effects both real and personal to the said Charles Samuel Pearse, Cornelius Benjamin Fox, Charles John Treffry and William Hayward Treffry their heirs executors administrators and assigns Upon Trust to sell and dispose of the same and invest the proceeds thereof upon such securities as Trustees are by law authorised to invest trust moneys and to pay the annual interest dividends and income thereof unto my Mother during her life and after her decease I direct my Trustees to divide my said residuary estate and effects equally between such of my Brothers and Sisters as shall survive me or if either or any of my Brothers and Sisters should die during my lifetime leaving Children then I direct that such Children (except the Son of my Sister Marianna Wilson to whom I hereby devise the sum of Five pounds) shall stand in their parents place and receive their parents Share but no Grandchild or remoter issue of my said Brothers and Sisters is to receive any benefit under this devise And I hereby declare that any female taking any benefit under this my Will shall hold the same to her separate use independently of any Husband to whom she may now or at any time be married   And I hereby appoint the said Charles Samuel Pearse Cornelius Benjamin Fox Charles John Treffry and William Hay-· ward Treffry Executors and Trustees of this my Will   In witness whereof I the said George Treffry have to this my last Will and Testament hereunto set my hand this fifth day of November One thousand eight hundred and Seventy eight — GEORGE TREFFRY — Signed and declared by the said George Treffry the Testator as and for his last Will and Testament in the presence of us both being present at the same time when at his request in his presence and in the presence of each other have hereunto subscribed our names as Witnesses — JOHN DAW Solr. Exeter — WILLm MORGAN his Clerk

I GEORGE TREFFRY do hereby declare this to be a codicil to my last Will and Testament dated the fifth day of Novr. 1878   I give & bequeath to my Cousin Amy Jane Treffry (G. T. Toulmin) the whole of my Goods and Chattles not otherwise disposed of in my Will to be by her distributed as she may deem fit and to Ann or Annie Staddon an additional Nineteen Guineas   As Witness my hand this 15th day of April 1880 — GEORGE TREFFRY —

Witness to the signature   Emma Moore
of the said George Treffry   Elizabeth Brewer

Note: Thomas Betty married Elizabeth Morcomb on 5 January 1719 in St Issey, and were parents of John, christened 24 June 1720; Elizabeth, christened 23 January 1721/22; Thomas, christened 24 November 1723; Mary, christened 6 August 1725; Humphry, christened 23 October 1727; Hannah, christened 9 July 1731; and Joseph, christened 31 July 1733. The Betty and Morcomb families are of early record in St Issey, Cornwall. Samuel and Elizabeth Betty Treffry named their first daughter Betty, the mother's maiden name; John and Thomas after two of her brothers; and another daughter Mary after her sister. There can be no doubt that Betty is Elizabeth's maiden name, and that John Betty of the indenture tripartite is her brother.

SELECTED BIBLIOGRAPHY

Adams, D. P., *Tudors and Stuarts 1485–1714* (Heineman, London, 1962).

Boase, G. C., and Courtney, W. P., *Bibliotheca Cornubiensis* (3 vols., London 1874–1882).

Britton, John and Edward Wedlake Brayley, *Devonshire and Cornwall, Illustrated,* H. Fisher and Co., London, 1832.

Brunskill, R. W., *Illustrated Handbook of Vernacular Architecture* (Faber and Faber, London, 1978).

Burke, Sir John Bernard, *A Genealogical and Heraldic History of the Landed Gentry of Great Britain* (11th edn., London, 1906).

Burke, Sir John Bernard, *A Genealogical and Heraldic History of the Peerage, Baronetage and Knightage* (102nd edn., London, 1959).

Carew, Richard, *The Survey of Cornwall 1602* (De Capo Press, Amsterdam. 1969).

Cornforth, John, 'Place, Fowey, Cornwall I', *Country Life* magazine, June 21, 1962.

Cornforth, John, 'Place, Fowey, Cornwall II', *Country Life* magazine, June 28, 1962.

Costain, Thomas B., *The Last Plantagenets* (Doubleday and Co., Inc., 1962).

Cunliffe, Barry, *The Celtic World* (McGraw-Hill Book Co., United Kingdom, Ltd., Maidenhead, England, 1979).

Cunningham, Allan, *The Life and Discourses of Sir Joshua Reynolds* (Sawyer Ingersoll and Co., Hudson, Ohio, 1853).

Daniell, S., *Cornwall's Churches* (Tor Mark Press, Truro).

Dickinson, W. Howship, M.D., *King Arthur in Cornwall* (Longmans, Green and Co., New York, 1900).

Douch, H. L., *The Cornwall Protestation Returns, 1641: revised transcript of R. M. Glencross. T. L. Stoate, ed. pub. (Lower Court, Almondsbury, 1974).

Fry, Edw. Alex., *Calendar of Wills and Administrations of Devon and Cornwall proved in the Court of the Archdeaconry of Exeter 1540–1799* (1908).

Gardner, A. H., *Outline of English Architecture* (B. T. Batsford, Ltd., London, 1949).

Gay, Susan E., *Old Falmouth* (Headley Brothers, London, 1903).

Getlein, Frank, 'New England Flowered Early', *Smithsonian* (June 1982, 106–113).

Gibson, J. S. W., *Wills and Where to Find Them* (Baltimore, 1974).

Gilbert, Davies, *The Parochial History of Cornwall* (4 vols., 1838).

Graham, Winston, *The Grove of Eagles* (Doubleday and Co., Inc., New York, 1964).

Halliday, F. E., *A History of Cornwall* (Garden City Press, Ltd., Letchworth, Hertfordshire, 1975).

Harvey, John, *The Plantagenets* (Charles Scribner and Sons, New York, 1979).

Hodgkin, L. V., *A Quaker Saint of Cornwall* (London, 1927).

Laing, Lloyd, *Celtic Britain* (Charles Scribner and Sons, New York, 1979).

Lysons, Daniel, Rev., and Samuel, Esq., *Magna Britannia: vol. 3, Cornwall* (T. Cadell and W. Davies, in *The Strand,* London 1814).

MacLean, Sir John, *Parochial and Family History of the Deanery of Trigg Minor* (Nichols and Son, London, 1876).

Mais, S. P. B., *The Cornish Riviera* (Great Western Railway Co., London, 1934).

Midgley, L. Margaret (ed.), *Ministers' Accounts of the Earldom of Cornwall 1296-1297,* vol. II (Offices of the Royal Historical Society, London, 1945).

Montross, Lynn, *War Through the Ages* (Harper and Bros., 1948).

Morris, John, *The Age of Arthur, A History of the British Isles from 350 to 650* (Phillimore and Co., Ltd., Chichester, 1977).

Norden, John, *Manuscript Maps of Cornwall and Its Nine Hundreds* (reproduced in facsimile, University of Exeter, 1972).

Oxford University Press, *Dictionary of National Biography from Earliest Times to 1900,* vol. XV (1895-6).

Phillimore, W. P. W., *How to Write the History of a Family* (published Boston, 1887, reprinted Cupples and Hurd, 1972).

Pine, L. G., *The Genealogist's Encyclopedia* (Collier Books, New York, 1977).

Polsue, J., *Lake's Parochial History of Cornwall* (vols 1-4, Lake 1867-1873).

Polwele, R., Rev., *Biographical Sketches in Cornwall* (London, 1831).

Prideaux, T. E. P., Esq., *Pedigree of the Family of Prideaux of Luson in Ermington, Devon* (Wm. Pollard and Co., Exeter, 1889).

Richardson, John, *The Local Historian's Encyclopedia* (Historical Publications, Ltd., New Barnet, Hertfordshire, 1981).

Rowse, A. L., *The Byrons and Trevanions* (St Martin's Press, 1977).

Rowse, A. L., *The Cousin Jacks, The Cornish in America* (Charles Scribner and Sons, New York, 1969).

Rowse, A. L., *Tudor Cornwall* (Jonathan Cape, London, 1941-1943; new edn., Charles Scribner and Sons, New York, 1969).

Dictionary of American Biography, vol. 7 (Charles Scribner and Sons, New York, 1927).

Selleck, A. D., *Plymouth Friends, A Quaker History* (Society of Friends, Plymouth).

Shirley, John, *Canterbury Cathedral* (Pitkin Pictorials, London, 1972).

Smith, A. S. D., *The Story of the Cornish Language, Its Extinction and Revival* (Camborne Printing and Stationery Co., Ltd., Camborne, Cornwall, 1947).

Stearns, Raymond Phineas, *The Strenuous Puritan; Hugh Peter 1598-1660* (University of Illinois, Urbana, 1954).

Steel, Don, *Discovering Your Family History* (British Broadcasting Corp., 1979).

Stoate, T. L. (ed.), *Cornwall Hearth and Poll Taxes 1660-1664* (Lower Court, Almondsbury, Bristol, 1981).

Thompson, W. Harding, F.R.I.B.A., *Cornwall, A Survey of its Coast, Moors, and Valleys* (University of London Press, Ltd., 1930).

Thorn, Caroline and Frank (eds.), *Domesday Book: vol. 10, Cornwall* (Phillimore and Co., Ltd., Chichester, 1979).

Todd, Arthur Cecil, *The Cornish Miner in America* (D. Bradford Barton, Ltd., Truro, Cornwall, 1967).

Tregellas, Walter H., *Cornish Worthies, Sketches of Some Eminent Cornish Men and Families* (Elliot Stock, London, 1884).

Vivian, J. L., *The Visitations of Cornwall (1530–1573, 1620) with Additions 1887* (Wm. Pollard, Exeter, England, 1887).

ADDITIONAL SOURCES OF INFORMATION

Unpublished records of:
> *Treffry, Joseph Thomas (Austin),* Memorandum Book 1848, various letters.
> *Treffry, Spencer Thornton,* 'The History of Fowey and the Treffry Family' 1891.
> *Treffry Pedigrees* (from charts at Place).
> *Treffry, John* (1778–1849), emigrant to Canada, diaries.
> *Treffry, Hannah Hayward* (1788–1879), letters to daughter Elizabeth.
> Letters and records from many descendants of John and Hannah Treffry.

Original research collections of
> *Jones, Mabel* (Mrs. E. Stanley).
> *Smith, Harriet Fröelich* (Mrs. Harvard).

Original parish records, wills, legal documents, directories, of
> *Society of Friends* (records used by permission of Library Committee)
> > Euston Road, London
> > Swarthmore House, Plymouth, Devon
>
> *Public Record Offices:* London
> *County Record Offices:* Plymouth, Devon; Exeter, Devon; Truro, Cornwall.
> *Society of Genealogists,* London.
> *Royal Institution of Cornwall,* Truro, Cornwall.

Genealogical Society of the Church of Jesus Christ of Latter-Day Saints, Salt Lake City, Utah.
> *Microfiche parish registers:* Devon, Cornwall, Lancashire, London, and other counties in England, Canada and United States.
> *Microfilm:*
> > Society of Friends Quarterly meetings, Devon, Cornwall.
> > Henderson Calendars for Cornwall.

INDEX

Compiled by Angela Tredell

ABBREVIATIONS USED IN INDEX

a. = alive
b. = born
ba. = baptised
bu. = buried

d. = died
da. = daughter
m. = married
s. = son

171